6/8/16   <+L

WILD
running

wild-running *(n.)*:

1. running in the wild or in the elements; escaping the modern world and reconnecting to nature.

2. running freely, with exhilaration; without limits or restrictions.

3. running to the peak of our evolutionary ability; running extraordinary distances and achieving the extraordinary.

D1421962

Jen Benson and Sim Benson

SWANSEA LIBRARIES

6000198263

WILD
running

Contents

Runs by Region

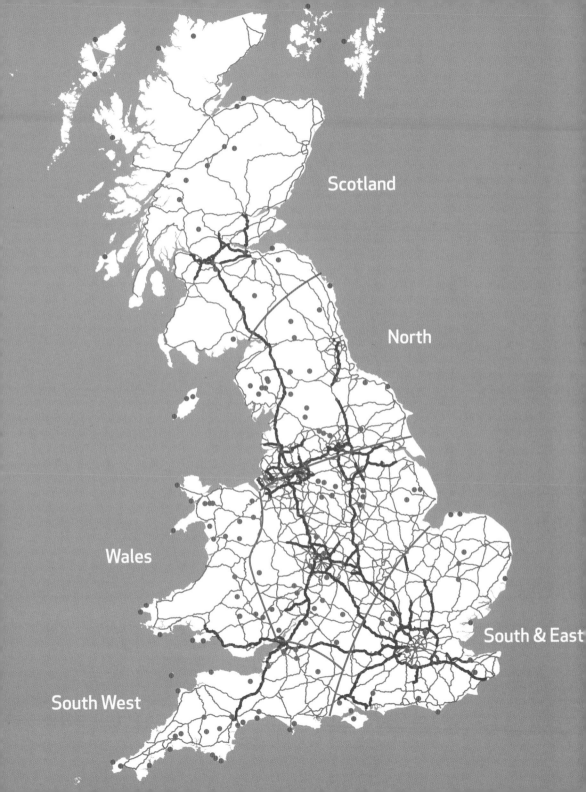

Scotland

North

Wales

South & East

South West

Introduction

After a long ridge run along the springy, wildflower-lined trails of the Cotswold Way we arrived at Broadway Tower. From here the route drops off the escarpment, soaring down a great, grassy hillside, perfect for fast, free running, with far-reaching views the whole way. We ran together, descending through field after field, the path winding ahead and drawing us down faster and faster, racing, laughing, barely in control but loving every exhilarating step...

Natural runners

Humans have evolved as runners. More specifically, we have evolved as wild runners – our ancestors taking to the plains and savannahs, rather than roads and treadmills. As unlikely as it seems now, as so many of us hunch over desks all day, humans are uniquely adapted to covering great distances without stopping; with our upright postures and ability to regulate our body temperature and refuel on the move, we are amongst the finest distance runners of all mammals. These adaptations enable us to track prey that would easily outrun us over shorter stretches. Indeed, in late 2013, a group of Kenyan farmers chased down cheetahs – the fastest mammals on earth – that were stealing their goats, tracking them for several hours in the midday heat, until they collapsed of exhaustion and could be safely moved from the area.

Of late, more and more of us are going back to our historic running roots. A survey by Sport England suggests that two million adults participate in athletics (including running) on a weekly basis. Running club membership and participation in races has also increased, with many major city marathons attracting tens of thousands of runners and being regularly over subscribed. Then there's the rise in different disciplines. Participation in trail running – runs along marked off-road routes – and fell running – taking to the wilder fells and dales – is booming, while it's estimated that five million people worldwide took part in some kind of obstacle race in 2013. More and more runners are pushing their boundaries, signing up for ultras (any

race longer than a marathon) and triathlons – which, according to British Triathlon, is the UK's fastest-growing sport, with participation increasing at a rate of 10 percent a year.

Why run wild?

Wild running might be defined as that which falls somewhere between, or perhaps even outside, the traditional disciplines, taking the best from each but not being constrained by rules and regulations. The essence of wild running is in the excitement, location and pure joy of running a route, rather than the surface it is run upon. Freedom, fantastic running terrain and the exploration of new and beautiful places are all key to a perfect wild running adventure.

Wild running takes you away from everyday life, providing the freedom to discover and explore fantastic new places. The experience of running in remote areas teaches us self-reliance, makes us fitter and stronger and encourages us to become better at finding our way. A wild running adventure can be as gentle or as testing as you choose to make it, and it can be different every time, but the key ingredients – an adventure somewhere amazing, with great running underfoot – are always there.

Running is a time-efficient and cost-effective means of getting and staying fit. It helps you meet new people, explore new places. It can fit in perfectly with a busy working lifestyle. It's even good for the mind, with evidence suggesting that running improves both mood and mental ability. Running is also unique in its simplicity: lace trainers; open door; one foot in front of the other; repeat. No need for fancy kit or lessons – it's something we've all been doing since childhood, when we ran for the pure unadulterated joy of self-propelled movement.

This simplicity lends running a freedom that's found in few other sports. It allows us to experience our surroundings through our interaction with them: feet skipping over rough ground and along winding trails; the tough, lung-wrenching struggles of hard ascents; the liberation of speedy descents; the ease and enjoyment of bounding over flat, soft turf; the uncomplicated satisfaction of getting yourself from A to B.

Our story

Sim and I love running together. We've entered some incredible races, from ultramarathon classics to epic self-invented

Did you know...?

A 2008 study by Stanford University found that regular distance running can slow the aging process, concluding that "elderly runners have fewer disabilities, a longer span of active life and are half as likely as aging nonrunners to die early deaths".

A 1991 study at the University of Zurich found runners had lower rates of illness and disease, better weight management, reductions in anxiety and depression and an increase in self-esteem compared with nonrunners.

A 2011 study at Exeter University found that "compared with exercising indoors, exercising in natural environments was associated with greater feelings of revitalization and positive engagement, decreases in tension, confusion, anger, and depression, and increased energy".

challenges; we relish discovering the wild, beautiful and often surprising places running takes us. Running has even shaped our careers and we have both worked extensively in the outdoor and fitness industries. My research has always focused on the sport, first looking at the biomechanics of running, and then at the characteristics and motivations of distance runners. Today, with the added challenges of a young family, we still train and race regularly, and together whenever possible.

Most of our running adventures have been around Britain, exploring its incredible diversity on foot. Our search for routes for this book has seen us revisiting favourite places to run and discovering new ones. With its dramatic coastlines, leafy woodlands, moorland expanses and rugged mountains, Britain provides a huge and varied playground for runners to explore. The country is criss-crossed by an extensive network of close to 150,000 miles of public rights of way, allowing access to many magnificent and inspiring places.

I view a new route like a new acquaintance; exciting and unknown, perhaps dependable but perhaps fickle and one that, if followed blindly, might lead me astray. A well-known path on the other hand is like a trusted friend; honest and familiar, offering sound guidance, and always there to turn to in troubled times. My regular routes are my comfort – never dull, for they change daily with the seasons and the weather; these are the places where I can connect completely with myself and my running, where I have my most lucid moments of thought and work through life's equations with clarity and objectivity. The known and the unknown complement each other perfectly, creating balance and variety, comfort and adventure in equal measure.

A run round Britain

We have been on many trips around Britain where we have run as a way to explore new places, challenge our physical limits and have enjoyable adventures, but have found few guides aimed specifically at runners. Walking guides gave us route directions; mountain bike guides focused on the terrain and the great ascents and descents. We felt that the perfect running book lay somewhere between the two: using pure human power to access and discover incredible and beautiful places while making sure the terrain encountered made for exciting, varied and enjoyable running.

Many of our runs combine several different types of terrain, as we felt it was important to prioritise the experience of running the route rather than to be restrictive about what lay underfoot. As a result there are some that include gentle running on quiet country lanes, fun muddy wading through boggy ground and scrambling over boulders and scree slopes alongside the more usual trails and paths. We strongly believe this adds to the variety and interest of the runs themselves.

This book leads you on a running journey around Britain. The routes included are deliberately diverse in their length, terrain and navigability, showcasing the variety of running on offer and providing runs to suit and challenge as many people as possible.

Starting in the South West, we take to the spectacular Coast Path, winding its way around the edge of the peninsula. The wild expanses of Bodmin, Exmoor and Dartmoor follow. The South and East section heads out across the rolling South Downs to the towering white cliffs at Beachy Head. East Anglia has wonderful beach running and access to the classic long-distance trails of the Peddars Way and Icknield Way, the latter stretching across the country to the Chilterns, a wonderful hilly escape from nearby London.

Central England is home to the Peak District, from the limestone trails of the White Peak to testing sections of the Pennine Way across the rugged and remote Dark Peak. Venturing into the North, the majestic Lake District offers the chance to scale some high-level traverses or relax on a gentler lakeside excursion. The moors and fells of Yorkshire offer wilderness and fascinating geological features, providing challenging and exciting running. Wales has a great variety, from the rolling, grassy hills of the south, along its rugged Coast Path to the towering mountains of Snowdonia in the north. Scotland takes altitude to a new level with challenging ascents, tours of the dramatic coastline and an escape to the remote and wind-swept Scottish islands.

Wherever you chose to go, our aim for this book is to inspire you to get out and try running in its most unadulterated form, experiencing fully our natural environment: on foot, as one with the landscape and the elements, using only the power of the body. This is where some of the most pleasurable, fulfilling and exhilarating experiences happen, and where running becomes truly wild.

Getting Started

One of the many great reasons to run lies in its simplicity and lack of need for complicated equipment. However there are items that will make running safer and more enjoyable if chosen with care. Each run is different, so carefully consider your requirements -and those of the run- before setting out.

Shoes A well-fitting pair of shoes appropriate to the terrain, and conditions of your run are essential. For hard-pack and road-based runs, a pair of road shoes will provide protection and cushioning for your feet. On trails and dry off-road surfaces trail shoes which combine a more rugged, grippy sole with some cushioning will give you traction and make running fast over uneven terrain easier. In wet, muddy conditions, a pair of fell shoes with deep lugs will grip the ground and stop you slipping and sliding as you run, greatly improving comfort, performance and safety. Many runs involve a combination of terrain so shoe choice is an important but not always straight-forward decision. And remember, good fit is key, so be prepared to try several.

Clothing Running generates large amounts of heat, even in cold weather, so it's a good idea to layer your clothing to allow for easy ventilation. A lightweight windproof jacket is invaluable, as it can be worn over other clothing when required or stashed easily in a pocket. Bear in mind that in cooler weather you will lose heat rapidly if you need to slow down or stop for any reason. Other than this, dress for the conditions you will encounter and the length of your run, from tights, long-sleeved base layers, hats and gloves in winter to shorts and a vest in summer; most choices are common sense. Well-fitting, supportive underwear is essential for comfort whilst running and worth time and effort to get right.

Socks! A good pair of running socks is essential, providing warmth, cushioning and protection and wicking away sweat from the skin to reduce the chances of blisters. Make sure they fit really well and don't ruck up in your shoes, and consider taking a change of socks on really long runs. Waterproof socks are a great investment for wet-weather running.

How to use this book

Directions: This book includes basic directions, overview maps and a lat long to OS grid reference conversion table (in the annex) to enable you to locate the routes. However, it is important to fully research each route, using our online resources at **wildrunning.net** where you will find detailed route descriptions, Ordnance Survey maps and downloadable GPX files. Simply enter the unique address provided for each run. Make sure you print out these maps before you leave home - or why not load the GPX files into one of many apps which turn your phone into a GPS device (e.g. ViewRanger, MemoryMap or EveryTrail). We always recommended that you plot your route on the relevant 1:25,000 map and take it with you on the run.

Grading: Each run is graded either 'easy', 'moderate' or 'challenging' for navigation and toughness to give you an idea what to expect. 'Challenging' routes will require good levels of navigational and/or running ability so consider these carefully before setting out.

Building fitness and technique

Routes have been included to provide for all levels of fitness and experience. Some of the longer and/or more mountainous routes require high levels of fitness and endurance to complete. Here are some tips for building fitness if you are just starting out:

Run regularly It is important to run regularly to allow your body to become conditioned to the forces exerted upon it during running and to maximize gains in fitness. Occasional hard runs interspersed by long gaps are more likely to leave you tired, sore and demotivated.

Build up gradually It's old advice but good. There's no proven maximum amount that you should increase by each week, and progress will be highly individual,

however take the time to increase the intensity and duration of your runs gradually to allow your body to adapt.

Find a training plan Having a set number and type of runs to complete each week is great for keeping your training fresh and varied. Make sure you listen to your body though, as no training plan will suit everybody all the time.

Enter a race Having a goal, such as race, on the horizon is great for motivation and helps get you out running even when the sofa seems like a much better option.

Technique Off-road running takes time and practice to perfect, and requires your body to work differently to road running. If you are new to running off-road, start with well-used trails and less

technically challenging terrain and work up to the more demanding routes. This will make them all the more enjoyable when you get there. As with most activities, the more you do the better you will get, but there are some specific areas to work on that will help you improve more rapidly:

Build strength Incorporate strength and conditioning work into your routine. Stronger muscles will make you more efficient in your running and protect against injury.

Practise balancing Good balance is key to running off-road successfully, yet it is something we rarely train ourselves to do. Incorporate balance work into your daily routine to increase body awareness and improve co-ordination.

Resources for Runners

There is a wealth of information and advice available for runners, from books and magazines to websites and forums. We have listed a few of our favourites:

Magazines such as Runners' World and Trail Running Magazine are fantastic resources for training and nutrition information, route ideas, injury advice and race listings. The Runners' World website also has a searchable events listing..

Local running shops are often an invaluable source of information on local routes, running clubs as well as footwear and running kit advice. Running clubs are excellent sources of guidance and motivation for all runners.

fellrunner.org.uk has a wealth of information on fell running and full details of all fell races, many of which aren't advertised elsewhere.

britishtrailrunning.co.uk is a great resource for trail running.

goodrunguide.co.uk has great content and database of routes, payment is required.

scottishrunningguide.com is great for running in Scotland.

Bags A light-weight rucksack or waist pack can be really useful for carrying spare clothing, food, water and safety kit. It can take many attempts to find the perfect one for you, so be prepared to try several and always take the time to adjust them to fit you properly to avoid discomfort, bouncing around and chafing. There are many different types on the market and much is down to personal preference. Those with easy-to-reach zipper pockets for food are great for longer runs. Water-carrying options range from side, rear and strap arrangements to integrated bladder pouches, all of which have strengths and weaknesses in terms of comfort, accessibility and ease of refilling, with most runners having a personal preference.

Food and drink Again, the need for carrying refreshments will depend hugely on the run you are doing and the availability of stops along the way. In general it is important to take supplies if you are running for more than about 90 minutes. Many runners drink energy drinks, however these may become unpalatable on longer runs and are often expensive and sugary. Plain water is perfectly adequate in most cases and straightforward to replenish. Drink to thirst and, on longer runs especially, make sure you also replace salts which are lost through sweating, either through electrolyte tablets which can be added to water or simply by eating little and often. Hyponatraemia is a serious condition caused by over over-drinking, and a far greater danger to distance runners than dehydration. Snacks should be easy to carry, palatable and easy to stomach and can range from expensive energy bars to a handful of dried fruit, depending upon taste. In general, runners find their preference for sweet foods declines as the run duration increases, so try out different foods and see what works for you.

Emergency items When venturing out on longer runs or into remote or weather-affected areas, even more careful kit consideration is required. Packing the right safety equipment can prevent a run becoming an epic and may save your own or someone else's life. Carrying, and being able to use, kit is an important part of being prepared. The following list is not exhaustive and intended as a guide only: route description, map, compass, mobile phone, money, food, water, warm clothing, waterproof clothing, hat and gloves, first aid kit, whistle, survival bag, head torch, sun screen. Clothing and equipment choices should always reflect the conditions and the route.

10 ways to be wild and safe

1 Take a compass and map and know how to use them, particularly when running in remote or unfamiliar places. Bring a mobile phone but don't rely on it.

2 Tell someone where you're going and when you'll be back.

3 Wear the right shoes. Enjoyable and safe off-road running requires shoes with good grip.

4 Dress right. When undertaking longer runs or venturing into remote or high areas, take extra clothing to allow you to keep warm should the weather deteriorate or should you need to stop or slow down.

5 Consider not wearing headphones, particularly if there are road crossings.

6 Ensure that you have enough food and water for the duration of your run.

7 Take a basic emergency kit on longer runs, and those in remote areas. Include a head torch, whistle, space blanket and emergency rations.

8 Research your run. Be prepared for the terrain, navigation and the weather involved. Find out where there are places to shelter, refuel and get information. We cannot guarantee that routes will still be in the condition described.

9 Run with a friend! A running adventure is a fantastic thing to share and is safer with company. Alternatively there are many running groups and guides with whom running in remote areas can be made safer and more enjoyable.

10 The routes in this book are described for fine, summer conditions only. In poor weather they may be vastly different, particularly those in high and mountainous areas, presenting a considerably tougher challenge or requiring specialist equipment and techniques and the skills and experience to use them.

Best for Beginners

Shorter runs on relatively level terrain with easy route-finding. Perfect for those beginning to venture into the world of wild running.

3 St Anthony Head	91 Bamburgh Castle
16 Lundy	92 Cragside
30 Tamsin Trail	82 Loughrigg Tarn
43 Wendover Woods	110 Ann Griffiths
72 Clumber Park	130 Chatelherault
57 Longshaw	147 Esha Ness
113 Llanddwyn Island	145 Deerness

Best for Coast & Beach

From sandy, wave-washed beaches to rocky scrambles on rugged coast paths, these runs showcase the best of Britain's coastal adventures.

1 Pendeen to St Ives	98 Peel to Port Erin
2 Penzance to Land's End	100 Three Cliffs Bay
8 Prawle Point	101 Rhossili Beach
26 Tour of Portland	107 Porthgain to Whitesands
33 Holkham Beach	114 Llŷn Peninsula
40 Beachy Head & Seven Sisters	129 Aberlady Bay
91 Bamburgh Castle Beach Run	134 Burghead to Lossiemouth

Best for Forest & Woods

Winding trails through lush woodland and scented pine forests.

6 Two Valleys Run	57 Longshaw
18 Heddon Valley	59 Wychwood Forest
21 Quantock Hills Greenway	70 Edwinstowe
29 The Forest Way	75 Woodhall Spa
43 Wendover Woods	110 Ann Griffiths
47 Lyndhurst Loop	131 Leannach Forest
44 Ashridge Estate	133 Badenoch Way

Best for Wild Swimming

A fantastic run followed by a relaxing, refreshing swim in a tranquil lake, a calm sea or a hidden pool… what could be better?

Best for Hard as Nails

Our toughest challenges – for those wanting to take their wild running adventures to the next level.

Best for Ascents & Descents

Tough climbs with rewarding views and fast, exhilarating descents.

Best for Urban Escapes

Easy escape routes from the hustle and bustle of urban life to the wild trails beyond.

Best for Families

Fantastic runs in family-friendly places, great for days out and holidays.

Best for Really Wild

Remote and removed from everday life, these routes are a true escape into the pockets of wilderness still to be found in Britain.

Best for National Trails

Wonderful routes taking in the best of Britain's long distance, National and Great Trails.

1 Pendeen to St Ives
2 Penzance to Land's End
25 The Undercliff
31 Brancaster Coast & Marsh
37 Box Hill
42 Butser Hill
49 Broadway Tower
55 Edale & Jacob's Ladder

58 The Ridgeway at Ashbury
66 Suckley Ridge
69 Offa's Dyke Switchback
87 Fountains Fell
102 Rhossili to Oxwich
107 Porthgain to Whitesands
136 Iveroran to Kinlochleven
150 Moray Coast Trail

Best for History & Culture

Wild runs through beautiful places of historical or cultural interest.

1 Pendeen to St Ives
5 The Hurlers & the Cheesewring
16 Lundy
22 Bath Skyline
24 Dyrham & Doynton
32 The Great Eastern Pingo Trail
49 Broadway Tower

53 Bakewell & Chatsworth
56 Kinder Trespass
92 Cragside Estate
68 Tintern Abbey
70 Edwinstowe
91 Bamburgh Castle
140 Dalwhinnie to Culra Bothy

Best for Wildlife

Perfect runs for spotting Britain's rich diversity of flora and fauna.

6 Two Valleys Run
12 Blackdown Hills
16 Lundy
18 Heddon Valley
25 The Undercliff
32 The Great Eastern Pingo Trail
34 Dunwich Heath
51 Slad Valley

75 Woodhall Spa
92 Cragside Estate
106 Stackpole
109 Elan Valley Trail
130 Chatelherault
134 Burghead to Lossiemouth
144 Urgha & Maraig
146 Tour of Papa Westray

Must do Wild Races

The OMM The Original Mountain Marathon is a two-day, self-reliant, navigational race held over the last weekend in October each year. Its location varies but is always somewhere wild and remote with plenty of scope for getting lost and muddy.

The Classic Quarter (Cornwall) Showcasing some of Britain's most spectacular coastline along the South West Coast Path from Lizard Point to Land's End, this 45-mile ultramarathon, held in the height of the summer, pushes the mind and body to their limits. Great trail running and breathtaking scenery throughout.

3 Peaks Race (Yorkshire) One of the all-time classic fell races, this tough challenge takes in the three highest peaks in Yorkshire: Pen-y-Ghent, Wernside and Ingleborough, a distance of around 24 miles.

Race the Train (Wales) A tough, muddy, 14-mile off-road run from the coastal town of Tywyn along the course of the Talyllyn Railway. The aim is to beat the steam train, packed with cheering spectators, which arrives back at Tywyn in around 1 hour and 48 minutes.

The Highland Fling (Scotland) A 53-mile ultramarathon along the West Highland Way Trail, this race passes through wonderful scenery from Glasgow to Tyndrum, in the Highlands. Free beer and a traditional Scottish Ceilidh await the finishers.

The Clarendon Marathon (Wiltshire) Along with a half marathon, this great race follows the Clarendon Way from Salisbury to Winchester and is known for its atmosphere and organization. The route is 90 per cent off road, winding its way along tracks and trails through peaceful countryside.

The Grizzly (Devon) An established classic, the charming and eccentric Grizzly takes in approximately 20 miles of muddy, hilly, boggy terrain around coastal East Devon, with a changing theme each year.

Trionium Picnic Marathon (Surrey) A tough, full-distance marathon through the scenic North Downs with over 1,800 metres of climbing, this race consistently scores high in the rankings for great races. There is also a half marathon option.

Lakeland Trails Marathon (Cumbria) A wonderful run through the breathtaking scenery around Coniston Water, Blea Water and Tarn Hows, with a great party at the finish!

Jura Fell Race (Scotland) A beautiful but challenging 17 mile run over seven mountain summits, including the Paps of Jura, with some 2,370 metres of ascent.

Prawle Point

South West

The south west of England has a fantastic variety of places to run and experience, from rugged coastal trails across wild, open moorland to gentle, rolling, tree-lined hills.

Highlights
South West

Our favourite runs include:

1 Tackle the spectacular Penwith Heritage coastline, traversing towering sea cliffs on your way to the picturesque artists' town of St Ives

8 Run around the southernmost point of Britain, and watch the sun set over the sea at Prawle Point

14 Climb to the remote tor of High Willhays, the highest point in southern England

25 Conquer the wild and inescapable jungle of the undercliff at Lyme Regis

St Anthony Head

West Cornwall

Cornwall offers a wealth of running adventures, with its heady mix of dramatic coastline, colourful fishing harbours, white sandy beaches and windswept moorland. Being a peninsula edged with some of the most spectacular sections of the 630-mile South West Coast Path, this area offers well-signed, exciting and varied running, with plenty of opportunities for a cream tea at the finish. In spring, the fields are ablaze with daffodils and the scent of gorse fills the air. Should you dare take your eyes of the path for a moment, seals can be spotted sunbathing on rocks and playing in the startlingly blue sea, buzzards wheel overhead and rare Cornish choughs with their glossy black plumage and bright red beaks perch high above the waves.

The cliffs that form the base of many of the routes in this section are granite, and the resulting terrain is often rocky, steep and strewn with large boulders. Many of the features of the coast path, such as the stepped ascents and descents, stiles, stream crossings and walls, are hewn from this rock and require some negotiating, especially on tired legs. Despite this, however, there is plenty of good, fast running to be found.

An early adventure of ours here was the Classic Quarter race, a 45-mile traverse of the southern coast of Cornwall from Lizard Point to Land's End, held each June. Lining up for the start, our excitement and that of the 200 or so others was tinged with trepidation at the thought of what lay ahead. For me it was as far as I'd ever run before, and over much more challenging terrain. After some words from the race organisers, we were off, the stunning Cornish coast stretching out ahead. The sun rose ever higher in a deep blue sky as we climbed and descended the rough trails, warming our bodies and waking our minds, still dazed and cold after a 3am start from the campsite to reach the start. The sea glinted and sparkled, ever present

1

2

1

to our left, its cool depths an invitation we found increasingly hard to decline as the day progressed. Approaching Lamorna, I was concerned I didn't have what it took: my body ached, I was thirsty and depleted, yet nausea stopped me from eating or drinking much. The little cove, a special place we'd been to before, lifted our spirits and we set off from the checkpoint feeling more positive. Shortly afterwards, we took a wrong turn and a brief tour inland and then, just a mile before the finish, a huge navigational error sent us up a steep path, across some gorse and then scrambling all the way back down again, losing us about half an hour and my third place in the race. It was a lesson that route finding is never a given in wild places, even on a trail like this which hugs the very edge of the land. And so, finally, ended ten hours of shared moments of pleasure and pain, and many lessons learned.

The north and south coasts of Cornwall have their own distinct characters. The Atlantic coast to the north is exposed and rugged, often feeling wild and remote, whilst the south has a somewhat gentler feel, with its pretty beaches and harbours. The routes in this section take in many jewels that this area has to offer the wild runner, from lush woodland trails alongside babbling streams to winding paths over bleak, open moorland, often utilising the South West Coast Path as it wends its way round the peninsula above classic sea cliffs. Is the stretch of Atlantic coast path between Pendeen and St Ives the most startlingly beautiful in south-west England? Its soaring cliffs border a wave-sculptured plateau that was once submerged beneath an ancient sea. It had to be included as a classic Wild Run (Run 1). The path here is the upper border of the Penwith region of Cornwall, which has one of the highest concentrations of archaeological sites in Europe, with a mild climate that produces plants and flowers little seen elsewhere in the UK. Our second route, Penzance to Land's End (Run 2) follows the southern length of the coast path, again taking in the hugely exciting landscape, terrain and fascinating history of the area. Run 3 takes in the rugged coastal tip of the Roseland peninsula at St Anthony Head, with its fine views and wonderfully varied running terrain.

West Cornwall

1 PENDEEN TO ST IVES

Distance:	13½ miles (22km)
Start:	Pendeen Lighthouse, TR19 7ED
Finish:	St Ives
Terrain:	Trail, rocky trail, track
Toughness:	Challenging
Ascent:	935 metres
Navigation:	Easy to moderate
Good for:	Coast, history
Route info:	wildrunning.net/01

A magnificent run along the Penwith Heritage coastline following the SW Coast Path. Access the path from the little car park by Pendeen Lighthouse, and follow the coast path eastwards all the way to St Ives. The path is tough and technical for much of the way with rocky trails, boulders and hilly terrain, but the stunning views more than make up for it. Bosigran Ridge (3 miles from the start) is a dramatic and classic rock climb which makes its way up a perfect granite spine from the turquoise seas that boom around Great Zawn, to the hillside above. The run concludes in St Ives, with its stunning white sand, palm-lined beaches and plenty of good cafés and restaurants. Return by bus to Pendeen via Penzance.

2 PENZANCE TO LAND'S END

Distance:	16½ miles (27km)
Start:	Penzance railway station, TR18 2LT
Finish:	Land's End, TR19 7AA
Terrain:	Trail, road, Coast Path
Toughness:	Challenging
Ascent:	791 metres
Navigation:	Easy to moderate
Good for:	Coast, history, culture
Route info:	wildrunning.net/02

A tough but rewarding coastal run with plenty of scenery and history. Steep steps and narrow paths make for exciting, technical running. Leave Penzance by the coast road to the west, through Newlyn and Mousehole, before following the SW Coast Path sign left out onto the rugged coast path. Continue along an undulating mixture of trail and granite steps to Lamorna. The secluded cove and café here, surrounded by bluebell woods in spring, provides a welcome spot for a rest. Climb steep steps to the cliff top, passing Treen's white sandy beaches and the Minack Theatre. In the final miles, grasslands make for easier running as Land's End beckons. Return by bus to Penzance.

3 ST ANTHONY HEAD

Distance:	5½ miles (9km)
Start/finish:	St Anthony Head car park, TR2 5EX
Terrain:	Coast Path, riverside footpath
Toughness:	Easy to moderate
Ascent:	256 metres
Navigation:	Easy to moderate
Good for:	Wildlife, coast, history
Route info:	wildrunning.net/03

St Anthony Head (NT) is situated at the southernmost end of the wild Roseland Peninsula. At its tip stands St Anthony's lighthouse, at the entrance to one of the world's largest natural harbours: Carrick Roads and the Fal River estuary. Superb views, and a wonderful place to spot birds and other wildlife, as well as a 19th and 20th century gun battery. The run is an anti-clockwise tour of the edge of the Roseland Peninsula, starting and finishing at its tip. Keep the sea to your R throughout. When level with Towan Beach, turn L and, skirting Porth Farm, cross the peninsula. Continue round to the start, with the water still on your right. NT café at the car park.

Bodmin

East Cornwall

Like the coasts to the west, those that border either side of east Cornwall differ distinctly in character. South-east Cornwall is easily accessible by the main line train, which runs through Plymouth to Penzance. The area has many family-friendly activities, such as the Eden Project, in close proximity to fantastic places to explore and run wild. The Eden Project marathon and half marathon, held in October, make full use of the hilly terrain surrounding the famous geodesic domes. The pretty fishing villages of Looe and Polperro make for an enjoyable day's exploration; or follow the Coast Path along from the sensational scenery at Rame Head to the area's stunning beaches, from the three mile sweep of Whitsand Bay, to the more peaceful Samphire Beach and Portnadler Bay. Dramatic Run 4 goes around Gribbin Head – one of many routes with literary associations in Cornwall – finishing at the historical town of Fowey. Further inland there are beautiful estates and woodland, crisscrossed by many wonderful running trails.

In contrast to the south coast, Cornwall's north boasts dramatic cliff tops interspersed with fantastic beaches, perfect for a post-run paddle or a play in the surf. Inland, the landscape is greener, with lush wooded vales and rolling hills edged by rugged coastline. We ran here in the spring, joyfully finding the best of the UK's weather and a whole week of sunshine. Cornwall was in full bloom – a striking, bright yellow sea of daffodils, vivid against a vast blue sky.

Away from the sea, the wide-open spaces of Bodmin Moor are punctuated with tors whose granite has been used for millennia to build the standing stones, burial chambers, Cornish hedges, clapper bridges, cottages and farms that dot its

5

5

6

rugged landscape. Inviting trails draw the runner in to explore and experience its wild delights. The forest at Cardinham, which borders the moor, has many easy-to-follow trails, perfect for some relaxed woodland running, along with a lovely café, play area and separate bike track. Run 6 links the valleys of the Loveny and the Fowey, crossing open moorland on the edge of the moor.

Several well-marked long distance trails provide excellent running in this part of the country. The Camel Trail runs along a former railway from Wenfordbridge to Padstow, including one of the oldest sections in the world from Wadebridge to Poley's Bridge which was opened in 1834. The Trail provides easy, straightforward running through a variety of magnificent and varying landscapes. It follows the course of the River Camel along its valley, home to the vineyard that produces the internationally renowned Camel Valley sparkling wine. There are large sections through lush, peaceful woodland, providing many opportunities for further exploration. The Trail skirts open moorland at Bodmin before plunging back into trees. The estuary provides outstanding views and is home to thousands of birds including widgeon, grebe, egret and oystercatchers which can be spotted as you run. Parking and bike hire are available at both ends of the trail and at Wadebridge, and there are cafés and toilets at regular intervals along the route, making it a great trail for a bike/run day out with the family.

The Camel Trail is part of The Cornish Way, a 180-mile link of six trails for cyclists and walkers/runners from Land's End to the county boundary in Bude. It was opened in 2000 as a combined project between the Countryside Service and the Sustrans National Cycle Network.

The Cooper Trail, a 60-mile circumnavigation of Bodmin Moor, can be run in 10-mile sections or joined together to create a longer run. The fantastic run at the Cheesewring (Run 5) takes in a particularly stunning part of the first section of this trail, from Minions to Drayne's Bridge. A short extension to this run reaches Golitha Falls, an area of woodland occupying a steep-sided valley gorge, where the River Fowey tumbles down the rocks in a series of tumbling cascades.

East Cornwall

4 FOWEY

Distance:	7 miles (11km)
Start/finish:	Readymoney Cove car park, Tower Park, near PL23 1DG
Terrain:	Field, path, Coast Path, lane
Toughness:	Moderate
Ascent:	329 metres
Navigation:	Easy to moderate
Good for:	Coast, views, woodland
Route info:	wildrunning.net/04

A spectacular run around the peninsula below Fowey, crossing the headland to the Coast Path as it loops its way from Polkerris, over dramatic cliffs and along St Austell Bay back to Fowey. From car park, run downhill towards the sea and Readymoney Cove. Climb steps to Allday's Fields before following road between Coombe Farm and Lankelly Farm. Follow track to Trenant and paths/fields to Tregaminion church. Follow Coast Path S around Gribbin Head and back to Readymoney Cove, turning L inland back to car park. The historic town of Fowey with its picturesque estuary and harbour is well worth a post-run visit. Refuel at the lovely Lifebuoy Café on Lostwithiel Street.

5 HURLERS & CHEESEWRING

Distance:	3½ miles (5km)
Start/finish:	Hurlers car park, Minions, a little SW of PL14 5LW
Terrain:	Path, track, open moorland
Toughness:	Easy to moderate
Ascent:	103 metres
Navigation:	Easy to moderate
Good for:	Moorland, views, history
Route info:	wildrunning.net/05

Bodmin Moor's bleak wilderness is peppered with stone circles and great tors. The Hurlers and the Cheesewring are among the best known. Starting near Minions, the highest village in Cornwall, follow tracks NW from car park past the three circles of The Hurlers. Continue on obvious path until you can bear R to the Cheesewring, a towering stack of a rock formed over thousands of years by glaciation and weathering. Scramble to the top for breathtaking views. Descend and follow paths NNW until back on the main path heading N. Great running towards Sharptor, bearing R at the road and following the old tramway back past Cheesewring Quarry to return to car park.

6 TWO VALLEYS RUN

Distance:	5 miles (8km)
Start/finish:	St Neot car park, near PL14 6NG
Terrain:	Quiet road, track, moorland
Toughness:	Easy to moderate
Ascent:	227 metres
Navigation:	Easy to moderate
Good for:	Woodland, history
Route info:	wildrunning.net/06

A run of contrasts, with woodland and open moor, between the Loveny and Fowey valleys. It is partially waymarked, with some peaceful country lanes. Leave the car park, cross a bridge and head up hill on quiet lanes out of St Neot, past Wenmouth Cross. Follow signs for Liskeard then Draynes, dropping down through Treverbyn into the Fowey Valley. Continue along the valley, until a track climbs through woodlands to Berry Down, with its Iron Age fort and views. Descend on quiet roads past Tremaddock and Hilltown Farms, bearing R at the crossroads to return to the car park. St Neot is a magical place to explore, with its pretty woodland, filled with bluebells in spring.

Prawle Point

The South Hams

The beautiful and varied south Devon coastline runs from Seaton on the dramatic Jurassic coast westwards, through the cathedral city of Exeter, to the picturesque South Hams. Dotted with the jewels of Dartmouth, Salcombe and Kingsbridge along the coast and Ivybridge on its borders with Dartmoor, the region has endless scope for running as well as plenty to explore with families or friends. The lighthouse-studded coastline, with its rocky promontories at Start Point and Bolt Head, provides adventurous and sometimes technically-challenging running along the South West Coast Path (Run 9); there are beaches to explore along the great sandy sweep of Start Bay, and the lower Avon and Dart valleys lead through secluded valleys lined with lush woodland (Run 7). The entire coast is designated an Area of Outstanding Natural Beauty, providing the inspiration for many a wild running adventure. Inland, the terrain is classic Devon countryside, with lush, green, rolling hills, hedgerows laden with blackberries in the autumn and many footpaths and bridleways to explore. There is an abundance of woodland to discover, and the Woodland Trust's MOREwoods initiative aims to plant some 30,000 new trees to increase this further. For a wonderful point-to-point run, the Dart Valley Trail is a 17-mile waymarked route, taking in both banks of the River Dart as it wends its way from Totnes to the South West Coast Path. It is a picturesque and sensory journey through varied landscapes of woodland, river and estuary along one of the country's most beautiful valleys.

Kingsbridge-based race organisers Endurancelife hold their annual South Devon coastal marathon starting and finishing at the pretty fishing village of Beesands every February. It is run over a fantastic course which takes in the spectacular coast path around Start Point and Prawle Point (overlapping our Run 8) before heading inland through Devon's mud and hills

8

7

8

to finally finish through Slapton nature reserve and along the iconic golden spit of Slapton Sands. One of the original classics of the Coastal Trail Series, the race now offers distances from 10km to ultra and is a superb way to see this part of the country with plenty of waymarkers and water stations along the way.

My own first visit to Slapton was during the final section of the Devon Coast to Coast Extreme, a 140-mile traverse of the south-west peninsula on foot, mountain bike and kayak. This was first year the event had taken place, and we set off at midnight to make our way from Foreland Point, Devon's most northerly point, with the aim of making our way to its southernmost tip at Prawle Point in under 24 hours. Our worlds reduced to a tiny tunnel of light from our head torches, we completed the initial run section and took to our bikes, winding our way up steep roads onto Exmoor. Pedalling down through mid-Devon, trying not to doze off on the longer descents, familiar places flashed by, strangely still and silent in the early hours. Dawn brought some much-needed daylight to our sleep-deprived brains and we eventually climbed onto Dartmoor, leaving our bikes at one point for a run up to a checkpoint on High Willhays, the summit of the moor. We reached the half-way point at Princetown, where those undertaking the race over two days would camp for the night, and stopped briefly to change to off-road tyres. At Totnes we abandoned our bikes and kayaked for 9 miles down the beautiful, tree-lined River Dart, the sun dappling the surface as our paddles beat their watery rhythm. The final 17-mile run took us out onto the coast path, where the winding, rocky terrain challenged our tired legs and brains in equal measure. Running along the seafront at Slapton we passed another runner, out for a jog in the evening sun. We laughed at ourselves, at the absurdity of having been on the go, non-stop, for nearly 20 hours. The final few miles, in the dark with a failing head torch, felt like an eternity as we made our way along the Coast Path, meandering its way around the land's edge. Finally we spotted lights high up on the cliffs and picked our way towards them, finishing in a little over 22 hours.

The South Hams

7 AVON ESTUARY

Distance: 8 miles (13km)
Start/finish: Bantham Beach car park, TQ7 3AN
Terrain: Footpath, green lane, road
Toughness: Easy
Ascent: 363 metres
Navigation: Easy (waymarked)
Good for: Coast, wildlife
Route info: wildrunning.net/07

A classic run, with a lung-busting ascent and a fast, technical descent along the way. Starting with a ferry ride (May to September, not Sundays) from Bantham slipway to Cockleridge Ham, this run traces the winding course of the river Avon from Aveton Gifford through beautiful, secluded valleys, rich with wildlife, to the sea. The route is waymarked with blue 'Avon Estuary Walk' markers. Burgh Island can be seen across the bay, topped with its famous Art Deco hotel. The sandy expanses of Bantham Beach are perfect for an early morning run and the surf is some of the best in Devon. Bantham has a village store and pub and, in summer, the Gastrobus in the car park sells good food.

8 PRAWLE POINT

Distance: 4 miles (6.4km)
Start/finish: The Green, East Prawle TQ7 2BY
Terrain: Green lane, Coast Path, field, road
Toughness: Moderate
Ascent: 228 metres
Navigation: Easy to moderate
Good for: Coast, history, wildlife
Route info: wildrunning.net/08

This picturesque run loops around Prawle Point, the most southerly tip of Devon, covering a fine mix of fast, flat running, and technical, rocky sections. A clear evening is a wonderful time for this run, as the skies ignite all around. A magical, tranquil place, Prawle Point is an SSSI and home to an abundance of wildlife. From the village green, take the lane that runs SE out of the village and follow a bridleway and footpath downhill to reach the Coast Path. Turn R and run around the headland at Prawle Point, passing Elender Cove and Maceley Cove. Take a footpath to the R, leading uphill along a footpath, green lane and then a quiet lane back to the start. The eccentric Pigs Nose Inn at East Prawle is definitely worth a post-run visit.

9 BOLT TAIL

Distance: 7 miles (12km)
Start/finish: Malborough Village Hall, TQ7 3BX
Terrain: Green lane, Coast Path, field, road
Toughness: Moderate
Ascent: 234 metres
Navigation: Easy to moderate
Good for: Coast, wildlife, history
Route info: wildrunning.net/09

A glorious run along ancient green lanes and peaceful tracks and out onto the spectacular coast path at Bolt Tail. It takes in a 500BC hill fort at Bolt Tail, and pretty Hope Cove, with its tiny beach, many fishing boats and history as a centre for smuggling. From Malborough, head south through Portlemore Barton before heading across fields to South Down Farm and then out onto the SW Coast Path at Bolberry Down. Follow the Coast Path around Bolt Tail and on to Inner Hope. Turn right on footpath signed 'Galmpton 1m', returning across fields and along Higher Town back to Marlborough. The coast here is a wonderful place to watch the sun set. In autumn the hedgerows are a feast of blackberries.

Exe Estuary

Exeter &
East Devon

The Exe estuary, from either shore, is a place of magical, sparkling views. I have spent many a summer afternoon, sometimes after a run, other times not, at the Turf Lock outside Exminster, a pub whose grassy gardens slope right down to the water's edge. The place is almost an island – it even has a ferry service with regular crossings to the pretty town of Topsham, where the Goat Walk out along the edge of the estuary can be run and looped around back into the town at the station, a pleasant couple of miles for a gentle jog or afternoon stroll. The annual 'Topsham to Turf' swim takes place each August, with entertainment and refreshments at the finish.

The geology of East Devon ranges from the Triassic sandstone pebble- bed heathlands in the west, where the running is on stony, gravelly paths, to the more fertile Jurassic and Cretaceous sandstones and limestones that underlie the green, rolling hills and expansive farmland in the east. The Old Red Sandstone typical of much of this area is sculpted into strange shapes by the sea along the dramatic coastline. The best examples are at Dawlish, where great arches and stacks line the coast, along which rumble the regular trains on Brunel's magnificent South Devon Railway. This line provides a scenic and restful return journey for the Exe Estuary run (Run 11) which heads out from historic Exeter Quay, taking in tranquil canal and estuary trails before tackling a steep climb and descent to a walkway above waves which reach almost your feet at high tide along the seafronts at Dawlish and Teignmouth. From Exmouth, on the opposite side of the estuary, the Jurassic coast stretches 96 miles eastwards to Old Harry Rocks near Swanage in Dorset, its cliffs documenting 180 million years of geological history.

The breathtaking coastline and varied inland landscape of this area has understandably excited many race organisers,

10

12

11

keen to test runners on its challenging terrain. Local club Axe Valley Runners host one of the most famous races in the south west, The Grizzly, held each spring over "twentyish muddy, hilly, boggy, beachy miles of the multiest-terrain running experience you will find this side of the end of time". This quirky race started as an 8-mile race from Beer Head in 1988 and has become something of a legend, with entry now only by lottery. The Exe to Axe 20-mile race is one of only a dozen or so fell races held each year in the south west (compared with several hundred in the north). It traverses the coast from Exmouth to Seaton (or some years in the opposite direction) with spectacular running, big climbs and descents and uninterrupted Devon scenery. Further inland, the Bicton Blister is a popular 10-mile multi-terrain race held on Woodbury Common in November and organised by the Exmouth Harriers.

The East Devon section of the Jurassic Coast falls within the East Devon Area of Outstanding Natural Beauty, a landscape characterised by tranquil woodland, vast areas of heathland, rolling grassy hills, fertile river valleys, breathtaking coastal views and dramatic clifftops. The East Devon Way (see Run 148) is a 40 mile route which samples much of this varied natural landscape. The Blackdown Hills AONB covers much of the border between east Devon and Somerset, a beautiful and remote landscape characterised by steep ridges, high plateaux and wooded valleys, networked by quiet country lanes and winding footpaths. Run 12 takes in a wonderfully varied loop, following the babbling River Yarty at its start and finish, interspersed with some of the area's highest hills.

Woodbury Common is an expanse of heathland, crisscrossed by many tracks waiting to be explored. The commons have far-reaching views over the Devon countryside and out to the sea towards Budleigh – indeed this position was utilised by the builders of Woodbury Castle, used first as an Iron Age hillfort, then as a Napoleonic lookout. The lovely Run 10 starts and finishes in the village of East Budleigh, climbing up to the commons and joining the East Devon Way before returning down a thrilling descent through coniferous and deciduous woodland.

12

Exeter & East Devon

10 EAST DEVON HEATHLANDS

Distance:	9 miles (15km)
Start/finish:	Sir Walter Raleigh Inn, East Budleigh, EX9 7ED
Terrain:	Path, track, trail, quiet road
Toughness:	Moderate
Ascent:	295 metres
Navigation:	Moderate
Good for:	History, views, woodland
Route info:	wildrunning.net/10

A fine run which starts and finishes in the pretty village of East Budleigh, climbing to the Pebble Bed commons with their wonderfully runnable network of paths and fantastic views over the surrounding countryside to the sea. Take the lane opposite the pub and follow up hill to Hayes Barton. Take footpath R, following fields and tracks through Yettington and up onto the Pebble Bed commons. Follow main track past Iron Age hill fort at Woodbury Castle to join East Devon Way. ⚠ Note two road crossings. Continue on the East Devon Way to loop back around to the B3180, descending from the common until you can turn L, leaving the Way to return to East Budleigh.

11 EXE ESTUARY

Distance:	16 miles (25km)
Start:	The Quay, Exeter, EX2 4AN
Finish:	Teignmouth sea front
Terrain:	Trail, Coast Path, road, path
Toughness:	Easy to moderate
Ascent:	231 metres
Navigation:	Easy
Good for:	Coast, families, wildlife
Route info:	wildrunning.net/11

This run follows the Exe from bustling Exeter to Dawlish. Pleasant canal-side running becomes a glorious winding pathway with stunning estuarine views, ending in an exciting run along the sea wall in Teignmouth. From Exeter quay on south side of river follow the canal towpath SE past the Double Locks pub. Cross main road at pedestrian crossing and continue along R side of canal to Turf Locks pub. Follow estuary to pedestrian level crossing with ⚠ fast, frequent trains and continue through Starcross and Dawlish before following Coast Path signs to Teignmouth. Catch a train ride along Brunel's masterpiece back to Exeter.

12 BLACKDOWN HILLS

Distance:	9 miles (14.5km)
Start/finish:	Kilmington village hall car park, EX13 7QZ
Terrain:	Track, trail, field, road
Toughness:	Moderate
Ascent:	279 metres
Navigation:	Moderate
Good for:	Views, history
Route info:	wildrunning.net/12

A peaceful and scenic run in the lush depths of the Blackdown Hills. From Kilmington head N crossing A35 ⚠ and continuing up lane for ½ mile. Turn R onto footpath and follow to cross River Yarty. Turn L to follow river NW to reach Yarty Farm. Turn L onto lane, recrossing river and following lanes towards Beacon Hill. Take footpath to pass S of Beacon Hill, crossing lane to pass Horner Hill on footpaths and quiet lanes, heading generally S to reach Danes Hill. Head E to recross river Yarty at Beckford Bridge, turning R to rejoin outward route and return to start. Alternatively continue on wonderfully tranquil lanes back to Kilmington.

13 Dartmeet Bridge near Princetown

Dartmoor

The open expanses of Dartmoor offer an entirely different world of adventure from the pretty, coastal routes of the South Hams. Well-worn tracks lead through windswept moorland and past ancient granite tors. The summit of High Willhays, the highest point on the moor at 621 metres, is the often mist-shrouded mid-point of an unforgettable tour of the wild and remote north moor, and is an iconic route for the runner (Run 14). The Princetown circular (Run 13) is a bracing, circular run, high on the vast open moorlands. By contrast, the south moor, with its picturesque views of the English Riviera, provides the setting for one of the most exhilarating runs in the area, along the Templer Way (Run 15).

The Templer Way trail is named after the Templer family, builders of the Haytor Granite Tramway and canal, which once carried quarried stone via the most direct route from Dartmoor to the coast at Teignmouth. From the springy grass of the open moorland to interesting rights of way, permissive paths and quiet country lanes to the sea, it's a predominantly downhill run with some fast descents and a wide range of stunning scenery including woodland trails, river valleys and canal workings, finishing along the foreshore of the Teign estuary, at Newton Abbot.

I first ran the Templer Way early one summer morning, tackling it the hard way, in reverse from coast to peak. After a short section of road leaving Newton Abbot, I was into the country, skipping along narrow, winding wooded trails, leaping fallen branches, brushing my legs through stinging nettles and ferns in the undergrowth on the sides of the path. At one point, I spotted a deer in this wood. I don't think it expected me to be moving so quickly, as I caught it unawares; I always see far more of these sights than I would on a walk.

Leaving the forest, I followed a couple of miles of quiet country road. Tall, deep hedges shaded me as I ran uphill until I finally

13

13

15

emerged out onto the moor itself. The short springy grass made for perfect running, even though initially it was so steep I wasn't really going much above a fast walk.

Every time I run this route, I reach the granite tramlines in a different place. The path isn't particularly distinct, but the direction is clear and you can't go far wrong. Once you reach them, the tramlines act as a perfect guide all the way to the old quarries. I like to put in a final sprint up the steep incline to the great bulk of Haytor at the very top, stopping gratefully to lean against its comforting rough walls, letting the oxygen fill my body, feeling the sharp crystals indenting my skin. After a few moments, I let gravity guide me back across open moorland toward the woods beyond and further still, just sparkling blue on the horizon, the sea. This was the really fun bit – downhill all the way home.

There are several great races here: the Dartmoor Discovery 32-mile ultra in June takes on the maze of hilly lanes which loop the moor, and the infamous 6-mile Haytor Heller sees a lung-busting ascent and breakneck descent of the hill at Haytor rocks. But Dartmoor's varying terrain offers mixed challenges for runners. Although there are some fantastically runnable parts, much of the moor, the south moor in particular, is filled with boggy, tussocky grasslands which are time consuming and uncomfortable to cross, breaking the feet and the will in equal measure. The moor's undulations, rolling and indistinct, add the extra challenge of navigational difficulty, as all features look similar. In 2010, the Original Mountain Marathon was held on Dartmoor, paying a rare visit to the south west and providing many with an unexpectedly tough challenge.

Dartmoor has plenty to keep runners and families entertained too, from scrambling on the tors to paddling in the rivers and picking bilberries. For a great day out with families, visit Lydford and the deep and beautiful, tree-lined ravine of Lydford Gorge. This is the area's deepest gorge and stretches about 1½ miles from the Devil's Cauldron whirlpool to the White Lady Waterfall, offering much to discover, including a lovely 3-mile run around its winding paths.

Dartmoor

13 PRINCETOWN CIRCULAR

Distance:	7 miles (11km)
Start/finish:	Plume of Feathers pub, Princetown, PL20 6QQ
Terrain:	Moorland tracks and lanes
Toughness:	Easy to moderate
Ascent:	187 metres
Navigation:	Easy to moderate
Good for:	History, moorland
Route info:	wildrunning.net/13

This heady, circular run, high on the vast open moorlands of some of the most remote areas of Dartmoor, follows the obvious track S from the car park of the Plume of Feathers pub, past the campsite, and up and over South Hessary Tor. Reaching a main path, bear L then R onto a lane. The lane becomes a moorland track, climbing through the remnants of Bronze Age history past ancient settlements and stone circles to Swincombe, before turning left onto the Dartmoor Way. This takes you back into Princetown, passing the Crock of Gold cairn and kistvaen (Bronze Age grave), one of the best preserved on the moor. ⚠ Navigation may be challenging if visibility is poor

14 HIGH WILLHAYS & YES TOR

Distance:	8 miles (12km)
Start/finish:	Meldon Reservoir car park, near EX20 4LU
Terrain:	Path, open moorland, bog
Toughness:	Moderate
Ascent:	467 metres
Navigation:	Moderate
Good for:	Moorland, summits, views
Route info:	wildrunning.net/14

This wonderful run takes in the highest point in England south of the Peak District, climbing gradually to the summit before crossing to the slightly lower Yes Tor with its panoramic views. Starting at the N end of Meldon Reservoir, cross the dam to follow the southern shore. Cross the footbridge and follow the E bank of West Okement river for just under a mile until the rocks of Black Tor appear up to your left. Make your way up to these and to the summit of High Willhays in the E. Then head N to the summit and trig point of Yes Tor, where a clear path leads down to a track along the E slopes of Longstone Hill to the start. ⚠ Military training area - check activity times with tourist information before running.

15 TEMPLER WAY

Distance:	17½ miles (28km)
Start:	Haytor Visitor Centre, TQ13 9XT
Finish:	Teignmouth
Terrain:	Moorland, trail, road
Toughness:	Easy to moderate
Ascent:	250 metres
Navigation:	Easy (waymarked)
Good for:	Moorland, woodland, coast
Route info:	wildrunning.net/15

Exhilarating run with breathtaking views, following the old winding granite tramway through woodland and river valleys, passing old quays and locks and finishing along the estuary foreshore. Follow waymarkers from visitor centre, crossing road and heading R around bottom of Haytor Rocks. Descend to beautiful Yarner Wood, to join main road at Edgemoor Hotel. Continue on original tramway through Brimley to the Ventiford Basin, through Stover Park and along quiet lanes. Follow Stover canal to Newton Abbot town quay then on to Teign estuary path to Teignmouth. ⚠ Only run the estuary path at low tide or take local lanes. Return by bus via Newton Abbot to Bovey Tracey.

Hartland

North Devon & Exmoor

Exmoor National Park covers 267 square miles of unique and varied landscape, including open moors and farmland, peaceful lakes, lush wooded hills, clear gushing streams winding their way through steep valleys and towering cliffs plunging into the Bristol Channel below. As a result, the running here is extraordinarily diverse, from tough, tussocky moorland and technically challenging coast path to gentle, gravelly cycleways, perfect for family days out.

Exmoor hosts many local races including the Exmoor Stagger (15 miles) and the Exmoor Stumble (6 miles), both of which start from Minehead, the Doone Run (10 miles) from Lynmouth and the Exmoor stage of the Endurancelife coastal trail series (10km, half/full marathon and ultra). The UK Ironman 70.3 is held annually in June at Wimbleball, with a fantastic dawn swim in the lake, a savage bike course on the hilly roads surrounding the area and a fine half marathon through the woods, over the dam and around the lakeside's many winding paths. Sir Ranulph Fiennes famously trained for many of his expeditions on Exmoor's tough terrain.

The island of Lundy sits in the Bristol Channel, 12 miles from the coast of north Devon. A solid lump of granite more than 50 million years old, it measures just 3 miles in length and ¾ mile across. Rich in wildlife, it is home to thousands of seabirds, including the chatty, clown-like puffins which, it is suggested, give the island its name, the old Norse word for puffin being *lundi*. Seals roll in the surf at the foot of sheer cliffs, and deer, Soay sheep and wild goats graze all over the island. There are 23 buildings ranging from lighthouse to manor house in which visitors can stay, and a campsite near the only pub, the Marisco

16

17

18

Tavern, which serves food all day, from huge bowls of steaming porridge in the morning to local produce in the evening. Running along the trail that carves its way along Lundy's longitudinal midline, I spotted a herd of Sika deer, watching me warily, their coats a soft dun against the autumn grasses. There isn't a huge choice of run routes on Lundy, the main out-and-back (Run 16) being the most obvious and straightforward, but the unique feel and setting of the place makes it a special, and definitely wild, place to run.

The north-Devon section of the South West Coast Path winds its way along rugged cliffs and up and down steep wooded gorges, past the towns of Lynton and Lynmouth with their resident goats, and out to the green and tranquil surrounds of Hartland (Run 17). We visited this area in autumn when the hedges were laden with blackberries, and flocks of geese, skuas and shearwaters filled the air, migrating south. Setting out early, admiring views out across the sea to Lundy, we made our way down through dew-soaked fields to the Coast Path and then scrambled down a steep, rocky gully. We emerged onto a deserted pebble beach, all greys and golds in the still-early misty air, and ran along strange rocky fingers reaching out towards the roaring sea, jumping rock pools and skidding on seaweed. These great, layered rocks, formed 320 million years ago, buckled under the forces of the two great continents of Laurasia and Pangaea colliding, forming the striking chevron-shaped rock formations that line this part of the coast.

On Exmoor, one of our favourite runs winds its way through the lush and romantic wooded valley of Heddon, beloved by Wordsworth, Coleridge and Shelley (Run 18). Nearby Wimbleball Lake has a 9-mile loop providing wonderfully scenic and varied running through woodland and across the towering dam. The path is also suitable for bikes, and there is a great variety of water and other sports available to entertain the family. Away from the rugged challenges of moorland and coast path, North Devon's Tarka Trail, which follows sections of disused railway line between Ilfracombe and Meeth, is a predominantly flat, paved trail and great for family days out on the bike.

North Devon & Exmoor

16 LUNDY

Distance:	5 miles (8km)
Start/finish:	The Marisco Tavern, Lundy Island, EX39 2LY
Terrain:	Trail, track
Toughness:	Easy
Ascent:	110 metres
Navigation:	Easy
Good for:	Coast, wildlife
Route info:	wildrunning.net/16

Lundy Island is a mere two-hour boat trip from the Devon mainland and was Britain's first statutory Marine Nature Reserve. This lovely, gentle run takes you straight along the centre of the island. Head N from the Tavern on the main path along the length of the island until reaching Lundy North lighthouse. Return the same way, enjoying a second glimpse of the magnificent coastal scenery, rare wildlife and feeling of being entirely removed from normal life. This run is especially beautiful with the backdrop of a spectacular sunrise or sunset. An alternative 10-mile (16km) loop of the island takes in Lundy's two surprisingly contrasting coasts. The island is free from access restrictions, so runners are free to roam wild.

17 HARTLAND POINT

Distance:	6½ miles (10km)
Start/finish:	Hartland Quay car park, EX39 6DU
Terrain:	Coast Path, footpath, road
Toughness:	Moderate to challenging
Ascent:	433 metres
Navigation:	Moderate
Good for:	Coast, views, geology
Route info:	wildrunning.net/17

This circular run starts and finishes on Hartland Quay with its impressive rock formations, and takes in the stunning Coast Path, unusual geology and abundance of flora and fauna of this area. A scrambly detour down to Blegberry Beach, with its sandy channels and clear, anemone-filled rockpools, is well worth the effort. From Rocket House, near to the attendant's hut at Hartland Quay, follow the Coast Path E then N, passing Hartland Point with its lighthouse. On reaching a car park below radar station tower, bear R up a lane. Pass heliport and follow signs to Blegberry, then Stoke. Pass L of the church, before following the footpath through fields and back to Hartland Quay.

18 HEDDON VALLEY

Distance:	6 miles (9km)
Start/finish:	The Hunters Inn, Heddon Valley, EX31 4PY
Terrain:	Coast Path, woodland trail
Toughness:	Moderate
Ascent:	488 metres
Navigation:	Easy
Good for:	Coast, wildlife, history
Route info:	wildrunning.net/18

This run takes in sensational coastal views, ancient oak woodlands and a Roman fortlet. There are vast numbers of sea birds along the coast, and buzzards and peregrines can be spotted wheeling high above. From The Hunters Inn follow the bridleway that runs alongside. Follow signs through woodland towards Woody Bay along a wide track called The Carriageway. Continue up onto the headland to be greeted by glorious views across the Bristol Channel to Lundy Island and Wales. Continue to follow signs for Woody Bay, following a quiet road until reaching a South West Coast Path sign on the left signposted to Hunters Inn. Follow the Coast Path back to the start.

Quantock Hills

Wiltshire & Somerset

Meaning 'the land of the summer people', Somerset is a county of great contrasts, from the wild moorland and wooded valleys of Exmoor in the far west, through the Blackdown and Quantock Hills and across the open grasslands of the Somerset Levels to the Mendips and the great limestone gorge at Cheddar. The Levels and Moors is a sparsely populated ancient coastal plain, abundant in history and wildlife. The are is mainly flat grass and wetland, punctuated by the former islands of Glastonbury Tor and the wonderfully-named Burrow Mump.

The Mendip Hills reach across Somerset from Frome in the east to Brean Down in the west. From steep, winding tracks to gentle slopes, the rewards for climbing to the tops are panoramic views out across the Levels. The grassy summits are interspersed by deep gorges filled with ancient woodland. The many paths which network the hills make them a perfect place for exploration. Run 20 takes in Mendip's woodland, grassy ridges and two of the most picturesque peaks in the area.

Wiltshire, in contrast, is characterised by high downlands and wide valleys, dominated by the great chalk plateau of Salisbury Plain. With 2,300 prehistoric sites and long history of military use, this is a vast expanse of grassland, often feeling wild and desolate, yet perfect for running (Run 19). The Megalithic stone circle at Avebury is the finishing point of the infamous Ridgeway Challenge, which is held annually on August bank holiday and challenges runners to complete the 95 miles and 2,743 metres of ascent from Ivinghoe Beacon in Hertfordshire.

The Quantock Hills run from the Vale of Taunton Deane in the south for about 15 miles to Quantoxhead on the Bristol Channel. This was England's first AONB, and boasts incredibly diverse landscapes of heathland, oak woodlands, ancient parklands and agricultural land. On a clear day, from the highest point at Wills Neck it is possible to see Glastonbury Tor to the

21

20

21

east, the Gower Peninsula to the north, Exmoor to the west and the Blackdown Hills to the south. The hills have been sculpted by their occupation since prehistoric times with Bronze Age round barrows and Iron Age hill forts marking the hillsides. The Quantock Hills Greenway is a 38-mile waymarked route taking a figure of eight around the area's beautiful and varied landscape. Run 21 takes in the northern half of the route. This can also be linked up with the West Somerset Coast Path and the Coleridge Way. This latter trail, walked by the poet Samuel Taylor Coleridge, is a 36-mile trail from Nether Stowey on the Quantocks finishing on the steep, 2½ mile descent to Porlock on Exmoor. It covers much of western Somerset's beautiful countryside and provides some excellent running.

The Parrett Trail is a 50-mile route following the River Parrett to Bridgwater Bay, where it joins the West Somerset Coast Path. Lonely and desolate at its conclusion at Steart Point, the Trail winds its way along riverside tracks, through (often muddy) fields, crossing drainage ditches common in this floodland area. The annual Parrett Trail Relays are held each October and see many local running clubs vying for the win and the coveted Eel trophy over its six-stages, the final (hilliest and highest-pressure) stage finishing sociably at the pub in Winyard's Gap, by the river's source at Chedington, in Dorset.

We visited the Quantocks in midsummer when the trees and grassy hillsides blazed bright green against a deep blue sky. Winding our way through the lanes outside Bridgwater we eventually started to climb up a long, leafy lane bordered by a sheer and sizeable drop. Reaching the top, we ran through sparkling, dappled woodlands where the sun made zebra stripes of the trees on the path ahead of us. Emerging from the woods onto open heathland dotted with grazing ponies, we picked up the pace and raced to the nearest summit, marked by a plateau of boulders. As we stood there, a Chinook helicopter rose over the hills and thunked its heavy passage across the valley below us. We watched until it vanished from sight, then turned and descended fast down a track back to the woods. Turning our backs to the sun, we made our way up a steep track to Wills Neck, racing the final steps to the trig point.

21

Wiltshire & Somerset

19 SALISBURY PLAIN

Distance:	5½ miles (9km)
Start/finish:	Car park at start of Chitterne Road, Tilshead, near SP3 4SB
Terrain:	Gravel track, grassy path
Toughness:	Easy
Navigation:	Easy to moderate
Ascent:	92 metres
Good for:	History, views
Route info:	wildrunning.net/19

Salisbury Plain is a strange, yet often, in its own way, beautiful landscape with superb running along tracks and trails through grassy chalklands. This run also passes near prehistoric long barrows, and a replica village and mock shanty town, used for military training (not open to the public). From the car park near the Tilshead end of Chittern Rd, follow the Imber Range Perimeter Path south, keeping the military training facility on your L. Return on path towards White Barrow and back to Tilshead. ⚠ This is within a military training area, but no live ammunition is used, so it is safe and legal to run on the land. Do not interrupt soldiers or touch any equipment.

20 MENDIPS – CROOK PEAK

Distance:	6½ miles (10km)
Start/finish:	Car park S of Compton Bishop
Terrain:	Field, path
Toughness:	Moderate
Ascent:	310 metres
Navigation:	Easy to moderate
Good for:	Ascents, descents, woodland
Route info:	wildrunning.net/20

Running on the Mendips is a wonderful experience: the short-cropped, springy grasses form clear ridge-top paths, with valleys either side carpeted in flowers in spring and early summer. From the car park on the main road W from Compton Bishop, cross the road, through fields and scrubland down to the village. Follow quiet lanes past the village church. Take track to base of Wavering Down, then through fields to village of Cross, turning L after a short road section to run through woodland at King's Wood. The route then ascends to the trig point at the top of Wavering Down and continues straight over Compton Hill and on to Crook Peak. A fantastic long descent, through limestone outcrops, brings you back to the start.

21 QUANTOCK HILLS GREENWAY

Distance:	19 miles (31km)
Start/finish:	Triscombe Stone car park, ½ mile NE of Triscombe, TA4 3HE
Terrain:	Trail, open moorland, quiet road
Toughness:	Moderate
Ascent:	891 metres
Navigation:	Easy (waymarked)
Good for:	Coast, woodland
Route info:	wildrunning.net/21

The 19-mile northern route of the Quantock Greenway enjoys green lanes, open moorland and woodland trails, with some sections winding along quiet country lanes. From the car park, head SW down lane to reach track junction. Head R, following waymarkers around the W edge of the hills, then continuing to follow waymarkers in a clockwise direction to loop the hills, returning to the car park. A shorter run takes 4 miles (6.5km) around Kilve, which follows some of the magnificent coast around East Quantoxhead and the wonderfully atmospheric, fossil-strewn Kilve Beach.

Clifton Suspension Bridge

Bristol & Bath

The city of Bath nestles in a sheltered valley surrounded by easily-accessed wooded hills and magnificent countryside, ripe for exploring. It is a UNESCO World Heritage Site, rich in Roman and Georgian heritage. The Kennet and Avon Canal runs to the heart of the city, winding its way past picturesque Cotswold villages with their honeyed stone cottages, to the small but perfectly-formed town of Bradford on Avon: an enjoyable run on the tow path, with lots of interest and easy access to trains at either end, and several stations en route. The Bath Skyline is a National Trust-maintained waymarked trail which tours the open spaces above the city, its views reaching out past the city to the rolling hills beyond. This run (Run 22) winds its way through hidden limestone valleys, meadows carpeted with flowers, and tranquil beech woodlands. The running is at times surprisingly challenging with some rough, steep ground; however, on reaching those hard-won high points, you are rewarded with breathtaking panoramas which open out beneath your feet as the sound of skylarks fills the air. The route also passes an Iron Age fort, Sham Castle on the outskirts of the University grounds and Prior Park Landscape Garden. With its rare Palladian Bridge, serpentine lake and paths and caves to explore, Prior Park is a great place for a family day out. There is a Bath Skyline 10km series over the winter, organised by Relish Running Races, based at the University's Sports Training Village.

Bristol, lying across the border between Somerset and Gloucestershire, is the most populous city in the south west. Within a short distance of the centre, there is much to delight the runner wishing to escape the urban jungle. Bristol is in

61

23

24

22

a limestone area, which runs from the Mendip Hills in the south and the Cotswolds in the north east. The rivers Avon and Frome cut through this limestone to the underlying clays, creating Bristol's characteristic hilly landscape. Run 23 follows the course of the river Frome out of Bristol and into the peaceful countryside beyond, on its journey to Old Sodbury in Gloucestershire. Running in and around Bristol is generally an undulating affair, with many challenging ascents and flying descents to be found. The Avon flows through the centre of Bristol and has cut through the limestone to form the impressive Avon Gorge, whose towering faces provide an abundance of rock climbs. At the top of the gorge, also accessed from the long incline of Whiteladies Road out of the centre, lie The Downs, a large, open, grassy area crisscrossed by many paths and great for a quick escape from the city, particularly at quieter times of day. The Downs and the nearby Leigh Woods have been protected from development, and this western fringe of the city provides the best scope for running adventure. To the north of the area lies Blaise Castle, an 18th century mansion house with 650 acres of accessible Grade II registered parkland, and free parking. Further south, Ashton Court estate is set out over 850 acres of woods and open grassland, with a 14th-century deer park where large herds of red and fallow deer and some resident wild roe deer roam. Much of the park is a Site of Special Scientific Interest and is home to the 700 year-old Domesday Oak.

The Cotswold Way enters its final miles as it approaches Bath, taking in the spectacular high ground around Dyrham Park and Bath Racecourse (Run 24). This part of the Way feels especially wild and windswept, particularly on a blustery winter's day. The feeling of removal from the busy necessities of every day life is enhanced by its elevated position, from where there are views for miles around, across rolling hillsides and down to the cities of Bath and Bristol below. The descent into Bath at the end of a run on the Cotswold Way is twisting and tortuous on tired legs, but the city's splendour and the finishing plaque at the entrance to the abbey makes it worth the journey.

22

Bristol & Bath

22 BATH SKYLINE

Distance:	6 miles (9km)
Start/finish:	Bathwick Hill, BA2 6JZ
Terrain:	Track, trail, grassland, road
Toughness:	Moderate
Ascent:	215 metres
Navigation:	Easy (waymarked)
Good for:	Families, urban escape
Route info:	wildrunning.net/22

The Bath Skyline is a National Trust-maintained, well-waymarked route over some very hilly terrain through a varied and interesting selection of the green spaces around the World Heritage city of Bath. There are outstanding views over the city and surrounding countryside, an 18th-century landscape garden with eccentric yet elegant follies, and paths through leafy, peaceful woodland. To access the run, stand on Bathwick Hill with your back to Cleveland Walk, take the path opposite that goes between the houses, through a kissing gate and diagonally across the field. From this point follow the regular waymarkers until emerging from Cleveland Walk, back onto Bathwick Hill.

23 FROME VALLEY WAY

Distance:	19 miles (31km)
Start:	Bristol Castle, BS1 3XD
Finish:	Old Sodbury, South Glos
Terrain:	Pavement, track, trail, field
Toughness:	Easy
Ascent:	303 metres
Navigation:	Easy
Good for:	Urban escape, wild swimming
Route info:	wildrunning.net/23

Starting in the very heart of the city of Bristol, this pleasant run follows the course of the River Frome in its entirety to its source deep in the Cotswolds. This is a real escape route, which tackles the urban landscapes of Bristol's parks, winds through Stapleton and Frenchay, briefly following the rumbling M32 which was built over the river, before diving under the M4 and emerging into the peaceful countryside and wooded valleys near Winterbourne Down. Continue to follow the river and well-marked path as it winds through a variety of landscapes and the villages of Frampton Cotterell, Yate, the medieval town of Chipping Sodbury and finally its finish at the river's source in Old Sodbury. Hourly buses to Yate then Bristol.

24 DYRHAM & DOYNTON

Distance:	7.5 miles (11km)
Start/finish:	Dyrham Deer Park car park, SN14 8ER
Terrain:	Trail, path, road
Toughness:	Moderate
Ascent:	373 metres
Navigation:	Easy to moderate
Good for:	Families, National Trail
Route info:	wildrunning.net/24

A fantastic loop taking in some of the truly wild-feeling spaces high above Bristol and Bath on the Cotswold Way. Dyrham Park (NT) is a great place to explore with the family. From start walk towards exit and into Whitefield. Turn R and run downhill to Sands Hill Lane. Turn L and follow lane to stile on R. Head across farmland and down steps to join Cotswold Way. Turn L and follow Cotswold Way markers to cross Gorse Lane ⚠. Leave Cotswold Way at Pennsylvania, turning R before the road and heading NW to Doynton to join the signed Monarch's Way. Follow this N until track junction allows R turn to return to Dyrham Park.

The Undercliff

Dorset

There are so few occasions in modern life when it is not possible to escape, to give up, give in, go home. The lack of options to quit, surely, must be one of the qualities of a place or a situation that is truly wild? "To find yourself...", as writer Primo Levi described it "...in the most ancient of human conditions, facing blind, deaf stone alone, with nothing to help you but your own hands and your own head." This feeling has found me several times: on long routes, both climbing and running, or in the middle of a long swim, far from the shore. This is when the situation seems so removed from daily life that I become completely alone and present only in the world I inhabit in that moment. There are no experts or search engines to consult, no one to hand over or delegate duties to. Nature is relentless and unyielding, taking no account of our history or place in society. At this point, we humans are all equal in terms of material wealth, reduced to our sinews and our instincts. This utter aloneness, this self-reliant state that could be called Wild, can be found in many places in Britain, both in the more obvious challenges of remote islands and mountains and in other, more surprising places where the situation feels precarious and escape is not an option.

Due to its other-worldly nature, completely removed from the seaside bustle of its bordering towns, and its hostile inescapability, the Undercliff at Lyme Regis, formed by a long history of landslips between Axmouth and Lyme Regis, has been described as being such a wild place by, amongst others, the great Roger Deakin. The path changes slightly each year, winding its way through the dense tangle of greenery, along cliff edges, steep steps and beside crevasses filled with bright green pools. A serious undertaking in its own way, the path is generally inescapable for this entire section of the South West Coast Path (Run 25).

25

27

27

John Fowles moved to a remote farm here in 1965 and, haunted by the image of a woman on the Cobb at Lyme Regis, staring out to sea, wrote *The French Lieutenant's Woman*. He describes his relationship with the Undercliff:

"I treasure it myself for its solitudes, its sheer beauty, its exuberance of growth, its memories of very different pasts and cultures. It is not for me primarily a fascinating area geologically, or a wonderful nature reserve, but quite simply one of those places one always thinks of as one does a poem or a piece of music; not quite of this world, or, of this world as it should be, but alas so largely isn't."

Dorset offers an incredible range of running, from the South West Coast Path which tours along its Jurassic coast, overlooking the wave-hewn limestone sculptures such as the great arch of Durdle Door, to the steep slopes of Golden Cap, which seem to rise straight out of the sea. The South Dorset Ridgeway, a former inland section of the Coast Path which is now a spectacular route in its own right (Run 27), is a fascinating place filled with history. This route takes in much of the diversity of the Ridgeway, showcasing its stunning landscape and fascinating history, from the ghostly White Horse to Iron Age hill forts and Neolithic barrows. Captain Hardy's Monument marks the highest point of the Ridgeway. This area has inspired many, including Thomas Hardy, who wove descriptions of this beautiful landscape throughout his work. Run 26 takes in another section of the Coast Path, round Portland's peninsula and part of the spit of Chesil Beach.

There are many wonderfully named races in Dorset, including the Stickler in October, the Puddletown Plod in June, The Beast in September and the Dorset Doddle 32-mile ultra (a walking event but runners are welcome) in August. Race organisers VO2 hold their Jurassic Coast Challenge here, taking in three tough, off-road marathons over three consecutive days from Charmouth, to Shell Bay, on the Studland peninsula. The tough but incredibly scenic Purbeck Marathon, first held in 2012, is run from Swanage in the autumn.

Dorset

25 THE UNDERCLIFF

Distance:	7 miles (12 km)
Start:	SW Coast Path, Seaton seafront
Finish:	SW Coast Path, Lyme Regis
Terrain:	Coast Path, clay
Toughness:	Moderate to challenging
Ascent:	311 metres
Navigation:	Easy (waymarked)
Good for:	Coast, wild
Route info:	wildrunning.net/25

A unique, surprisingly challenging run, passing through the Axmouth to Lyme Regis Undercliffs National Nature Reserve, a highlight of the Jurassic Coast. This is a wild area of landslides, rocky coastline and lush vegetation. It is a delightful route in spring, when the woodland is carpeted with bluebells and the air is filled with birdsong and the heady scent of wild garlic. From Seaton seafront follow Coast Path signs up a steep track, across a golf course and along a lane until reaching the Undercliff. Follow the coast path on technical, vegetated terrain, emerging high above the sea at Lyme Regis. ⚠ If continuing: there are no exit paths off the Undercliff until reaching Lyme Regis.

26 TOUR OF PORTLAND

Distance:	12½ miles (20km)
Start/finish:	Chesil Visitor Centre, DT4 9XE
Terrain:	Coast Path, trail, shingle beach
Toughness:	Easy to moderate
Ascent:	422 metres
Navigation:	Easy
Good for:	Coast
Route info:	wildrunning.net/26

Due to its prominent position on the south coast, the Isle of Portland is scarred by many years of military presence and quarrying for its much sought-after white limestone. Yet, despite this, it retains many natural riches, from abundant wildlife to rugged cliffs and hidden coves. The long shingle ridge of Chesil Beach provides tough but interesting running at the start and finish. Park at the visitor centre car park, by Ferrybridge. Tour along the coast path on fantastic, runnable paths with breathtaking scenery for much of the way. Follow the pebbly spit of Chesil Beach SE until reaching the SW Coast Path signs and the island of Portland itself. Follow well-defined paths around the perimeter of the island, returning either back along the beach, or the road and cycle way.

27 THE SOUTH DORSET RIDGEWAY

Distance:	13½ miles (21km)
Start:	The Sunray, Osmington, DT3 6EU
Finish:	Abbotsbury, DT3 4JR
Terrain:	Trail, grass
Toughness:	Easy
Ascent:	499 metres
Navigation:	Easy (waymarked)
Good for:	History
Route info:	wildrunning.net/27

The Ridgeway itself was the route of the original South West Coast Path, which now runs through Weymouth instead. Although inland, this is a peaceful, rural alternative and a fine run with spectacular views. From the pub, head N through the village, emerging to run across fields and climb up to White Horse Hill. On reaching the ridge, head W, following the clear, treeless ridge and the Ridgeway waymarkers. Head S on reaching White Hill to descend to the pretty village of Abbotsbury. The local delicacy, Dorset apple cake, makes for a great post-run treat. Occasional buses run from Abbotsbury straight back to Osmington.

Beachy Head

South & East

From the grand parks of London's buzzing metropolis to the desolate expanses of the Essex marshlands, rolling Kent downs and dramatic coastlines, England's south east holds a fantastic variety of landscapes. In peaceful East Anglia, the flat wilds of Norfolk's Broads give way to Suffolk's picturesque countryside and pebble beaches.

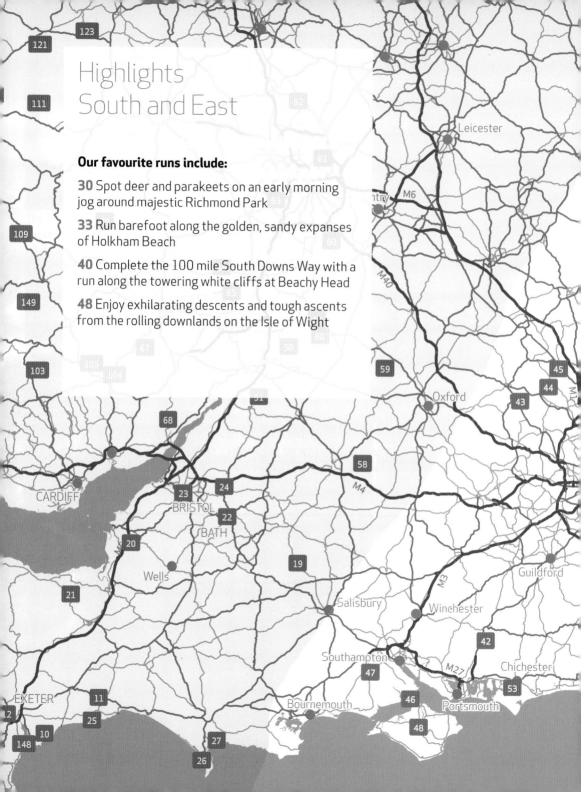

Highlights
South and East

Our favourite runs include:

30 Spot deer and parakeets on an early morning jog around majestic Richmond Park

33 Run barefoot along the golden, sandy expanses of Holkham Beach

40 Complete the 100 mile South Downs Way with a run along the towering white cliffs at Beachy Head

48 Enjoy exhilarating descents and tough ascents from the rolling downlands on the Isle of Wight

Richmond Park

London & Essex

Away from –or sometimes even hidden within– the hustle and bustle of the city, the potential for escape to beautiful and runnable places from London and its surrounding areas is often surprising. Hundreds of parks and green spaces filled with unexpected flora and fauna, ancient woodlands, salt marshes and historical intrigue lie within an hour's journey of the centre. A well-timed visit, avoiding the prime times for the commuting and sight-seeing masses, opens up a whole new world of exciting places to run.

Discovering Run 30, I stayed with friends in nearby Putney, catching a train to swanky Richmond to jog up the long hill through its railinged streets to the park. My first glimpse of the place was just as the morning mist had begun to rise through the trees, the warm, autumnal hues of the leaves ignited by the early sun into a blaze of scarlets and golds. The chilly morning air held scents of coffee and fresh bread mingled with the grassy, horsey tones of the park. Deer grazed in plain sight of the gate and I stopped for a few moments just to watch them, to feel their gentle peace, so close to the city's endless roar. Running along the 7-mile Tamsin Trail, the gravelly path crunching pleasantly beneath my feet, lost in my own world, the monotone drone of overhead jets was the only reminder of my proximity to the capital. Switching off the nagging voices of my training schedule, my weekend itinerary and yet another looming deadline, I spent an idyllic hour following this gentle trail around the very edge of Richmond Park, taking in everything it showed me, leaving the exploring to another day and simply being in and enjoying each moment.

29

30

30

Epping Forest covers 10 square miles of ancient woodland, heathland, grassland and wetlands, bordering the north-eastern edge of greater London and Essex. There are many trails and paths to explore within the Forest itself and the surrounding area. The Forest Way (Run 29) is a well signed, 25 mile route which takes in ancient forest, rolling countryside and part of the historic network of green lanes. It is a true urban escape, starting at Loughton underground station and heading straight into the woods, passing many points of historical interest, from the Iron Age hill fort of Loughton Camp to the ruins of the former medieval manor of Copthall (Copped Hall).

Further out of town is the Dengie Peninsula (Run 28), to the east of Chelmsford and formed by the tidal rivers of the Crouch to the south and the Blackwater to the north. The North Sea edges the east of the peninsula, creating the great expanses of the Dengie salt marshes. A flat, sparsely populated area, this is a place where sky, land and sea often seem to stretch endlessly in all directions. The area has a rich history from Iron Age settlers to Roman fort-builders and the Saxons who gave the peninsula its name. A military airfield existed here from 1942–1945, the remains of which can still be seen, and the long sea wall is punctuated with pillboxes, defending the land from invasion via the sea. There are some fine runs across beautiful countryside that often feels remote and other-wordly, particularly when bordered by the sea on three sides. Dotted around the area are pretty, weather-boarded villages separated by stretches of farmland and edged by vast, flat salt marshes – a haven for wildfowl.

There are many great races to be found in and around the capital, from the obvious challenges of the London Marathon and British 10km to many races, on and off-road, held in its parks and green spaces. The 50km Royal Parks Ultra in October is a recent but popular addition to the ultra calendar, along with the revived London to Brighton race, now an off-road challenge on trails and footpaths, held in September. Capital Runners organise a 10km race series in Bushy Park and Richmond Park, perfect for a traffic-free Sunday morning outing.

London & Essex

28 BRADWELL COCKLESPIT

Distance:	6 miles (10km)
Start/finish:	East End Road, Bradwell-on-Sea, CM0 7PW
Terrain:	Sea wall, mudflat, track, trail
Toughness:	Easy
Ascent:	29 metres
Navigation:	Easy to moderate
Good for:	Coast, wildlife, urban escape
Route info:	wildrunning.net/28

Looping the Dengie Peninsula, this run has a wild, remote and isolated feel. Flat expanses of agricultural land and salt marshes sweep away in all directions, with spectacular views across to the Maldon salt marshes and the watery horizons of the North Sea, kept from claiming the land by the sea wall. The run passes the disused Bradwell nuclear power plant, pale and innocuous. From the car park follow lane NE to reach the sea. Turn L, following waymarkers along the exposed sea wall anticlockwise around the peninsula. On reaching the Green Man Pub, cross over the road to locate waymarker, heading SE across fields to reach Bradwell. The main village road leads back to East End Road and the car park.

29 THE FOREST WAY

Distance:	25 miles (40km)
Start:	Loughton tube stn, IG10 4PD
Finish:	Hatfield Forest Park
Terrain:	Pavement, woodland path, track
Toughness:	Easy
Ascent:	369 metres
Navigation:	Easy (waymarked)
Good for:	Woodland, families, urban escape
Route info:	wildrunning.net/29

This run covers the historic hunting grounds of Epping and Hatfield Forests, along picturesque forest tracks and meandering trails through the rolling Essex countryside. From Loughton station, head N up Station Rd and then Forest Rd. Cross into Epping Forest, following waymarked footpaths past Loughton Camp. Continue to follow signs N, crossing the M25 to reach the peaceful Copthall Green. A wonderful section through fields and green lanes leads to Parndon Wood reserve. Enter Latton Wood before joining Latton and Harlow commons. Head E at Hobbs Cross on field paths to Matching Tye. The Way ends at Hatfield Forest. Train from Bishops Stortford.

30 TAMSIN TRAIL, RICHMOND PARK

Distance:	7 miles (11km)
Start/finish:	Richmond Park, TW10 5HS any entrance
Terrain:	Path
Toughness:	Easy
Ascent:	113 metres
Navigation:	Easy
Good for:	Urban escape, families
Route info:	wildrunning.net/30

This gentle jaunt around picturesque Richmond Park is one of the most straightforward routes, following the perimeter, and equally enjoyable in either direction. From any of the main entrances, join the Tamsin Trail, clearly signed as it crosses your path, heading left and right. There are plenty of opportunities to leave the track and explore grassy trails through the woods, lakes and rolling parkland. From King Henry's Mound, near to Pembroke Lodge, there is a fine, protected view all the way to St Paul's Cathedral. Cafés and ice-cream sellers are plentiful, and the affluent areas surrounding the park are abundant with places to relax and refuel post-run. The park closes at dusk.

Holkham Beach

Norfolk

The relentless erosion of the soft chalk and clay earth of the East Anglia coast by the North Sea is a concerning prospect; since the North Sea flood of 1953, millions of pounds have been spent on building flood defences to keep the people and land safe. Yet, the specific conditions on this part of the coast, with its expansive network of rivers and lakes, grazing marshes, reed beds and wet woodlands, have also created the Broads, a beautiful, protected area abundant with wildlife. Once thought to be natural features, the Broads were in fact created as a result of medieval peat excavations by the local monasteries - the cathedral alone taking some 320,000 tons of peat per year. The signature landscape of this area lends itself to running that, in its own way, feels uniquely wild.

My early memories of Norfolk are of caravanning with my grandparents: long days running around the golden expanse of Holkham Beach (Run 33), digging through the clean yellow sand to the oily messiness below, iron-smelling seaweed between my toes, evenings filled with laughter, spearing dressed crab and vinegary cockles with a toothpick, sides of brown bread and butter, bedtime in the caravan with the wind gusting outside and the roar of the gas lamp with its kerosene smell. And bright, clear mornings barefoot in the dewy grass with fat grey pigeons cooing loudly from the trees. When we arrived back, after an absence of nearly 30 years, the first thing I did was demand to stop and buy crab from a van right by the shore. The seller was ruddy and cheery, and handed over two red-brown crabs, expertly prepared, in a brown paper bag. We sat looking out over marshes and lobster pots, boats

33

31

33

jangling gently in the breeze, and hungrily ate our sweet, crabby breakfast with our fingers – the reality even better than my memory had served.

Early next morning I set out in search of the combined miles of the Peddars Way and the Norfolk Coast Path that loop their way out and back between the coastal towns and villages that dot the coast (Run 31). I found a vast land of salt marshes, the tide out so the sea is just visible far away on the horizon. Climbing some wooden steps, I headed out onto a raised path that ran as far as I could see between the marshes, guiding travellers safely through the treacherous, boggy terrain. The path took me far out from the mainland, to a place so quiet and still that the only noise I could discern was of seabirds calling and the rhythmic crunch of my feet as they carried me along. For half an hour or more this is all I experienced, a strange, limbo world as I was guided by the path in a wide arc towards a hidden village somewhere ahead. There was no way off this path, my only options being to turn back or continue and hope that I would indeed be returned to civilization. Although my rational brain which read the map before I set out told me that it could not be much further, this did little to stop the doubts creeping in that perhaps this path might continue forever and I would be consigned to spend the rest of my days wandering the great, flat expanses of the Norfolk marshes. Presently, a windmill came into view and a branch inland led me past a field full of grazing cattle to a quiet lane and my route back to the start. The Norfolk Coast marathon and 62-mile ultramarathon take place along this fascinating stretch of coast path.

Pingos are the wonderfully-named shallow depressions found in the Brecklands of Norfolk and Suffolk. They were formed during the last Ice Age by bubbles of underground ice which expanded, forcing the soil upwards. Centuries of weathering created craters, now filled with water to create pools that teem with wildlife. Run 32 is a chance to explore the weird and wonderful pingos on a peaceful run around the wooded, sandy Breckland around Thompson Water and the nature reserve.

Local races include the North Norfolk Marathon, taking in scenic sections of the Coast Path in May.

Norfolk

31 BRANCASTER COAST & MARSH

Distance:	6 miles (10km)
Start:	The Ship Hotel, Main Road, Brancaster, PE31 8AP
Finish:	Burnham Overy Staithe
Terrain:	Trail, coast path
Toughness:	Easy
Ascent:	14 metres
Navigation:	Easy
Good for:	Coast, wildlife
Route info:	wildrunning.net/31

This run takes you through vast, flat saltmarshes before heading out for several miles of fantastic, uninterrupted running along a raised embankment. Head down Broad Lane from the church towards the sea and turn right onto the coast path. The route follows a section of the waymarked Norfolk Coast Path, just a short section of the 93-mile National Trail which links the Peddars Way with the Norfolk Coast Path. ⚠ Marshes before Burnham Deepdale may become submerged during a spring tide. Looping back inland it passes a fine windmill before arriving at the little harbour nestled at the foot of the village of Burnham Overy Staithe. Regular buses back to Brancaster.

32 GREAT EASTERN PINGO TRAIL

Distance:	7 miles (11km)
Start/finish:	Great Eastern Pingo Trail car park, Stow Beadon, near NR17 1DP
Terrain:	Track, trail
Toughness:	Easy
Ascent:	53 metres
Navigation:	Easy
Good for:	Wildlife
Route info:	wildrunning.net/32

This peaceful route on well maintained trails, including a former railway, explores the eastern edge of the Norfolk Brecks, taking in the fascinating pools of the Pingos, created during the last Ice Age. From the car park take the path straight ahead, aiming SW through woodland to a ruined cottage. Turn R onto Peddar's Way Circular Trail then R onto main Peddars Way. Pass Thompson Water before R turn into Thompson Common Nature Reserve, following waymarkers. Cross two bridges and Thompson Carr, with its resident Shetland ponies, following signs through woodland back to the start.

33 HOLKHAM BEACH

Distance:	9 miles (14km)
Start/finish:	Lady Anne's Drive, Holkham (turn opposite NR23 1RG)
Terrain:	Sandy beach, path
Toughness:	Easy
Ascent:	92 metres
Navigation:	Easy
Good for:	Coast, beach running, families
Route info:	wildrunning.net/33

A spectacular alternative to the Coast Path run between Holkham and Wells-next-the-Sea, this run simply follows the broad, white, sandy beach from where you emerge from tall pine trees on a boardwalk leading from Lady Anne's Drive down to the beach all the way to Wells. To return, winding through the streets of Wells to reach a lane into Holkham Estate, entering the estate to run through cool, peaceful woodland and past the Hall, ice house and lake to the main entrance, before returning to the start. Alternatively, either follow the wonderful beach back, running in the shallow water at the edge of the vast North Sea, or head up and down the dunes which line the beach. Other return routes can be found along the Coast Path.

Suffolk

It is said that, given a quiet day and a certain tide, the bells of the churches can still be heard echoing from the submerged old town of Dunwich on the Suffolk coast. Formerly a large and important Anglo-Saxon seat, the town and the area surrounding it, and indeed much of this stretch of the east coast have been, and continue to be, claimed piece by piece by the relentless pull of the sea. Most of the buildings that were present in the 13th-century have disappeared, including some eight churches, leaving present day Dunwich as a small coastal settlement. There remains a strong connection to the past, and the remains of a 13th century Franciscan priory and a leper hospital can still be seen.

Suffolk's quiet lanes, dotted with honesty boxes selling produce from the fertile land, wind their way through its gently rolling, green hills. A contrast from the flat lands of Norfolk, there is a comforting, familiar Englishness to the place. On our first visit here, we headed for Dunwich Heath, finding a vast heathland ablaze with a carpet of different hues of purple heather, edged with delicate silk ribbons of silver birch. We set off across the wide, open heathland (Run 34), aiming for a pine plantation on the horizon, the springy, peaty earth forming itself into many paths ahead of us as we ran. We ran for an hour, looping the heath, stopping occasionally to watch huge flocks of geese making vast V's in the sky on their September voyages to warmer climes. Our circuit complete, we headed for the beach, a long jumble of multi-coloured pebbles rolled musically by a gentle sea. Post-run, we sat and gazed out at the unchanging horizon, enjoying the massage of the stones, allowing the time to pass unhurried, an easy silence occasionally punctuated by a find of a fossil or unusual stone to show to the other.

36

34

35

The Breckland, familiarly known as The Brecks, covers an area of 392 square miles of open, gorse-covered sandy heathland and tranquil forest in the north of Suffolk and across the border into Norfolk. A haven for wildlife and a place whose heritage stretches back to the Stone Age, it is also a geologically fascinating area. There is a wealth of trail to explore on the Brecks, with several waymarked long-distance routes crossing the area, including the Icknield Way, the Angles Way and the Iceni Way. There are many circular routes, descriptions for which are available in a booklet from the Brecks Countryside Project. Or, spend a wonderful day simply exploring the many trails, paths and tearooms the area has to offer. Our Run 36 follows the route of the River Ouse through the tranquil Thetford Forest.

The Stour Valley Path is a 62-mile waymarked footpath starting in Newmarket, Suffolk, and ending in Cattawade, Essex. Linking the Icknield Way with Sudbury and the Essex Way, the path passes through an area of beauty and tranquillity that inspired many of the great works of the English landscape painters. Run 35 passes through much of the equally picturesque scenery of the Suffolk countryside., finishing at the grassy mound of Clare Castle.

The Stour Valley Path 100 Ultra Run, held in August, covers almost the entire length of the well-marked trail, and is one of the longest point-to-point races in East Anglia. The winning men complete the course in around 10 hours and the women in 13–14 hours. There are many road races in Suffolk, taking advantage of the many miles of relatively quiet roads and lanes, but also plenty to get stuck into off-road. The popular Mud & Mayhem series has a Thetford round, and the Great Barrow Challenge is a series of races throughout the year with a main four-day event held in September covering over a marathon a day in distance.

Suffolk

34 DUNWICH HEATH

Distance:	9 miles (14km)
Start/finish:	Vulcan Arms, Sizewell, IP16 4UD
Terrain:	Field, path, track, road
Toughness:	Easy
Ascent:	88 metres
Navigation:	Moderate
Good for:	Coast, wildlife, woodland
Route info:	wildrunning.net/34

Despite a good stretch of (quiet) road, this run is included due to the wonderful variety of scenery and landscape it passes. From the pub, take the stile opposite, crossing fields to reach the Coast Path, passing the power station. Pass Minsmere Bird Reserve before climbing up to the row of white coastguard cottages. Here the route heads inland across the beautiful expanse of Dunwich Heath and through woodland before following the road into Eastbridge village. Passing the Kenton Hills nature trail, the run follows blue waymarkers, heading across the Sizewell Belts and Leiston Common. Finally markers lead through more woodland, crossing Sandy Lane and then turning R on another Sandy Lane, returning to Sizewell.

35 BURY TO CLARE

Distance:	18 miles (29km)
Start:	Nowton Park, Bury St Edmunds, IP29 5LU
Finish:	Clare Castle, Suffolk
Terrain:	Trail, track, some surfaced road
Toughness:	Easy
Ascent:	267 metres
Navigation:	Easy (waymarked)
Good for:	Wildlife, history, families
Route info:	wildrunning.net/35

A picturesque run over the gently undulating downs and wolds of West Suffolk, this fully waymarked route links the St Edmund Way/ Lark Valley Path at Bury St Edmunds and the Stour Valley Path at Clare. This run changes with the seasons, each providing its own rewards and challenges. It takes in some magical paths through fields high with crops, wildflower meadows, green lanes, peaceful villages and ⚠ two larger road crossings. From Nowton Park follow waymarkers SW on lanes, then fields to Park Lane. Turn L and follow lanes and fields through villages of Hawstead, Whepstead and Somerton, finishing at medieval Clare Castle. 3-4 buses daily back to Bury.

36 THE LITTLE OUSE PATH

Distance:	10 miles (16km)
Start:	Brandon rail station, IP27 0BA
Finish:	Thetford
Terrain:	Towpath, footpath
Toughness:	Easy
Ascent:	109 metres
Navigation:	Easy (waymarked)
Good for:	Wildlife, woodland
Route info:	wildrunning.net/36

This route, although starting in Norfolk, predominantly runs through the countryside of northern Suffolk. A fully waymarked trail, it follows the lazily winding River Ouse from Brandon to Thetford, through picturesque landscapes and tranquil woodland, including Thetford Forest park. The route is entirely off-road, following the original towpath for much of the way. There are many opportunities for a paddle in the river, a very welcome respite particularly if undertaking the route as an out-and-back. From Brandon Station head S on High Street. Just before the bridge, turn L down Riverside Way. Little Ouse Path is waymarked from the first turning R, which takes you straight to the river. Frequent trains back to Brandon.

Swale Estuary

Kent

Kent is often referred to as England's garden for its abundance of orchards and agriculture and its mild climate and fertile soil. Amongst its many borders, the county has some more unusual ones: with France, halfway through the Channel Tunnel, and with Essex in the middle of the Thames Estuary. Kent's location between London and continental Europe has led to it being in the front line of several conflicts, including the Battle of Britain during World War II when its eastern parts were known as Hell Fire Corner. The geology of the area dictates the changes in landscape and therefore the running here. The Weald Dome, centred around Tunbridge Wells, is formed from layers of limestone, sandstone and clay, whilst the North and South Downs that flank the Dome are of the chalk for which the area is famous, forming the iconic White Cliffs of Dover from which France can be seen on a clear day.

The running here is varied, from the green lushness of the forests and rolling hills in the west, to the vast solitude of the salt marshes in the east. Parts of the North and South Downs Ways pass through the county, and there is an abundance of other waymarked trails for great running days out. The 100 mile South Downs Way is challenging and picturesque, offering outstanding views and a real sense of escape (Runs 37-38). The North Downs, although perhaps less wild in character than their southern relatives, are much more easily accessible from the centre of London. The North Downs ridge is a range of chalk hills that run from Farnham to the White Cliffs of Dover, passing through two Areas of Outstanding Natural Beauty, the Surrey Hills and the Kent Downs. The North Downs Way

39

38

37

follows these hills for 153 miles, winding its way through areas rich in wildlife and history. Two of our Runs, 37 and 38, explore different parts of these beautiful hills.

Although the channels which once made their separation more obvious are now silted up, the Isle (formerly isles) of Sheppey comprises three land masses: Sheppey itself, Harty and Elmley. Harty, with its vast views across the Swale estuary to mainland Kent and out to sea past Whitstable Bay, lies at the south-eastern tip of the island. It is home to an 11th-century church which, as described by Sir John Betjeman, sits in "splendid isolation, with sea birds wheeling by and the Thames so wide as to be open sea, and air so fresh as to be healthier than yoghurt (unflavoured)". This is a remote and almost strangely quiet place, with just a few buildings dotted about and the pub – the Ferry Inn –with its gardens sloping right down to the water's edge. Vast numbers of birds fill the land, sky and sea, and by night the chilling shriek of a barn owl echoes through the stillness. Across the Swale, the route of the former Harty Ferry, lie the Oare Marshes, a nature reserve and home to abundant wildlife and thousands of seabirds. Thames sailing barges, with their great red-brown sails, can often be seen at the mouth of the Swale, awaiting the tides that will allow them passage (Run 39).

The area also has a strong running heritage – the North Downs 30km race, held annually in June by Isted & Ifield Harriers, has been run for the past 30 years and has been described by Runners' World magazine as "a swaggering mudslinger that can lay claim to the title 'the toughest race in the South East'. Challenging hills, exhilarating trails, scenic views, excellent marshalling and a decent swag bag make it a favourite". For those wishing to see a little more of the Way, the North Downs 100 is a 100-mile continuous trail run along the Way, organised in August each year by Centurion Running (who also hold 100 milers on the South Downs Way, the Thames Path and even a hard-as-nails winter version) and is a qualifying event for the classic international ultramarathons, the Ultra Trail du Mont Blanc and the Western States 100.

37

Kent

37 BOX HILL

Distance:	9 miles (15km)
Start:	Box Hill and Westhumble station car park, RH5 6BT
Finish:	Merstham
Terrain:	Woodland path, trail
Toughness:	Moderate to challenging
Ascent:	440 metres
Navigation:	Easy (waymarked)
Good for:	History, ascents, urban escape
Route info:	wildrunning.net/37

A challenging but rewarding section of the North Downs Way. From the station, head S on Westhumble Street to a subway under the road, from where the Way is fully waymarked. The run starts by hopping across the River Mole on stepping stones (or bridge if the river is high), before heading up Box Hill. The spectacular views are worth the effort. A fast, fun descent through woodlands and another steep ascent up Brockham Hills, with fine prospects. Juniper and Colley Hills, and Reigate Hill with its Victorian fort, follow, each with its own challenges and great views. From Reigate Hill the path descends through school grounds and a golf course to Merstham.

38 WYE DOWNS

Distance:	4½ miles (7km)
Start/finish:	Coldharbour Lane, Wye, 400m N of TN25 5HE
Terrain:	Trail, field, path, track, paved
Toughness:	Easy
Ascent:	143 metres
Navigation:	Easy to moderate
Good for:	Urban escape
Route info:	wildrunning.net/38

This exhilarating run along inviting trails through quintessential English countryside follows the North Downs Way, winding along the chalk ridge of the North Downs, providing great running underfoot, including challenging ascents and fast descents of the picturesque Wye Downs, with their steep-sided chalk valleys. From parking area, cross road and proceed through two kissing gates. Head downhill on grassy paths and steps, following waymarkers to reach Amage Road. Head NW along wonderful trails to Wye Village, joining the North Downs Way in the village centre and following this through woodlands and along Wye Downs to Broad Downs before returning over fields through rolling green countryside to the start.

39 OARE & THE SWALE

Distance:	8 miles (13km)
Start/finish:	Faversham market, ME13 7AG
Terrain:	Field, track, sea wall, paved
Toughness:	Easy
Ascent:	74 metres
Navigation:	Easy to moderate
Good for:	Coast, wildlife, history
Route info:	wildrunning.net/39

This gentle, varied run is full of intrigue as it tours the peninsula around the Oare Marshes Nature Reserve and the Swale estuary, enjoying views across wide open marshland and farmland and over to the Isle of Sheppey. From the market place, head along West Street and turn R up Davington Hill. Continue into Oare. Turn R at Castle Inn, at the head of the creek. Keeping creek on R run through fields to Oare Marshes Nature Reserve. Follow the sea wall past Harty Ferry. At Dan's Dock, head SW inland, following tracks and field paths to Luddenham Court. Head E over fields back to Oare. A longer run of around 10 miles starts in Oare itself, following the Swale Heritage Trail to Conyer before branching R onto the Saxon Shore Way to return to Oare.

Beachy Head

The South Downs

The South Downs is a range of chalk hills that extends across the south-eastern coastal counties of England from the Itchen Valley of Hampshire in the west to Beachy Head, near Eastbourne, in the east. These open, rolling downs are covered in old chalk grassland, the fine, springy, close-cropped turf created by centuries of grazing by sheep and rabbits, and pure joy to run on. The South Downs National Park includes several National Nature Reserves. The yew forest at Kingley Vale, near Chichester, contains trees that are amongst some of the oldest living things in Britain. There are also many important archaeological sites and protected habitats for the region's abundant wildlife. Lullington Heath, on the northern fringe of Friston Forest, is one the largest areas of chalk heath in Britain. Friston Forest itself, through which the Beachy Head and Seven Sisters run (Run 40) passes, has many trails to explore on foot or mountain bike.

The South Downs Way runs for 100 waymarked miles from Winchester to Eastbourne. The Way has been travelled by humans for some 8,000 years, winding along the high ground of the chalk downs, safely above the surrounding lowlands. The trail follows the downs' northern escarpment from where there are extensive views across the Weald to the north and over the rounded hills and dry valleys to the sea in the south. There are several steep ascents when crossing the valleys of the River Cuckmere at Alfriston, the Ouse at Southease, the Adur south of Bramber and the Arun at Amberley. Between Eastbourne and Alfriston, there is an equally lovely coastal alternative to the inland route, running along the cliff tops with spectacular views to Beachy Head and the Seven Sisters. This option then turns inland along the Cuckmere Valley to rejoin the main route at Alfriston. Our Run 41 goes along some of the loveliest sections of the South Downs Way, linking two iconic features: Ditchling Beacon, one of the highest points on the

41

42

42

South Downs, and the Devil's Dyke, a large, dry valley carved out in the last Ice Age.

The South Downs lend themselves well to exploring on foot, and there are many fantastic places to run and visit, including the chalk figure of the Long Man of Wilmington, Iron Age hill forts and barrows and the iconic white faces of the Seven Sisters. Aside from running, there are many other enjoyable things to do, including kite flying, paragliding and indulging in the South Downs Food and Drink Trail.

The South Downs Marathon is held in June each year, starting at Slindon College and following fantastically runnable, undulating trails to the Queen Elizabeth Country Park near Petersfield. There are also half marathon and relay categories. There is an annual ultramarathon, organised by Centurion Running, with distances of 50 and 100 miles. The 100-mile event takes in the entire length of the South Downs Way. Course records at the time of writing, both set in 2013, are 15 hours, 43 minutes and 53 seconds for men (Robbie Briton) and 16 hours, 56 minutes and 38 seconds for women (Jean Beaumont). For a lower key, mountain marathon-style adventure, the National Trust runs a backpackers' campsite at Saddlescombe Farm on the Devil's Dyke Estate, just off the South Downs Way, from April to September. There is no vehicle access, preserving the peaceful tranquillity of the place, and lending itself perfectly to a two-day exploration of the Way and stunning countryside and coast in the surrounding area with a mid way camp in between. Butser Hill lies just outside the Queen Elizabeth Country Park on the South Downs Way. The infamous Butser Hill challenge, which is a Grade B fell race, has been held since 1978 and involves three ascents and descents of the hill. Our Run 42 goes up Butser Hill, but only once, before following the South Downs Way through wood and nature reserves.

The Clarendon Way links with the South Downs Way, and is a 24-mile trail joining Salisbury and Winchester. The fantastic Clarendon Marathon, which is 90 percent off-road, follows its course, with a few extra twists and turns. It is held every October.

Wilmington Long Man

The South Downs

40 BEACHY HEAD & SEVEN SISTERS

Distance: 15 miles (24km)
Start/finish: Beachy Head Countryside Centre, Eastbourne, BN20 7YA
Terrain: Track, trail, field, paved sections
Toughness: Moderate
Ascent: 581 metres
Navigation: Moderate
Good for: Coast, families, woodland
Route info: wildrunning.net/40

This spectacular route takes in the iconic white chalk cliff tops with their precipitous drop into the sea below, lush woodland, a meandering river and shingle beach. From the start, head N, joining the South Downs Way shortly after the B2103. Follow waymarkers to Jevington. Leave the SD Way here and head SW through Friston Forest to Westdean. Follow tracks S along the edge of the Seven Sisters Country Park to reach the SD Way again, now heading E along the coast. Follow waymarkers, past Birling Gap, all the way back to the start. The area is great for families with plenty of activities nearby. Friston Forest has excellent mountain biking trails, nature trails, bushcraft, barbeque areas and camping.

41 DITCHLING BEACON

Distance: 6 miles (10km)
Start: Ditchling Beacon, Ditchling Road BN1 9QD
Finish: Devil's Dyke
Terrain: Trail, track, path
Toughness: Moderate
Ascent: 223 metres
Navigation: Easy (waymarked)
Good for: National trail
Route info: wildrunning.net/41

This wonderful run along the cropped, springy turf of the South Downs chalk ridge passes through some of the best landscape on the South Downs Way to link Ditchling Beacon and the Devil's Dyke. There are regular buses from Brighton to Ditchling Beacon and a car park on site. From the foot of the Beacon, ascend to the summit on the South Downs Way. Follow the blue acorn waymarkers W until the Devil's Dyke is reached. This route can be run as a point-to-point, with a return to Brighton on the bus, or as a very pleasant out-and-back. There is also an enjoyable circular run of 5 miles (8km) from Ditchling Beacon E to Blackcap.

42 BUTSER HILL & WETHER DOWN

Distance: 13½ miles (21km)
Start/finish: Buriton village centre, GU31 5RT
Terrain: Downland trail, track, road
Toughness: Moderate
Ascent: 464 metres
Navigation: Easy (waymarked)
Good for: Wildlife, ascents, national trail
Route info: wildrunning.net/42

Another iconic section of the South Downs Way with wonderful running over the rolling terrain of the downs' chalk ridge. Butser Hill, home to the infamous Butser Hill race, is the highest point on the main ridge of the South Downs. From the duck pond in Buriton, follow footpath up through Buriton Chalk Pit Nature Reserve. At road crossing, head straight up hill on track. Go under the A3 and up grassy slope to the summit of Butser Hill. Follow Limekiln Lane SW and join the South Downs Way. Follow waymarkers over Tegdown Hill, Hyden Hill and Wether Down, returning by the same route. The route passes through Queen Elizabeth Country Park, with its 20 miles of trails for exploring, café and lush woodland.

The Chilterns

Overlooking the Vale of Aylesbury in Buckinghamshire are the magnificent Chiltern Hills. The well-marked trails winding through this Area of Outstanding Natural Beauty make for great running. The Chilterns form part of a system of chalk downs which run throughout eastern and southern England, formed between 65 and 95 million years ago. This 'Chalk Group' runs through Salisbury Plain, Cranborne Chase, the South Downs and the Isle of Wight in the south, whilst continuing northeastwards across north Hertfordshire, Norfolk and the Lincolnshire Wolds, finally arriving in a prominent escarpment at the Yorkshire Wolds. One of the most heavily wooded parts of England, the area is also home to stunning open heath and commons, and picturesque gardens and parkland, making for a great variety of high quality runs. There are some challenging ascents, and enjoyably fast descents but nothing too steep - it's a good run up to the stone monument on the wooded summit of Haddington Hill, the highest point of the Chilterns at 267 metres (Run 43).

I had long wanted to visit Ivinghoe Beacon, the hallowed start point for the two great long distance trails of the Ridgeway and the Icknield Way. We set off from the campsite which sits right at the foot of the Beacon, heading up the slippery clay and chalk path towards the trig point, visible at the top. The human desire to achieve a summit receives almost instant gratification here, but the delight is no less for it. The Chilterns may be small relative to many of the more famous ranges, however they are perfectly sculpted and provide wonderful running across sweeping valley, with regular climbs and

44

45

45

descents between. From the trig point at the top of the Beacon we headed down into the Ashridge Estate, following winding paths through gentle countryside bordered by ancient trees. We explored some of the many winding paths here before making a wide loop back to the Beacon. A fast, exhilarating descent down one of the steeper sections of the hill, slipping and sliding our way down the clay to the bottom, provided a fine finish to a wonderful run. Later that evening we again climbed the beacon to watch a spectacular sunset blaze its way across the sky. This is a high-point of both Runs 44 and 45, the first circling the fantastic Ashridge Estate, the second running between the Ridgeway and the Icknield Way.

The Icknield Way, starting on Ivinghoe Beacon, is said to be Britain's oldest road, following the pathways of our prehistoric ancestors. Its chalky 110 miles wind their way, as Edward Thomas described in 1913, like a "white snake on a green hillside" from the Chilterns to Knettishall Heath in Norfolk. For much of its length the Way remains a rough path or a bridleway, preserved for the recreational traveller and accessible only on foot, horse or bicycle. In other places it has been surfaced into winding country lanes, and often, when it descends from the hills and ridges and back into civilisation, it disappears beneath the concrete, engulfed by the urban landscape. Cars, lorries and buses now follow its route: the most obvious way across the land. A mark of progress? In some ways perhaps. The Icknield Way does still exist in these places, but in an altered, unrecognisable state, more suited to the journeys of modern humans.

The prominent green wedge of Ivinghoe Beacon is also the starting venue for the Ridgeway Challenge, an 85-mile race organised by the Trail Running Association in August each year. Including some 2,743 metres of ascent, the race passes through the Chilterns, the North Wessex Downs and Barbury and Liddington hill forts, before finishing at the World Heritage Site of Avebury with its Neolithic barrows and Henge. Many of the aid stations en route are manned by local running clubs.

45

The Chilterns

43 WENDOVER WOODS

Distance: 6½ miles (10km)
Start/finish: Wendover Station, HP22 6BN
Terrain: Trail
Toughness: Easy
Ascent: 204 metres
Navigation: Moderate
Good for: History, woodland
Route info: wildrunning.net/43

An enjoyable run on well-maintained trails through the ancient beech woods covering Haddington Hill above Wendover, the highest point in the Chilterns, and Boddington Hill, site of an Iron Age hill fort. From the station head L along the High Street. After the final shop take R turn signposted 'ridgeway'. Follow ridgeway signs until reaching Wendover Woods. Leave ridgeway L then turn R onto bridleway. Continue on track downhill to reach road back to Wendover. Wendover Woods are also a great place for simply exploring or for families, with activities such as Go Ape, orienteering, a fitness trail assault course and an extensive children's play area.

44 ASHRIDGE ESTATE TRAIL

Distance: 17 miles (27km)
Start/finish: Ashridge Estate Visitor Centre, HP4 1LT
Terrain: Trail, path
Toughness: Moderate to challenging
Ascent: 397 metres
Navigation: Easy (waymarked)
Good for: Wildlife, history, families
Route info: wildrunning.net/44

This run has just about everything, and is only a short trip from the centre of London. Following steep, uneven tracks with plenty of muddy fun when wet and gloriously runnable when dry, it is a well-signed tour of the spectacular and varied landscapes of the NT Ashridge Estate. From Ivinghoe Beacon there are panoramic views over the estate and the Vale of Aylesbury. From the Visitor Centre, ascend to Wellington Monument. From here take the path N into woods. Follow green circular waymarkers clockwise around the estate, returning to the Visitor Centre. Nearby Whipsnade Zoo is great for a family outing.

45 ICKNIELD WAY – RIDGEWAY LINK

Distance: 7½ miles (12km)
Start: Chilterns Gateway Centre, Dunstable Downs, LU6 2GY
Finish: Ivinghoe Beacon, nr LU6 2EG
Terrain: Paths, trail
Toughness: Moderate
Ascent: 194 metres
Navigation: Easy (waymarked)
Good for: Families, national trail
Route info: wildrunning.net/45

An enjoyable, well-signed run through spectacular Chilterns countryside. From the start, follow circular 'Ridgeway Link' waymarkers along the upgraded path of the Icknield Way, wonderfully runnable in the dry and wonderfully muddy the rest of the year. It passes Whipsnade Zoo and Whipsnade Tree Cathedral which, with Ashridge Estate, offer great opportunities for exploring with the family, too. The final climb up Ivinghoe Beacon is rewarded with spectacular views across the Vale of Aylesbury; a wonderful place to watch the sun set. Car parks at both ends of the trail, and buses from Ivinghoe and Whipsnade.

Tennyson Trail

The New Forest & the Isle of Wight

Created as a royal forest for deer hunting by William I in the 11th century, the New Forest covers 150 square miles of broadleaved woodland, tree plantations, heathland and pastureland. The National Park extends even further (218 square miles), making it the largest area of unsown vegetation in lowland Britain. Several rivers run through the forest and drain to the nearby sea. The Forest is a fantastic place to run, with 143 miles of immaculate trails gently winding and undulating their way through stunning landscape, from deep within the leafy woodland to out on the wide, open heathland grazed by native ponies. Our circular Run 47, from Lyndhurst, showcases some of the fantastic scenery and history of this area. Run 46, where the New Forest meets the Solent, gives the runner the pleasure of seabirds, pine-fringed meadows and sea views.

There are many waymarked walking trails provided by the Forestry Commission, all of which are under 3 miles in length and perfect for a family day out or some gentle exploring. Several long-distance paths also pass through the area, providing a great, often well-signed means of journeying further afield. One of these paths, and great way to explore the coast, is the Solent Way, a 60-mile waymarked coastal route from Milford-on-Sea through bustling seaside towns, quiet harbours and deserted salt marshes to Emsworth Harbour. The route has recently been changed following the withdrawal of access rights at Browndown – details can be found on the Solent Way page of Hampshire County Council's website. The New Forest Marathon, held in September each year, is a hugely popular multi-terrain race which has been established for over 30 years. The area boasts its own running festival, held in Linwood in March, with six races to enter, from 10km to 50km.

47

48

47

On a recent trip to the New Forest, we ran some wonderful trails in the autumn, as the shortening of the days began to turn the trees from lush greens into fiery golds. The summer's discarded robes lay many layers deep on the trails, and we ran through the rustling, crunching leaves, kicking them up around us as we passed. We have visited at all times of the year, and each season brings with it a specific magic: spring, with its fresh, lime-green shoots and carpets of bluebells; summer, when the forest stands in verdant glory, the warm, bright sunlight filtering through and dappling the paths below; and winter, when crisp leaves crunch beneath our feet and a dusting of snow makes the dark trees stand like charcoal on paper.

England's largest island, the Isle of Wight, briefly held independent status in the 15th century. Of its 984 square miles, slightly over half is a designated AONB. The wildest and most peaceful areas are in the west of the island, with its dramatic coastlines and chalk downland ridge which runs across the whole island and ending in the iconic Needles stacks, whose knife-like edges slice out into the sea. The Tennyson Trail (Run 48) follows much of this ridge. Red squirrels flourish here, and bats, dormice and wild deer can also be found. The Isle of Wight Coastal Path is a 67-mile loop that takes in the spectacular chalk cliffs, rolling terrain and fine sea views. The northern section ventures inland fairly frequently, but the remainder provides continuous coastal running for many miles. There are many beautiful inland trails, all of which lend themselves brilliantly to running. They include the Stenbury Trail (10 miles), Hamstead Trail (7 miles), Worsley Trail (13 miles), Bembridge Trail (11 miles), Nunwell Trail (8 miles), Shepherds Trail (7 miles) and Freshwater Way (5 miles).

The island has a rich sporting history, from the sailing that draws Dame Ellen MacArthur to live here, to cycling (the island was listed in the Lonely Planet's top 10 cycling destinations world-wide) and distance running. The Isle of Wight Marathon is Britain's oldest continuously held marathon, having been run every year since 1957. Starting and finishing in Ryde, runners pass Newport, Shanklin and Sandown with a total climb of 459 metres.

The New Forest & the Isle of Wight

46 THE LEPE LOOP

Distance:	5 miles (8km)
Start/finish:	Lepe Country Park, SO45 1AD
Terrain:	Footpath, gravel track, shingle
Toughness:	Easy to moderate
Ascent:	48 metres
Navigation:	Easy to moderate
Good for:	Coast, woodland, families
Route info:	wildrunning.net/46

This is a great circular run with plenty of variety. There are lovely views out over the Solent, abundant with seabirds, pine-fringed cliffs and summer wildflower-filled meadows. It starts in Lepe Country Park with fine coastal views. Head W out onto the coast path, keeping the sea on your L until reaching quiet road. Follow uphill to where the road takes a sharp L. Turn R inland on footpath to fine paths across farmland and winding wooded trails. Cross road and head E to East Hill Farm; return S via the long row of slate-fronted coastguard cottages, to the country park. ⚠ Check tides first, as there are low-and-high tide alternatives. The country park itself is great for families, with wildlife, a café and the mile-long beach to explore.

47 LYNDHURST LOOP

Distance:	4.5 miles (7km)
Start/finish:	Bolton's Bench Forestry car park, nr SO43 7NL
Terrain:	Road, grass track, trail,
Toughness:	Easy to moderate
Ascent:	60 metres
Navigation:	Moderate
Good for:	Woodland, history, wildlife
Route info:	wildrunning.net/47

This wonderful and varied run starts on the atmospheric White Moor, dotted with remnants of military history. It follows the old Salt Way, passing medieval earthworks and a Bronze Age barrow before emerging onto spectacular heathland, ablaze with heather and gorse in summer. The route then follows the Beaulieu River at Longwater Lawn, a trickle during the summer months that becomes a gushing watercourse in winter. From Bolton's Bench, follow tarmac road to cemetery, turning L and following wall to reach the edge of Mallard Wood. Cross open heathland to Beaulieu River. Follow E until bridge crossing, heading S to Matley Wood. On reaching road, bear right along track to return to Lyndhurst.

48 TENNYSON TRAIL I. OF WIGHT

Distance:	14½ miles (23km)
Start:	Carisbrook, Newport, PO30 1NR
Finish:	Alum Bay
Terrain:	Ancient lane, track, trail
Toughness:	Moderate to challenging
Ascent:	547 metres
Navigation:	Easy (waymarked)
Good for:	Coast, forest, wildlife
Route info:	wildrunning.net/48

A challenging, scenic run across the Isle of Wight, starting from Newport, in the island's centre and heading out over hills and through the picturesque Brighstone Forest to the Needles and around to Alum Bay. Follow High St (B3401) W, then turn L onto Nodgham Lane, following waymarkers for the Tennyson Trail and passing Carisbrook Castle and Bowcombe Valley. The route climbs over Bowcombe Down, Brighstone Down, Mottistone Down, Compton Down, Tennyson Down and High Down, each with its own tough ascent and fast descent. Finally, the route descends to end at Alum Bay. This fantastic ridge provides extensive views across the island and out to sea.

Central

Home to a surprising diversity of landscapes, from the parklands of the Midlands, through the rolling countryside of the Cotswolds and the Welsh Borders, to the Peak District's craggy edges and remote moorland, central England has an abundance of exciting trails to explore.

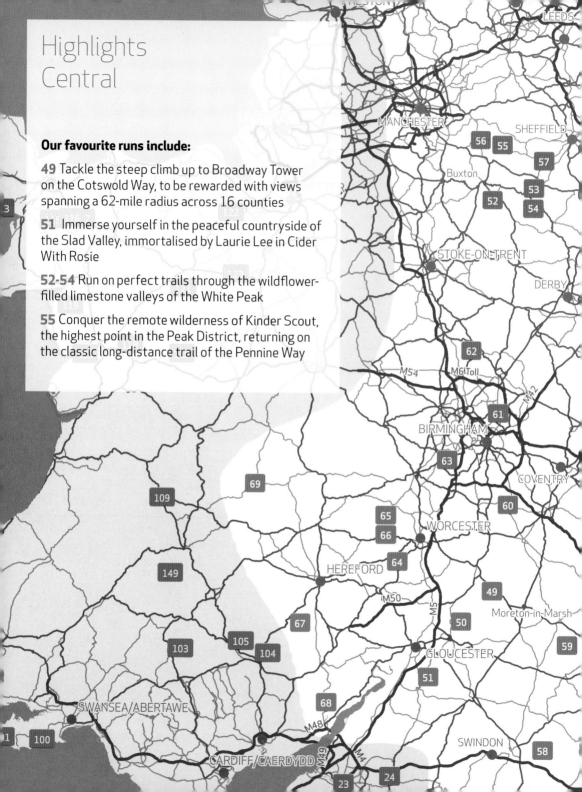

Highlights
Central

Our favourite runs include:

49 Tackle the steep climb up to Broadway Tower on the Cotswold Way, to be rewarded with views spanning a 62-mile radius across 16 counties

51 Immerse yourself in the peaceful countryside of the Slad Valley, immortalised by Laurie Lee in Cider With Rosie

52-54 Run on perfect trails through the wildflower-filled limestone valleys of the White Peak

55 Conquer the remote wilderness of Kinder Scout, the highest point in the Peak District, returning on the classic long-distance trail of the Pennine Way

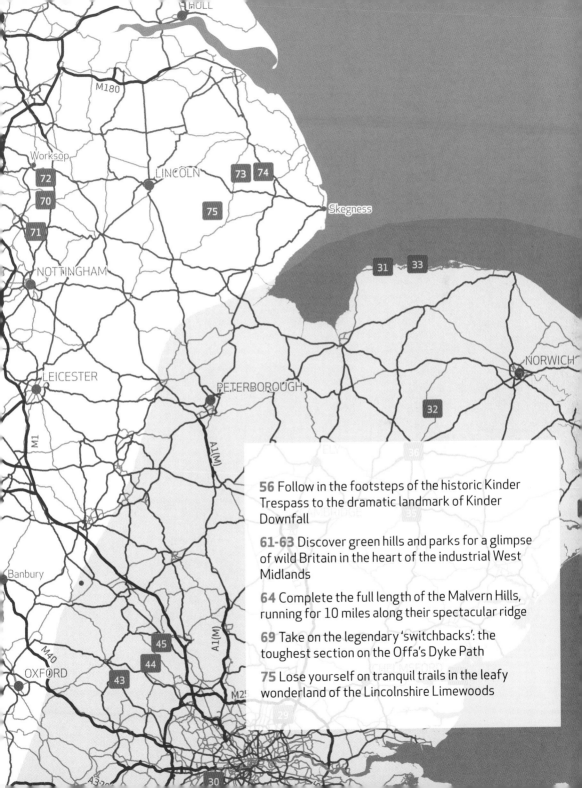

56 Follow in the footsteps of the historic Kinder Trespass to the dramatic landmark of Kinder Downfall

61-63 Discover green hills and parks for a glimpse of wild Britain in the heart of the industrial West Midlands

64 Complete the full length of the Malvern Hills, running for 10 miles along their spectacular ridge

69 Take on the legendary 'switchbacks': the toughest section on the Offa's Dyke Path

75 Lose yourself on tranquil trails in the leafy wonderland of the Lincolnshire Limewoods

Cotswold Way

The Cotswolds

The Cotswolds are a range of hills running diagonally from south-west to north-east through six counties including Gloucestershire, Oxfordshire and Warwickshire. They cover an area 25 miles across and 90 miles long, with the highest point being Cleeve Hill at 330 metres. The northern and western edges of the Cotswolds are marked by the steep, limestone escarpments of the Cotswold Edge down to the Severn valley and the Warwickshire Avon. The eastern edge is bounded by Oxford, and the west by Stroud. To the south-east, the upper reaches of the Thames Valley are often considered to mark the limit of this region, whilst to the south the Cotswolds reach to the World Heritage City of Bath.

The area is deservedly designated an Area of Outstanding Natural Beauty and this, along with the striking limestone landscape, provides varied and exciting running along exposed ridges, through lush green fields and wildflower meadows and along country lanes and through the attractive towns and villages built of the Cotswold stone, a yellow oolitic limestone.

The Cotswold Way runs along the Cotswold escarpment for 102 miles to its southernmost conclusion at the circular marker created by local artist Iain Cotton outside Bath Abbey. The running is varied, from quiet lanes through honey-coloured villages to steep climbs and inviting trails. Being practically all within an AONB there are few parts of this designated National Trail that aren't abundant in Wild Running treasures. The Cotswold Way is well signposted and can be run in sections or used as part of circular routes, many of which are also waymarked, or even run in its entirety. Its start is in Chipping Campden, a picturesque town filled with touristy shops and plenty of choices for a post-run meal or snacks to fuel you on your way. The Tourist Information Office here can also supply you with a card to have stamped along your way, should you wish to complete the full route.

49

51

50

Our own plan, devised, as so many of the best plans are, in the comfort of a warm pub after a pint or two, was to run the Cotswold Way over four consecutive days, carrying everything we'd need other than food and water, which we'd pick up at the towns and villages we passed en route. At a little over 25 miles a day, this seemed like a testing but achievable challenge. Winding our way up to the escarpment from Chipping Campden early on day one, rucksacks bulging with almost everything that we'd need for a little over 100 miles of running and three nights out on the hills, we were full of optimism. Well-marked paths and soft, springy grass underfoot on the run through fields down to the picture-perfect village of Broadway further buoyed our spirits. By dusk on day three, with aching bodies and blistered feet, we chanced upon a bed and breakfast and succumbed to its hot water and comfy beds. We completed our final day in torrential rain, stopping for lunch in Chipping Sodbury in an attempt to stop the shivering, before heading back out across fields, eventually winding our way down towards the finish in Bath.

The current official Cotswold Way record is held by Darryl Carter of Teddington, Middlesex who, on 22 July 2012, ran from Bath to Chipping Camden in 20 hours and 36 minutes. There are several races on the trail, with a Cotswold Way Century in September and a Broadway Tower marathon and half marathon in November, both organised by Cotswold Running.

Two of our runs, 49 and 50, follow fantastic sections of the Cotswold Way. Run 51 dives into the glorious Slad Valley, following the waymarked Wildlife Way through beautiful countryside and visiting three nature reserves en route. Slad was the home of Laurie Lee and the setting for his classic *Cider with Rosie*. A run here in midsummer, with the ground carpeted in wild orchids, the birds in full song and the bees buzzing lazily in the valley's captivating warmth, transports you straight into the author's world and his magical descriptions of the area:

"The valley was narrow, steep, a channel for the floods and a jungly, bird-crammed, insect-hopping sun-trap whenever there happened to be any sun."

The Cotswolds

49 BROADWAY TOWER

Distance:	3½ miles (6km)
Start/finish:	Broadway High Street, WR12 7AP
Terrain:	Field, path, small road section
Toughness:	Moderate to challenging
Ascent:	175 metres
Navigation:	Easy to moderate
Good for:	National trail, ascents, history
Route info:	wildrunning.net/49

A short and fantastic run, starting in the pretty Cotswold village of Broadway and making its way unrelentingly up the Cotswold Way across a series of fields to the 18th-century Capability Brown folly of Broadway Tower at the very top. The Cotswold Way is signposted on the R as you make your way up High Street from the village centre. Follow waymarkers as far as the tower. On reaching the top, either turn around and re-trace your steps – the run back through the fields is fantastic, good underfoot, fast and with stunning views – or turn R past The Rookery, and follow paths and track to Coneygree Lane before making your way through fields to Broadway. Broadway itself is abuzz with cafés.

50 CLEEVE HILL

Distance:	6 miles (10km)
Start/finish:	Quarry car park, GL52 3PW
Terrain:	Track, field, path
Toughness:	Moderate
Ascent:	249 metres
Navigation:	Easy to moderate
Good for:	Wildlife, ascents, national trail
Route info:	wildrunning.net/50

A great run, with breathtaking views, taking in the highest point of the Cotswold Escarpment at 330 metres. Wonderfully varied terrain and scenery, from open limestone grasslands of Cleeve Common, rich in wildlife, to winding trails through tranquil woodland and beside babbling streams. The route follows the Cotswold Way for much of its length: fine running on well-maintained paths with plenty of interest and some good, challenging ascents. From the start, follow the Cotswold Way E downhill, across a stream and up a steep climb through woodland. After the woods, leave Way R on track which climbs uphill towards masts. Rejoin the Way and head N, following waymarkers over the summit of Cleve Hill and back to the start.

51 SLAD VALLEY

Distance:	5½ miles (9km)
Start/finish:	Bulls Cross Common, Longridge, on B4070
Terrain:	Track, field, quiet lane
Toughness:	Easy to moderate
Ascent:	213 metres
Navigation:	Easy to moderate
Good for:	Wildlife
Route info:	wildrunning.net/51

Immortalised by Laurie Lee, the limestone grasslands of the magical Slad Valley lie deep within the Cotswold Hills and are carpeted with wildflowers in summer. This run follows the route of the Slad Valley Wildlife Way, a scenic, sporadically-waymarked tour of this wonderful area. From the car park, follow main road N for 200m before turning R down track. Follow waymarkers heading NE to Snows Farm Nature Reserve. Exit reserve at a stream crossing at SW corner, continue through woodland to the distinctive 'double bump' of Swift's Hill and the Elliott Nature Reserve. From here head generally N across fields and quiet lanes to Frith Wood Nature Reserve. Exit at NE corner to reach road and start.

53 Longstone Moor

The Peak District – The White Peak

The Peak District is an upland area, lying mainly in northern Derbyshire but also reaching into Cheshire, Greater Manchester, Staffordshire and Yorkshire. An area of great diversity, it is split by its geology into the northern Dark Peak, characterised by areas of open moorland and gritstone crags and quarries, and the southern, limestone-based White Peak, with its rolling, forested hills. Run 54 joins the two, a varied and spectacular run on well-maintained trails, offering adventurous running from Bakewell in the White Peak to Hope on the southern edge of the Dark Peak.

Running in the Peak District is challenging and rewarding in equal measure. Many days out on the fells and moors here have taught me that the weather dictates the mood in this part of the country. Cloud brings a sombre air to the place, making the grey of the gritstone even greyer, the walls and stony tracks reflected and magnified by gunmetal skies. I have more than once felt very much alone on a late afternoon run in the depths of winter as the inky darkness begins to creep in at the very edges of the moor. Yet on a clear, sunny day, the mood is light and the fells are welcoming, with bright colours standing out in brilliant contrast. Orchids and cowslips line the path as I wind my way up through pastureland, clambering over the stone-stepped stiles that scale the drystone walls here. Skylarks burble overhead on the open moorland; dark, wet peat underfoot, pale purple flowers on maroon heather carpeting the ground in every direction. At each turn a new view opens out below: patterned, stone-walled fields, gritstone edges or high moorland stretching out into the distance.

Most of the villages in the Peak National Park are within the White Peak, making it popular with tourists, particularly in the summer months. Access to the spectacular countryside

54

53

53

in this part of the Peak is wonderfully easy, with footpaths, bridleways and green lanes forming a vast network of runnable trails to explore. Half an hour's run from any of the busier areas will take you to beautiful wild places where few others are seen, from remote high moorland overlooking patchworks of medieval strip fields to grassy, tussocky hillsides and picturesque limestone valleys filled with wildflowers such as those found on Chrome Hill, Run 52. Many of these valleys are nature reserves where the native flora can been seen in abundance, changing as the seasons pass: snowy wood anemones in early spring, bright yellow cowslips and woodland-filled bluebells in early summer and blazing purple orchids as the sun's warmth arrives.

The Chatsworth estate is a runner's playground of winding country lanes, peaceful trails alongside the sparkling river Derwent and pleasant running through lush deer parks bounded by great mixed forest. It's worth the long climb up to the wooded hilltops for some exploring in the tree-lined valleys beyond, followed by the careering, crashing descent back down again (Run 53). It is fast, exhilarating and joyous, as the magnificent Chatsworth House and gardens appearing below. Payment is required to visit the house and gardens, but the thousand-acre park is free to enter and provides a vast and characterful example of nature's playground. Passing right through the estate, the Derwent Valley Heritage Way is a 55 mile waymarked trail providing enjoyable and varied running along the Derwent valley from the picturesque waters of Ladybower Reservoir through the Derwent Valley Mills World Heritage Site to the historic inland port of Shardlow, ending at Derwent Mouth where the Derwent flows into the River Trent.

Several other long-distance trails provide many opportunities for anything from a short, waymarked excursion to an epic, multi-day run. Many are also suitable for cycling and horse riding, lending themselves well to family trips. These include the Limestone Way (46 miles) and the Pennine Bridleway (190 miles completed to date), and former railway tracks such as the Monsal Trail, the High Peak Trail, the Tissington Trail and the Manifold Way.

The Peak District – The White Peak

52 CHROME HILL

Distance:	5 miles (8km)
Start/finish:	The Quiet Woman pub, Earl Sterndale, SK17 0BU
Terrain:	Trail, track, short road section
Toughness:	Moderate
Ascent:	302 metres
Navigation:	Moderate
Good for:	Ascents, wildlife
Route info:	wildrunning.net/52

This great run to the top of Chrome Hill and its shorter but steeper neighbour, Parkhouse Hill, showcases some of the best running the area. Inviting trails lead over rounded, grassy hills and through dry valleys carpeted with flowers in spring and summer. Leave the village, via a slightly obscure route through the pub's recycling centre and down an alley; soon cross fields and then a quiet lane where you will find waymarkers directing you to Chrome Hill. The main ridge path over the hill rewards you with views out over the surrounding countryside of this beautiful part of the Peak District. The ascent of Parkhouse Hill includes some easy scrambles over limestone outcrops, but these can be slippery in wet conditions.

53 BAKEWELL & CHATSWORTH LOOP

Distance:	15 miles (24km)
Start/finish:	Bakewell station car park, Station Road, DE45 1GE
Terrain:	Trail, field, path, road
Toughness:	Challenging
Ascent:	541 metres
Navigation:	Moderate to challenging
Good for:	History, ascents, families
Route info:	wildrunning.net/53

Woodland and riverside trails, majestic deer park and a tough ascent up to Longstone Edge with far-reaching views. From the car park turn L onto Station Road then first L over bridge. Continue straight up steep track through woods to Ballcross Farm. Turn R along track. cross fields and turn L at track junction down through woods to reach Chatsworth Estate. Exhilarating descent through deer park to join Derwent Valley Heritage Way. Follow waymarkers N through Baslow and along lane, leaving the Way at sharp L corner. Continue on lane to cross B6001 ⚠. Follow steep track up to Longstone Moor, descending to Pack Horse pub. Then cross fields to Monsal Trail and turn L to head back to start.

54 THE WHITE TO DARK

Distance:	27½ miles (44km)
Start:	Bakewell Bridge car park, Coombs Road, DE45 1AQ
Finish:	Hope, Derbyshire
Terrain:	Path, moorland, track, trail, road
Toughness:	Challenging
Ascent:	1270 metres
Navigation:	Moderate (partially waymarked)
Good for:	History, hard-as-nails
Route info:	wildrunning.net/54

The trail is 27 miles long, but divides well into three sections: Bakewell-Litton (7 miles), Litton-Hathersage (9 miles) and Hathersage-Hope (11 miles). The running is brilliantly varied, from the paved sections of the Monsal Trail through stunning limestone valleys, across open moorland and along the top of the famous Stanage Edge. Finally the trail winds through conifer woods before ending in the pretty village of Hope. Although waymarked, the White to Dark discs are not frequent enough to run from these alone. It is only marked in a S to N direction. From car park turn L onto quiet road and cross Bridge Street to enter fields. Follow waymarkers from here.

The Peak District
– The Dark Peak

The Dark Peak forms the higher, wilder northern part of the Peak District, lying mainly in Derbyshire and South Yorkshire. On these high moorland plateaux, the underlying limestone is covered by a cap of Millstone Grit, creating a dark and brooding landscape, often peaty and waterlogged underfoot. The famous gritstone outcrops, fantastic for climbing and bouldering, form an inverted horseshoe shape around the lower limestone White Peak. The highest points of the Dark Peak include Kinder Scout at 636 metres and Bleaklow at 610 metres, separated by the steep, winding road of Snake Pass, and Black Hill at 582 metres. The high land and often-harsh weather of the Dark Peak have contributed to many aircraft crashes, and the wrecks of these ill-fated wartime planes still remain on the high moorland to be stumbled upon by those exploring the area. These findings have led to tales of ghostly sightings and visitations, particularly from those who have taken items from the wreckage sites.

Sometimes known as the High Peak (although the exact geography of the two areas differs slightly) the area is also home to the High Peak Marathon, a 42-mile navigational challenge for teams of four. The 'challenge' is enhanced by it being held at night in March, when snow often lies thickly on the ground, gales blast across the open moorland and driving rain brings added misery to those lonely pre-dawn hours.

It is winter in the fells. All around a soft whiteness muffles the world, making every familiar journey and view new and strange. At each step the snowy mantle briefly holds and then gives way, plunging my foot unexpectedly to the firmer ground below. The landscape I have come to know is entirely changed. Wind-channelled drifts pile as high as the gates on the old packhorse trails and the wall-lined lanes now gallery huge sculptures, undercut like rollers, more akin to a frozen sea than

55-56

57

56

a snowy landscape. The whiteness fills the hills, the moor, the valley below: a great white blanket marked into neat rectangles by long, dark, drystone walls. The land high up is flattened out by the wind-blown drifts; deep-filled holes become man traps awaiting the unsuspecting step. Though one might think the paths would be less obvious in such conditions, it seems they are somehow more defined, even more visible in this cold hour of need. Freshly covered and as yet undisturbed, I see the path shine out distinctly ahead of me, its smooth, flat ribbon distinct from the tussocky underlay of the surrounding land. Either side of the path the snow is uneven, with black fingers of heather here and there reaching up through their snowy blanket, fringing the smooth, white pathways whose delicate web clearly and intricately nets the moor.

The Kinder Trespass marks the location of one of the first demonstrations against the closure of moorland to walkers. Access was granted in 1932, paving the way for future generations of walkers and runners to explore the wilds of the Peak District. Run 56 follows the route of the Trespass from the banks of the river Kinder, winding its way upwards to reach the Pennine Way at Ashop Head. Dramatic views open out over wild moorland and rugged gritstone cliffs. Kinder Downfall, often a waterfall which crashes down the rocks to the left, can be scrambled when completely dry – we visit this waterfall also in Run 55, along part of the Pennine Way, over stunning open moorland, passing Kinder Scout, the highest point in Derbyshire. A long, fast descent across trackless pastured spur, picking off stiles and gates, provides exhilarating running. Easier is Run 57 in the Longshaw Estate, where it's possible to get happily lost along the many wandering paths. We've run here many times and never managed the same route twice!

The Dark Peak lends its name to a running club which has gained fame through both its performances at local and national level and its association with Richard Askwith's book, *Feet in the Clouds*, the Dark Peak Fell Runners. Formed in 1976 to provide a meeting point for local fell runners, the club continues to flourish and now has over 300 members. A full and amusing history of the club can be found on its website.

The Peak District – The Dark Peak

55 EDALE & JACOB'S LADDER

Distance:	10 miles (16km)
Start/finish:	Edale village, S33 7ZN
Terrain:	Trail, moorland, bog, path
Toughness:	Challenging
Ascent:	518 metres
Navigation:	Moderate (if visibility good)
Good for:	Ascents, national trails
Route info:	wildrunning.net/55

A spectacular route taking in moorland, the waterfalls at Kinder Downfall, a section of the Pennine Way and the short but steep descent of Jacob's Ladder. From Edale ascend steeply up the path of Grinds Brook, following it upstream across Edale Moor and all the way to Kinder Downfall on the Kinder Scout plateau for breathtaking views out across the Peak National Park. The path here is on lush, springy ground providing wonderful running, although it does get very muddy in winter. Continue on great running terrain, following the Pennine Way S to Edale Cross, down Jacob's Ladder and all the way back down long, sweeping trails into Edale village. Edale is on the Hope Valley train line, with regular connecting services to Manchester and Sheffield.

56 KINDER TRESPASS

Distance:	8½ miles (14km)
Start/finish:	Bowden Bridge car park, Kinder Road, Hayfield, SK22 2LH
Terrain:	Track, slabbed path, moorland
Toughness:	Challenging
Ascent:	536 metres
Navigation:	Moderate (if visibility good))
Good for:	Ascents, national trails, history
Route info:	wildrunning.net/56

Run in the footsteps of the 500 Kinder Trespassers who secured rights of access to open country for all. The challenging route passes the classic gritstone outcrops for which the area is famous and the beautiful Kinder Downfall waterfall, often a frozen tumble of icicles in winter. From the higher ground on a clear day, there is panoramic and utterly breathtaking high peak scenery, with far-reaching views. From Bowden Bridge car park follow Kinder Road NE to Booth Bridge. Take path up to White Brow, continuing along William Clough until R turn on Pennine Way to Sandy Heys. Follow Pennine Way past Kinder Downfall and over Kinder Low, to Edale Cross. Turn R on path and follow downhill to return to Hayfield.

57 LONGSHAW

Distance:	5 miles (8km)
Start/finish:	NT Longshaw Estate Visitor Centre car park, S11 7TY
Terrain:	Trail, path, rock
Toughness:	Easy
Ascent:	205 metres
Navigation:	Easy to moderate
Good for:	Families, woodland
Route info:	wildrunning.net/57

Scenic trail running around the spectacular Longshaw Estate. This run follows the 'long route' marked in green on the maps available at the visitor centre. Waymarking is sparse, so take directions with you if you want to stick to the trail, or do as we did on our first run here and lose yourself in the Estate's splendour. In autumn the estate is a sensory overload of multi-coloured trees, fiery bracken, and shards of golden sunlight. There are spectacular views of the Derwent Valley from White Edge Moor, part of the gritstone edge which also forms Stanage and many other famous climbing venues in the area. There are many child-friendly activities at Longshaw.

Oxfordshire & Southern Warwickshire

The counties of Oxfordshire and Warwickshire are home to some of the most quintessentially English countryside, towns and villages. They also provide inspiration for many hidden wild running gems, and as such deserve their own chapter.

Oxfordshire boasts a fantastic network of footpaths and bridleways, winding through the pretty countryside to connect its populated areas. These paths are the result of an interesting history, from trade and industry links to a legal requirement in the past for all residents to have access to churches. There is plenty to discover here, from the open vistas of the Vale of the White Horse to leafy beech woodlands and dense forested areas. Unspoiled Wychwood Forest has only one permitted path through it, our Run 59. Warwickshire is a land-locked county with a densely populated north and a rural, sparsely populated south. There are many great places to run here, with grassy hilltops that offer spectacular views of Burton Dassett and the extensive rolling countryside that borders Oxfordshire.

We ran the Heart of England Way, a 101-mile route from the Cannock Chase AONB to the Cotswolds AONB, over a series of winter weekends. Snow lay on the trails quite thickly in places, blanketing the surrounding landscape and falling in heavy clumps from tree branches as we passed. We started early in the mornings, usually just after dawn when the world was still a murky blue, the main light seeming to emanate from the sheer whiteness of the snow. We would begin sleepily and reluctantly, feet and knees complaining as we invariably ran too fast too soon in an attempt to warm up as quickly as possible. By mid-morning we were well warmed-up but tiring and ready for a second, or even third breakfast, either finding a café to thaw

59

58

58

the tips of our toes and wrap our fingers, stiff from the cold, around a warm mug, or, if no such luxury materialised, a hurried stop for water and flapjack. This trail is wonderfully varied and took us through many landscapes we would otherwise never have experienced.

The Thames Path National Trail runs for 184 miles from its source in the Cotswolds, through London and almost to the sea at the Thames Barrier in Greenwich. Passing through peaceful water meadows, unspoilt rural villages and historic towns and cities, it is a fantastic long-distance trail, either to run as a challenge or to pick up here and there as a means of exploring an area. It is a particularly enjoyable way of entering Oxford, winding your way right into the heart of the city. For most of its length, the Thames Path is for pedestrians only, with no cycling allowed, and as a result the going underfoot is often more yielding and interesting than paved cycleways. The popular Thames Path Challenge (25km/50km/100km), raising funds for the Hunger Project, runs from Putney to Henley in September, and the GB Ultra Thames Trot in February sells out months in advance. The Ridgeway Challenge 85-mile ultramarathon also runs through this part of the country en route to Avebury in Wiltshire. Our Run 58 includes a waymarked, classic section of the Ridgeway national trail, perfect as a reconnaisance run for those considering the full challenge. The Oxfordshire race calendar is packed, with a huge selection of road and off-road races at all conceivable distances, from marathons and half marathons to cross-country and multi-terrain and multi-sport events.

There are several long-distance routes that cross Warwickshire, including the 100-mile Millennium Way, the 98-mile Centenary Way and the wonderfully varied Heart of England Way. This 101-mile waymarked trail curves through gently undulating farmland, lowland heath, woodland and riverside paths. The Arden Way is a circular route which links with the Heart of England Way, forming a 26-mile loop (Run 60). There are also several lovely circular runs from Henley, including a great 5-mile loop heading out on the Millennium Way and retuning via an anticlockwise loop through Preston Bagot.

Oxfordshire & Southern Warwickshire

58 THE RIDGEWAY AT ASHBURY

Distance: 7½ miles (12km)
Start/finish: Car park at B4000 / Ridgeway junction, ¾ mile SE of Ashbury
Terrain: Track, field, path, quiet lane
Toughness: Moderate
Ascent: 185 metres
Navigation: Easy (waymarked)
Good for: Wildlife, national trail, history
Route info: wildrunning.net/58

This run is one of several waymarked round routes on the Ridgeway National Trail. The setting is the N Wessex Downs AONB, where wildlife-rich trails lead through classic chalk countryside with stunning views across rolling downland and the Thames Valley. Start where the Ridgeway National Trail crosses the B4000. Head NE on the Ridgeway, past Wayland's Smithy, a Stone Age long barrow. Leave Ridgeway R at next track, following Ridgeway Circular Route waymarkers. Run through woods and fields to Ashdown House (NT), taking the minor road L of the house. Head up through fields passing the Iron Age hill fort of Alfred's Castle before rejoining main Ridgeway path. Turn R and follow back to the start.

59 WYCHWOOD FOREST

Distance: 8 miles (13km)
Start/finish: Charlbury station, OX7 3HH
Terrain: Field, track, woodland path, road
Toughness: Easy
Ascent: 192 metres
Navigation: Easy to moderate
Good for: Woodland, history
Route info: wildrunning.net/59

Starting and finishing in the pretty town of Charlbury, this run loops out into the countryside, taking in the majestic Cornbury Park, and following the only permitted path through private Wychwood Forest, once a Royal Forest covering most of W Oxfordshire. Pleasant, runnable trails lead you through unspoilt woodland, dazzlingly green in summer and a blazing rainbow in autumn. From station, turn R to Dyer's Hill, R to Church Lane; follow track R of church. Turn R to Park St and follow pavement until driveway R into Cornbury Park with public footpath sign. Head S in park to reach Finstock, where short road section takes you back into park. Follow tracks NW for Chilson, then bridleway signposted Shorthampton, heading E back to the station.

60 THE ARDEN WAY

Distance: 27 miles (43km)
Start/finish: Henley-in-Arden station, B95 5JQ
Terrain: Footpath, bridleway, paved
Toughness: Easy to moderate
Ascent: 449 metres
Navigation: Easy (waymarked)
Good for: Urban escape, woodland
Route info: wildrunning.net/60

This circular run, of an almost perfect marathon distance, takes you on a tour of the beautiful Forest of Arden in Warwickshire. The route starts and ends near Henley-in-Arden station. From Station Road, turn L onto Bear Lane from where the Arden Way is waymarked in both directions. An anticlockwise loop leads through Ullenhall before heading towards Studley, passing the impressive 19th century Studley Castle. The route follows the River Arrow to Coughton and the 16th-century Tudor house, Coughton Court. Finally it winds through the market town of Alcester, the woodlands at Oversley and Spernall Park and returns to Henley-in-Arden.

The West Midlands

The West Midlands is a landlocked county which has only officially existed since 1974. Bordered by Warwickshire to the east, Staffordshire to the north and west and Worcestershire to the south, it is a heavily populated area, second in the UK only to London. However, exploring outside its cities brings unexpected glimpses of wilderness, carefully preserved in its parks and green spaces and an abundance of natural habitats in the form of 23 Sites of Specific Scientific Interest. Sutton Park, home to our first route (Run 61), is a National Nature Reserve and one of the largest urban parks in Europe, covering 2,400 acres. It is a wonderful escape from the busy cities that surround it and amazingly diverse, from ancient forest and open heathland to wetlands, marshes and lakes. Easily accessible by public transport, it is a perfect day out to explore the trails and take in the peacefulness and diversity of wildlife on offer. Cannock Chase, a designated AONB, is also a fantastic place to explore, either on foot or mountain bike, with many miles of woodland and heathland trails just a short journey from the city sprawl (Run 62). The area even has its own running club, the Chase Harriers. For GPS users who fancy something completely different, the new 22-mile Geotrail at Cannock takes in much of the fascinating geological history of the area and is a fun (and challenging!) day out with a twist on traditional orienteering. It's also great undertaken in sections with kids.

The Clent Hills lie 10 miles south-west of Birmingham city centre, strictly within Worcestershire, although their closest towns of Stourbridge and Halesowen both lie within the West

61

63

61

Midlands conurbation. There are many miles of footpaths, bridleways and trails to explore here, with breathtaking panoramic views over the Cotswolds, Shropshire Hills and Welsh borders. A run up to Walton Hill (Run 63), the highest point of the Clent Hills at 316 metres, is rewarded with wonderful views across to the Malvern Hills, Wenlock, Kinver Edge and the Clee Hills. On a clear day you can even spot the Black Mountains and the edge of the Peak District. Walton Hill is a little off the beaten track and a more tranquil area than some of the busier, more accessible parts. There is abundant wildlife, with protected breeding areas for birds and insects. For a slightly longer excursion, The North Worcestershire Path Highlights trail is an 8-mile linear route from the Clent Hills to the Lickey Hills, taking in some of the best bits of the North Worcestershire Way en route. Early morning is a wonderful time to run here, watching the sun rise with the world to yourself.

There is a vibrant running scene in the West Midlands, with well-supported races such as the Birmingham and Black Country Half Marathon, which follows the canal towpath, the Wolverhampton Marathon in September, the Birmingham Half and the Coventry Half all attracting large numbers of runners. There are many off-road and multi-terrain races and series to get involved in, through parks and green places in the area. The Grand Union Canal Race is a 145-mile ultramarathon which runs along the Grand Union Canal, from Gas Street Basin in the centre of Birmingham, to Little Venice in the centre of London, in May of each year. It is a brilliantly supported event and an established classic on the ultrarunning calendar. Competitors have a 45-hour time limit to complete the run, can choose to use their own support crew or the race support and must not stop for more than 40 minutes at a time, the current record of 25 hours and 37 minutes is held by Pat Robins (2011). In 2013, Mimi Anderson, multiple world record holder for incredible feats of running endurance, ran an out-and-back of the GUCR course, finishing the 290 miles in a combined time of just over 78 hours. At the time of writing, she was the only person to have completed the double.

The West Midlands

61 SUTTON PARK

Distance:	7½ miles (12km)
Start/finish:	Sutton Park Visitor Centre, Sutton Coldfield, B74 2YT
Terrain:	Footpath, track, parkland road
Toughness:	Easy
Ascent:	162 metres
Navigation:	Easy
Good for:	Urban escape, wildlife, families
Route info:	wildrunning.net/61

A gentle run through the National Nature Reserve of Sutton Park, 2,400 acres of green escape just 6 miles north of central Birmingham. Cattle and wild ponies roam freely, and fish lurk in the deep lakes. The run takes in the unexpected diversity of the park, skirting lakes, through ancient oak woodland and across grassy areas. From the start, turn L onto the road and run NW past Keeper's and Blackroot Pools before running on a pleasant woodland track through Upper Nut Hurst. Bear R, skirting around the E edge of Bracebridge Pool. Head S on the W edge of the park to reach Banners Gate. Return to Visitor Centre passing N of Powell's Pool and Wyndley Pool. Nearest station is Sutton Coldfield, a few minutes' walk away.

62 CANNOCK CHASE

Distance:	7½ or 12 miles (12 or 19km)
Start/finish:	Cannock Chase Visitor Centre, Hednesford, WS12 4PW
Terrain:	Trail
Toughness:	Easy
Ascent:	184 or 300 metres
Navigation:	Easy (waymarked)
Good for:	Woodland, urban escape
Route info:	wildrunning.net/62

This trail takes in the picturesque Sherbrook Valley with its mixture of woodlands and open heathland. There is a choice of routes, the shorter Pepper Slade loop and the longer Abraham's Valley loop. The Chase is a great place to explore, with plenty of activities for families and a café at the visitor centre. From the start follow waymarkers NW along the Sherbrook Valley. For the shorter of the two routes turn R at the third waymarker, running SE to reach parallel path which follows the E edge of the woods then S back to the start. For the longer route continue along the valley to reach stepping stones at the N edge of the woodland. Turn R to reach path which heads S through Abraham's Valley, and back to the start.

63 CLENT HILLS

Distance:	3½ miles (6km)
Start/finish:	Nimmings (NT) car park, Wood Lane, Hagley, B62 0NL
Terrain:	Woodland path, tracks, road
Toughness:	Moderate to challenging
Ascent:	345 metres
Navigation:	Easy to moderate
Good for:	Urban escape, ascents
Route info:	wildrunning.net/63

This short but sweet run tackles Walton Hill, the highest point on the Clent Hills at 316 metres, where panoramic views across the cityscapes and rolling countryside await. The run then loops around the surrounding hills, taking in the lush woodland of the Country Park. From the car park cross the road and descend on L hand path through fields to St Kenelm's church. After a short road section cross fields SW to ascent to trig point atop Walton Hill. Continue WSW, descending to Clent. Follow fields and tracks ascending from Clent into the Clent Hills Country Park, heading NE through Nimmings Wood to return to start.

Worcestershire & the Malvern Hills

The Malvern Hills are formed from some of the most ancient rocks in England, some 680 million years old, with their highest point being the Worcestershire Beacon (425 metres). Their distinctive shape, a 9-mile undulating ridge arising from the lower surrounding areas, is visible from many miles around. This is a designated Area of Outstanding Natural Beauty and a Site of Specific Scientific Interest, with open grassland and heathland on higher areas whilst the lower hillsides and valleys are wooded with ancient broadleaf. The Hills are fascinating to explore, with many iconic features such as the distinctive Iron Age earthworks of British Camp. Many tracks and trails offer great running with spectacular views, both on the hills themselves and in the surrounding countryside. The ridge of the hills, with views in every direction, is a wonderful place to watch the sun set of an evening. The vast deer park of Eastnor Estate and castle, really a Georgian country house, is fantastic for running and provides many activities for the family too. The Malvern Hills consist of the 15 summits of North Hill, Sugarloaf Hill, Worcestershire Beacon, Summer Hill, Perseverance Hill, Jubilee Hill, Pinnacle Hill, Black Hill, Herefordshire Beacon, Broad Down, Hangman's Hill, Swinyard Hill, Midsummer Hill, Raggedstone Hill and Chase End Hill. The end-to-end run included (Run 64) gives you the opportunity to visit all of them, whilst Run 65 makes a shorter tour of the northernmost Malvern Hills.

Worcestershire is a county of variation with many great places to run, from picturesque riverside runs through the Severn Valley's rolling countryside to the large woodland areas in the

64

66

66

north. The Worcestershire Way is a 31-mile fully waymarked trail which runs from Bewdley to Great Malvern, taking in some of the most scenic parts of the Worcestershire countryside. It passes through wooded valleys and copses, alongside babbling streams and through limewoods where russet-coloured muntjac, or barking deer, graze on the young shoots. Its final passage takes you through the Teme valley and the beautiful limestone landscape of Suckley Ridge with views out across the surrounding countryside (Run 66). We undertook the Way over a weekend, running the 16 miles from Bewdley to Martley with a stop at Abberley on day one, followed by the 18 miles from Martley to Great Malvern with a stop at Longley Green on day two. It was a pleasant challenge. The route is very well waymarked and designed to take in many beautiful areas, and would certainly also be possible in one go, or split into three sections of 10, 12 and 12 miles. There are several circular routes along the Worcestershire Way, including one that takes you through Abberley village and a similar loop at Martley. The Black Pear Marathon, bearing the same name as local running club, the Black Pear Joggers, is an anytime challenge of 24 miles which starts and finishes at the New Inn in Noutards Green, Stourport, providing a great circular route taking in some of the best bits of the Worcestershire Way. From the city of Worcester itself there is some wonderful towpath running along the canals to Birmingham (31 miles in total) or Stafford (46 miles in total).

Unsurprisingly, there are several notable races in this area, with race organisers drawn to the obvious challenges of these splendid hills. The Worcestershire Beacon Race is a tough 6½-mile run from the Rose Bank Gardens in Great Malvern to the top of the Beacon and back. The Malvern Hills Ultra is held in May and offers various race distances from 8 to 52 miles, with a 100-miler promised for 2015. Elsewhere in the county, the Worcester Marathon and Half are recent but well-reported additions to the road racing calendar and the Broadway Marathon and Half are tough, off-road races run on sections of the Cotswold Way, where the cold, muddy November conditions simply add to the fun and challenge of the event.

64

Worcestershire & the Malvern Hills

64 MALVERN HILLS END TO END

Distance: 10 miles (16km)
Start: North Quarry car park, North Malvern Road, WR14 4LX
Finish: Hollybush car park, Chase End Hill
Terrain: Path, trail, track, some paved
Toughness: Challenging
Ascent: 664 metres
Navigation: Easy
Good for: History, ascents
Route info: wildrunning.net/64

A hugely rewarding run for the full length of the Malvern Hills, N to S, including all 15 summits. The Malverns are highly runnable, with trails from wide, gravelled paths to barely-visible tracks to some of the lesser-visited tops. Only primary summits are included here. From the start, follow zigzag path up North Hill. Follow ridge due S over Worcs Beacon before descending to cross road at Upper Wyche. Continue over Jubilee Hill and Black Hill, down to cross another road before summiting Herefordshire Beacon, Hangman's, Swinyard and Midsummer Hills. Finally, head to Eastnor Park for final summits of Raggedstone, Chase End Hills. ⚠ Main road crossings.

65 NORTH MALVERNS CIRCULAR

Distance: 6 miles (10km)
Start/finish: North Quarry car park, North Malvern Road WR14 4LX
Terrain: Rock, path, paved sections
Toughness: Moderate
Ascent: 441 metres
Navigation: Easy to moderate
Good for: History, ascents
Route info: wildrunning.net/65

This fantastic run combines two shorter walking loops to make a wonderful tour of the northernmost Malvern Hills, including its highest point, the Worcestershire Beacon. The Beacon's summit is worth a moment's pause, to catch your breath and to admire the panoramic views. The route takes the broad path up from North Quarry car park and follows it S past St Anne's Well, with its tiny café, and around the southern edge of Earnslaw Quarry. It contours around the Worcestershire Beacon before heading N and over its summit. Continuing N, the route scales Sugarloaf Hill before taking in a clockwise loop around Table Hill and North Hill, finally winding its way back down to the start.

66 SUCKLEY RIDGE

Distance: 4½ miles (7km)
Start: A44 junction at Knightwick
Finish: Main Street, Longley Green
Terrain: Quiet road, bridleway, field
Toughness: Easy to moderate
Ascent: 187 metres
Navigation: Easy (waymarked)
Good for: Ascents, wildlife
Route info: wildrunning.net/66

This was our favourite and the most picturesque section when we ran the 31-mile Worcestershire Way over 2 days. Wonderful running along clear paths and wooded tunnels leads along the limestone ridge of the Suckley Hills. From lush lime woodlands, the trail emerges onto the ridge with spectacular views to Hereford and Worcs. Shy muntjac deer graze among the trees; in spring and summer, wild flowers illuminate the woodland floor. From parking by the start ⚠ cross A44 and take L signed Lulsley. Ascend the ridge and follow waymarkers S along the ridge. Finally descend into Longley Green. Buses back from here, but an out-and-back run of 9 miles gives twice the opportunity for deer spotting.

Herefordshire, Shropshire & The Marches

Herefordshire and Shropshire form much of the border between England and Wales, often referred to locally as the Marches. They are sparsely populated counties, characterised by thriving market towns, rolling agricultural land, river valleys, woodland, ridges and hills. The abundant natural features make this a fantastic place to run with a network of green lanes, bridleways, footpaths and quiet lanes to explore, contrasting with the wilder, open landscapes of the rugged uplands.

We ran a loop around Tintern (Run 68) in late summer, the grey stone of the abbey's ruins standing out against a deep blue sky. We followed the babbling River Wye along a pleasant, runnable path before crossing a road and climbing up and up through damp, green woodland to the Devil's Pulpit. At its towering limestone pillar we stopped to catch our breath and survey the spectacular views out across the Wye Valley and down to the abbey. A fantastic, flying descent through fields and past a ruined barn eventually brought us back down to the bottom of the valley, and we jogged back companionably along the river. Our afternoon was spent exploring the ruins and then watching the sunset turn the sky gold and crimson.

There are many well-maintained, well-marked, long-distance paths which wind their way through the Marches, providing a great way to explore the wonderful countryside in easily navigable sections. The Herefordshire Trail is a circuit of the county; our Run 67 follows a section with panoramic views. The Wye Valley Walk is a 136-mile waymarked trail that stretches between Chepstow Castle in Monmouthshire and Hafren Forest in Powys. It is a route of startling contrasts, from ravine gorges and steep valleys cloaked in woodland through rolling

68

68

69

farmland, wildflower meadows and orchards, to rugged and remote uplands. The route follows the course of the River Wye through the battle-scarred Anglo-Welsh borders to its rocky, mountainous source at Plynlimon in mid-Wales (Run 111). The Wye Valley Walk website lists just some of the highlights of the trail: Chepstow Castle, some of the most important woodlands in Europe, Tintern Abbey, Yat Rock viewpoint, Goodrich Castle, Capler Camp hill fort, Hay-on-Wye and its bookshops, Penddol Rocks rapids, Gilfach medieval longhouse, not to mention the bats, buzzards, bluebells, peregrine falcons and red kites.

Offa's Dyke National Trail runs for 177 miles from Sedbury Cliffs, on the Severn Estuary near Chepstow, to the North Wales resort of Prestatyn on Liverpool Bay. About 70 of these miles follow the course of the 8th-century Offa's Dyke earthwork. The path has recently been named by Lonely Planet as one of the best wall walks in the world. Its varied route crosses high, open moorland, and weaves in and out of England and Wales through wide river valleys and ancient woodland trails, rich in flora and fauna. On its way it passes through historic towns and isolated hamlets, hill forts, castles, abbeys and surviving remains of former occupants of the beautiful corridor of the path. The fastest running of Offa's Dyke path is by Michael Wood in 47 hours and 25 minutes. Two of our routes take in sections of the path – Runs 68 and 69 – with the latter tackling what is generally agreed to be the toughest section of the path, from Knighton to Brompton Crossroads, the 'Switchback' section.

Being an area with so much scope for wonderful runs, there are some great races here, many with a decidedly muddy theme. The Muddy Woody 6 in cold, wet February is a well-organised trudge around the undulating tracks of Haugh Woods, near Hereford, with tea and doughnuts for afters. The Mud Runner starts near Ledbury, on the edge of the Malvern Hills, and the Magnificent Eastnor Castle 7 takes in the stunning surrounds of the deer park at Eastnor Estate. In Shropshire, the popular Ironbridge Half Marathon is generally off-road and the Over the Edge marathon and half take in the spectacular Shropshire Hills AONB at Wenlock Edge.

Herefordshire, Shropshire & The Marches

67 GARWAY HILL

Distance: 7½ miles (12km)
Start/finish: Garway Hill Methodist Chapel, HR2 8EY
Terrain: Quiet lane, path, bridleway, road
Toughness: Moderate
Ascent: 332 metres
Navigation: Moderate
Good for: Descents, woodland
Route info: wildrunning.net/67

This wonderful run follows part of the Herefordshire Trail, a 154-mile circuit of the county. From the Methodist Chapel follow Herefordshire Trail waymarkers SW to Garway Hill, climbing the short-cropped grassy hillside towards the WWII radio tracking station, visible at the top. From the summit there are panoramic views of up to 70 miles on a clear day. Continue to follow waymarkers, running SE to Little Castlefield Farm across the springy turf of Garway Common. Head W, then NW, descending into the Monnow Valley to Kentchurch. Winding woodland trails heading N through Charlotte's Wood eventually lead to a lane. Leave Herefordshire Trail here, turning R to follow lane back to the start.

68 TINTERN ABBEY - DEVIL'S PULPIT

Distance: 6½ miles (10km)
Start/finish: Tintern Abbey, NP16 6SH
Terrain: Trail, track, short road section
Toughness: Moderate
Ascent: 352 metres
Navigation: Moderate
Good for: National trail, history
Route info: wildrunning.net/68

A hugely enjoyable run starting at the beautiful and atmospheric ruins of Tintern Abbey and heading into the lovely Wye Valley, taking in woodland trails and a section of Offa's Dyke Path. The route follows the Wye downstream. Head away from Tintern with river on R, crossing a bridge before climbing steeply up to the waymarked Offa's Dyke Trail. The path leads to the Devil's Pulpit, a narrow limestone pillar on the edge of the gorge: magnificent views back down to the abbey. Continue through woods, descending on wonderfully runnable fields and green lanes down into the Brockweir village. A former railway leads back to a pleasant riverside path, reaching Tintern Parish Church on the main road, which is then followed back to the Abbey.

69 OFFA'S DYKE: SWITCHBACK

Distance: 15 miles (24km)
Start: Cemetery Road car park, Knighton, near LD7 1EW
Finish: Brompton Crossroads
Terrain: Trail, track, field path
Toughness: Challenging
Ascent: 987 metres
Navigation: Easy (waymarked)
Good for: National trail, ascents
Route info: wildrunning.net/69

Offa's Dyke Trail journeys through 177 miles bordering England and Wales, with picturesque and spectacular landscapes. This 'switchback' section has a reputation, as it rises and falls through the Shropshire Hills AONB. Considered the toughest on the path, this run has lots of tough ascents and fun descents; but the tranquillity and views make the tough parts worthwhile. From car park, follow river NW. Cross Kinsley Road, joining waymarked Offa's Dyke path. Head generally N, following waymarkers along the dyke, climbing Llanfair Hill (432m) before descending to Newcastle. Continue, passing Churchtown to reach the end of this section at Brompton Crossroads.

Sherwood Forest

Sherwood Forest

Home to the 800 year-old Major Oak, hiding place of Robin Hood and his Merry Men, Sherwood Forest is a National Nature Reserve and, away from the popular tourist areas, can be a wonderfully peaceful and remote place to lose yourself, running through the trees. The Forest is divided into three sections, each with its own character. In the north of the forest is The Dukeries, which includes the lovely National Trust Clumber Park (Run 72), Welbeck Abbey and Creswell Crags, some of the old Ducal estates, characterised by rolling countryside dotted with charming villages. There are many quiet lanes and tracks on which to explore this part of the forest. The second area is the Heart of the Forest, including Edwinstowe (Run 70) and Sherwood Forest, Rufford and Vicar Water Country Parks. This is the historic and classic ancient Forest where small towns and parks surround the National Nature Reserve, within which lie the Royal Wood of Birklands and Budby Forest. At nearby Kings Clipstone, the 'Royal Heart of Ancient Sherwood Forest', can be found the remains of King John's Palace and the Royal Hunting Park. There is an extensive network of paths and tracks on which to explore this part of the forest. The final, third, area is Byron Country – the southern forest, home to Blidworth (Run 71), Newstead Abbey and Bestwood Country Park. This was the former Royal Forest and the west face of the ruined Newstead Abbey, a former Augustinian priory which became the ancestral seat of Lord Byron. There are strong Robin Hood connections in this part of the forest, from the Rainworth Water valley, Thieves Wood and Harlow Wood through to the village of Blidworth itself. The runs described take in each of these areas, showcasing the great running and unique characteristics each one has to offer.

133

71

70

70

There are many waymarked and unmarked trails to explore within the forest. We have found that heading away from the main visitor centre and Robin Hood-themed areas provides the best opportunity for wild running, enjoying the woodland, heathland and history of the place, far away from roads and crowds. For a family day out that also has great running potential, the National Trust-owned Clumber Park is a wonderful place to explore. Clumber is a beautiful expanse of picturesque parkland, open heaths, peaceful woodland and a magnificent lake covering more than 3,800 acres. Once the country estate of the Dukes of Newcastle, it still retains reminders of its past, from the Gothic-style chapel to the Walled Kitchen Garden. The loop around the vast, man-made lake is 5 miles in length, all on level, easy-access paths. Clumber Park is a fantastic place for walks, picnics and wildlife spotting, a stone's throw from the busy East Midlands.

There are many great races in the area, many themed around the forest such as the Legends of Sherwood 10k and the Robin Hood Half Marathon. The impeccably organised Worksop Half Marathon, seemingly an unlikely venue for a picturesque race, soon heads out of the town's streets and into the beautiful local countryside, taking in a loop of Clumber Park which is a lovely place, if only you could stop for a moment to admire it. There is the popular Towpath and Trail 10k at Shireoaks, enjoying scenic countryside and runnable trails alongside the Chesterfield Canal. Finally, for those looking for longer distances, there is the Dukeries Ultra in May. The race offers two distances of 30 or 40 miles, following a waymarked loop, and passing though the area's pretty sandstone villages and historical sites. Starting in the heart of Sherwood Forest and keeping mostly to forest trails and footpaths, the route passes charming lodges, runs through Cresswell Crags and skirts the Welbeck Estate. It crosses Clumber Park and through peaceful farmland before looping back past the Thoresby Estate and returning to Sherwood Forest.

Sherwood Forest

70 EDWINSTOWE

Distance:	7½ miles (12km)
Start/finish:	Edwinstowe Youth Hostel, Mansfield, NG21 9RN
Terrain:	Forest trail
Toughness:	Easy
Ascent:	114 metres
Navigation:	Easy
Good for:	Woodland, families
Route info:	wildrunning.net/70

An enjoyable, flat, circular run along leafy forest trails into the heart of the National Forest. This is classic Sherwood Forest country, with ancient, gnarled oaks standing majestically all around. The route starts on some of the busier trails but soon heads out along a quiet track around the edge of the Forest. From start, head NW along path, continuing around the S edge of the forest. The route passes a Chantry chapel and hermitage, dedicated to King Edwin of Northumberland. After Ladysmith Plantation, the route emerges on to the open heathland of Budby South Forest and the heart of the original forest, Birklands. Return to the start passing the wonderful, vast structure of the Major Oak on the way.

71 BLIDWORTH FULL ROUND

Distance:	8 miles (13km)
Start/finish:	Car park off Mansfield Road (B6020), Blidworth, NG21 0LR
Terrain:	Forest track, quiet road
Toughness:	Easy
Ascent:	189 metres
Navigation:	Easy to moderate
Good for:	Woodland, families, history
Route info:	wildrunning.net/71

Blidworth is a small village in the south of Sherwood Forest, well served by footpaths leading out into the countryside. It has its own Druid Stone, a rocky outcrop over 4 metres high and 25 metres wide, with a hollow large enough for a person to pass through. Variations to this route include a ½ round and ¾ round but this is the full version and worth the effort, incorporating wonderful parts of Byron Country. From car park, head E through Tippings Wood Nature Reserve. Run SE through Boundary Wood, crossing Dale Lane. Follow clockwise loop through Haywood Oaks, looping around to Old Blidworth. Cross Main Street and follow footpaths NW, looping back around to Old Blidworth and back to the start.

72 CLUMBER PARK

Distance:	6 miles (9km)
Start/finish:	Clumber Park (NT) car park, Worksop, near S80 3AZ
Terrain:	Trail, path, some quiet road
Toughness:	Easy
Ascent:	112 metres
Navigation:	Easy to moderate
Good for:	Families
Route info:	wildrunning.net/72

A wonderfully peaceful run in the 3,800 acre Clumber Park estate, escaping the popular (but enjoyable) 5-mile lake loop and heading out into the wilder parts of the park. The route creates a larger circuit around the lake, taking in peaceful woodland, open heath and parkland on perfect running trails. From the car park, run SW to the lake, and head down a wide path through woods to reach the 18th century Clumber Bridge and 19th century grotto. Pass Drayton and Normanton Gates, 2 of the 7 park entrances, and cross open farmland alongside woodland with views down to the lake and weir. After Hardwick village the route returns to the lake, the Pleasure Ground and Lincoln Terrace before ending back at the car park.

Juicetrump Hill

Lincolnshire Wolds

The Lincolnshire Wolds Area of Outstanding Natural Beauty is a range of hills continuous with the Yorkshire Wolds. Running along the North Sea coast from the River Humber in the northwest to the town of Spilsby in the southeast, they are the highest area of land in eastern England between Yorkshire and Kent. This is a truly wonderful place to run, with miles of footpaths and trails through spectacular, green rolling countryside and on perfect trails through leafy woodland. Runs 73 and 74, Juicetrump Hill and South Orsmby Circular, allow the runner to absorb the tranquillity of the Wolds.

Tennyson, born in Somersby in the Lincolnshire Wolds, is said to have drawn inspiration from the landscape for some of his most famous works. In *Maud* he writes of lakes, meadows, sands and *"a bed of daffodil sky"*:

"From the meadow your walks have left so sweet
That whenever a March-wind sighs
He sets the jewel-print of your feet
In violets blue as your eyes,
To the woody hollows in which we meet
And the valleys of Paradise."

Lime, or linden, trees were once abundant in Britain's woodlands and have been a part of the country's landscape for millennia. Some ancient examples still exist, including a lime coppice in Westonbirt Arboretum near Bristol estimated to be 2,000 years old. The Lincolnshire Limewoods, inspiration for Run 75, are some of the few remaining predominantly lime woodlands, also rich in history as they hide the remains of medieval abbeys and numerous archaeological sites. In summer, the air is rich with the lime flowers' heady, honeyed incense and the small, bright green leaves spreading their dense canopies over the paths create a wonderful dappled

137

74

74

75

place, luminous with sun. The Lincolnshire Limewoods Project has worked for several years to create better access to the woodland, through the creation of many great new trails, the management of the ancient woodlands and the planting of areas of new trees. They also aim to provide education about this treasured part of the English countryside.

The Lincolnshire Wolds Black Death Challenge is a 26 mile anytime challenge set by prolific walker and writer of guidebooks, John Merrill. The route starts and finishes at Louth's 'Cathedral of the Wolds' St. James Church. Rich in history, the route passes the sites of seven medieval villages, mostly depopulated as a result of the Black Death. The route works brilliantly as a tough one-day challenge, or a pleasant long weekend, and is a delight throughout. It tours the wildest parts of the wolds, taking in the Hubbard Hills and the best of the area's unspoilt graceful, rolling landscape with all its spectacular scenery and wildlife. Some of the running is tough going in winter, but this just adds to the challenge; there is plenty of straightforward running too. A full guidebook to the route, devised for walkers but perfect as running challenges is available from the John Merrill Walk Guides website. The Saleby Jogging Centre website is also a fantastic resource for runners looking for inspiration for some of the longer local challenges.

The Viking Way is a long distance path, running for 147 miles across a varied and interesting route from Burton-upon-Humber to Oakham in Rutland, taking in the Lincolnshire Wolds and the limestone escarpment of Lincoln Cliff en route, at Oakham it links with the Macmillan Way and the Hereward Way. The Viking Way Ultra is a non-stop race taking in the full 147 miles of the trail. The Grim Reaper Ultra is rapidly becoming a classic, now in its 5th year. Starting from Grimsthorpe Castle, runners have 26 hours to complete courses of 40, 70 or 100 miles, either in solo or team categories. For a slightly shorter but fantastic introduction to the brilliant running the area has on offer, the Gruesome Twosome Half Marathon is run over a challenging, multi-terrain course in the Lincolnshire Wolds around Caistor.

Lincolnshire Wolds

73 JUICETRUMP HILL

Distance: 4½ miles (7km)
Start/finish: Bluebell Inn, 1 Main Road, Belchford, LN9 6LQ
Terrain: Path, trail, track
Toughness: Easy to moderate
Ascent: 103 metres
Navigation: Easy (waymarked)
Good for: Wildlife
Route info: wildrunning.net/73

A lovely circular run, deep within the Lincolnshire Wolds AONB, that is fully waymarked to allow you to simply enjoy running in this beautiful part of the country. The amazingly named Juicetrump Hill (which sadly has no public access) is passed on your right as you leave the village. Its strange shape was once thought to be due to its use as a Neolithic longbarrow; however, it is a result of geology – a limestone outcrop formed by the weathering of the softer rock to leave the harder roach stone exposed. The outward half of the route follows the Viking Way as it winds its way across Lincolnshire. Leaving the Way at the footpath, follow field tracks and bridleways W and S, taking in the spectacular views.

74 SOUTH ORMSBY CIRCULAR

Distance: 8 miles (13km)
Start/finish: The Massingberd Arms, South Ormsby, LN11 8QS
Terrain: Field path, track, trail, road
Toughness: Moderate
Ascent: 170 metres
Navigation: Moderate
Good for: Wildlife, woodland, ascent
Route info: wildrunning.net/74

For a feeling of total immersion in the peace and tranquillity of the area, this wonderful run follows miles of inviting trails through the spectacular and varied landscape of the Lincolnshire Wolds. From the Massingberd Arms, footpaths lead W to Moor Holt woods and great running along a bridleway to a lane leading S to Harden's Gap. The bridleway continues past woodland at Willow Bank and Snake Holt before leading to a quiet lane and then a track upwards to Sutterby Holt woods and further great views. The route then drops down to Driby before crossing fields to the remains of the medieval church of St Andrew. Finally, run alongside the stream and through woodland to return to the Massingberd Arms.

75 WOODHALL SPA

Distance: 7½ miles (12km)
Start/finish: Royal Square, Woodhall Spa
Terrain: Woodland trail, field, road
Toughness: Easy to moderate
Ascent: 66 metres
Navigation: Easy to moderate
Good for: Woodland, wildlife
Route info: wildrunning.net/75

This great run explores the rare and wonderful Lincolnshire limewoods and National Nature Reserve, which lie between Wragby, Bardney and Woodhall Spa. It is a fantastic place to spot rare birds, butterflies, dormice and grass snakes. Starting in pretty Woodhall Spa, leave Royal Square, heading E to reach a church, then N to run around the edge of the golf course and out into the wilds. Continue N through Halstead Wood, looping around to Stixwould Wood, before heading S into the village of Stixwould, once home to a Cistercian nunnery. Winding through mature woodland on wonderful trails, the route then follows the Viking Way. This waymarked trail leads you through stunning Scots pinewoods and silver birch coppice to return to the start.

The Howgills

North

England's North has some of the best running terrain to be found anywhere, along with a vibrant fell running scene. Explore the fantastic diversity of the area, from the vast, open moorlands of the North Pennines to the deserted beaches of Northumberland and the craggy fells and majestic waters of the Lake District.

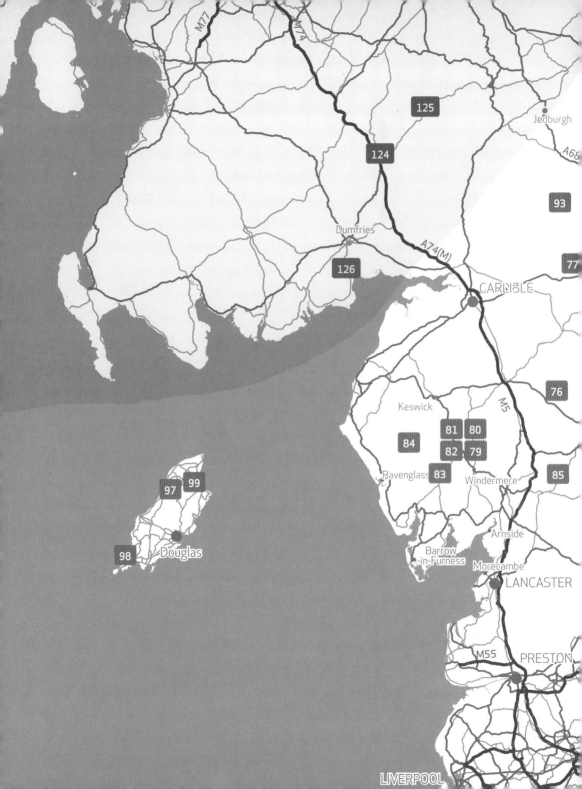

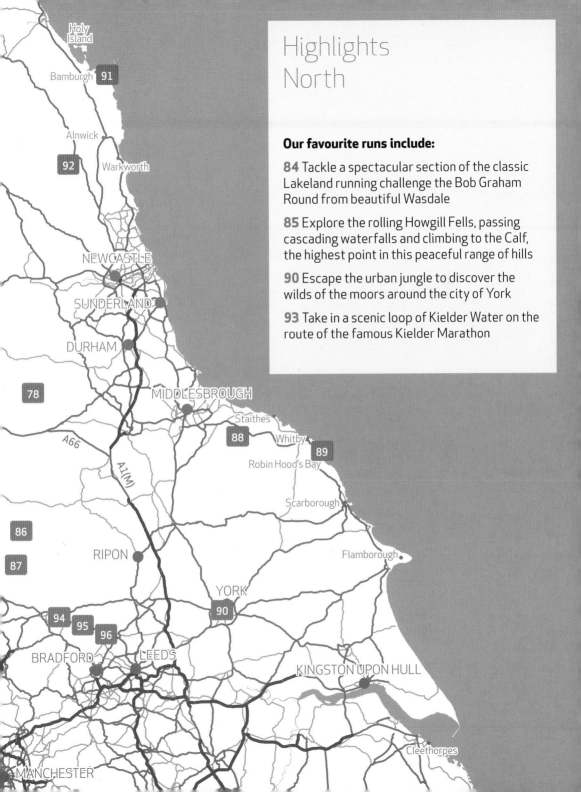

Highlights North

Our favourite runs include:

84 Tackle a spectacular section of the classic Lakeland running challenge the Bob Graham Round from beautiful Wasdale

85 Explore the rolling Howgill Fells, passing cascading waterfalls and climbing to the Calf, the highest point in this peaceful range of hills

90 Escape the urban jungle to discover the wilds of the moors around the city of York

93 Take in a scenic loop of Kielder Water on the route of the famous Kielder Marathon

North Pennines, near Hadrian's Wall

The North Pennines & Hadrian's Wall

The North Pennines was designated as an Area of Outstanding Natural Beauty in 1988 for its spectacular moorland scenery which, although wild and untamed in appearance, is in fact the product of centuries of farming and lead-mining. At 770 square miles it is the second largest of the 49 AONBs in the United Kingdom. The landscape of the North Pennines is one of open heather moors rising between deep dales, upland rivers, hay meadows and stone-built villages, many of which still hold the legacies of a mining and industrial past. Described by Roland Smith, author of *On Foot in the Pennines*, as "England's last great wilderness" this is an area of great contrast where, away from the scars of its industrial history, there is great, wild beauty and fantastic, varied running to be found. From the strange barren moonscape of Cross Fell to the wildflower meadows of Upper Teesdale and the breathtaking scenery of the Pennine Way, running here will not disappoint.

The Pennine Way is a 268-mile trail which runs along the backbone of England from the Peak District, through the Yorkshire Dales and over Hadrian's Wall to the Cheviots. Devised by Tom Stephenson, the Way is described (again by Roland Smith, whose beautifully photographed and written book is worth a read prior to visiting) as "sticking roughly" to the route of the Pennines themselves - an "epic long-distance footpath... rough is the right adjective for this toughest of mountain marathons". It is the subject of Mike Cudahay's classic book *Wild Trails to Far Horizons* which, in poetic detail, describes his own attempts to break the Pennine Way record.

77

78

76

Cudahy's record was broken in 1989 by his great ultrarunning rival Mike Hartley, whose incredible time of 2 days 17 hours 20 minutes and 15 seconds still stands at the time of writing. Runs 76 and 78 both offer 8-mile microcosms of the Pennine Way through some of its most dramatic and iconic landscapes.

Hadrian's Wall stretches across the north of England from Bowness-on-Solway, ½ mile from the Scottish border, to Wallsend near Newcastle, 68 miles from the border. This huge, winding structure with its many gateways, milecastles and turrets was built as a defensive fortification in Roman Britain. It marked the northernmost part of the then-vast empire of Rome, and building began in AD122 under the rule of Hadrian. The 84-mile National Trail that follows the wall runs along the river in Tyneside, through farmland and then climbs up and onto the remote and spectacular upland section dominated by the great dolerite escarpment of Whin Sill. Passing Crag Lough and the meeting point with the Pennine Way, the trail then gradually descends to the rich, rolling green pastures of Cumbria and finally the salt marshes of the Solway Estuary.

There is concern over erosion and damage to the wall and a 'User Code of Respect' asks visitors to keep to signed paths, particularly in poor weather. Circular routes, such as our Run 77, take in the wonderful countryside and heritage of the area, whilst minimising the impact upon the wall itself. The Moss Troopers' Trail is another alternative to traditional paths along the Wall. "This is a route for dreamers, drovers, revivers and rogues", suggests its creator, eco walker and author Mark Richards. It takes in the spectacular countryside and scenery to the north of Hadrian's Wall, avoiding the tourist trails and offering excellent and varied running terrain. The route is linear but can be linked up with the Hadrian's Wall path at several points to create a shorter, circular run. Passing the remote wilderness of Thirlwall Common, the run skirts Wark Forest and Haughton Common before heading south to Newborough, crossing Hadrian's Wall on the way. This route provides a wonderful run, on varied terrain and ever-changing scenery. A guide-book to the trail, with 10 percent of profits going to conservation projects, is available at markrichards.info.

The North Pennines & Hadrian's Wall

76 HIGH CUP

Distance:	8 miles (13km)
Start/finish:	Billysbeck Bridge (S entrance to Dufton), 500m S of CA16 6DB
Terrain:	Moorland, track, trail
Toughness:	Challenging
Navigation:	Moderate to challenging
Ascent:	178 metres
Good for:	Views, national trails
Route info:	wildrunning.net/76

This spectacular run out along the Pennine Way to the breathtaking High Cup Nick and back along High Cup Gill takes in everything this wonderful area has on offer, from the verdant Eden Valley to the extraordinary rock formations of the Nick itself, the apex of a huge, horseshoe-shaped glaciated valley high on the W edge of the North Pennines. This is a properly wild place, exhilarating, and the running is a perfect mix of fast trail, challenging ascents and technical descents. Start by joining the Pennine Way, heading E and over a long stretch of the classic route as far as High Cup Nick, running over Peeping Hill and Narrowgate Beacon on the way. Turn sharp R to head SW down High Cup Gill to reach quiet road. Turn R to return to start.

77 HADRIAN'S WALL LOOP

Distance:	10 miles (16km)
Start/finish:	Peel car park, Melkridge, 500m N of NE47 7AN
Terrain:	Track, trail
Toughness:	Moderate
Navigation:	Moderate
Ascent:	300 metres
Good for:	History, wildlife, national trails
Route info:	wildrunning.net/77

A fantastic run with a great stretch of the historic Wall path, before winding over open commons and splashing through babbling Caw Burn. Pass the fantastic organic farm and B&B at Gibbs Hill before looping stunning Greenlee Lough, returning on the Pennine Way and then Hadrian's Wall path. From the car park run W along Hadrian's Wall, turning R at milecastle 41 to follow path across Melkridge Common. Ford Caw Burn and continue on path N until reaching obvious junction. Head E to Gibbs Hill and then NE, running clockwise along the edge of the plantation around Greenlee Lough NNR. On reaching the Pennine Way, head S to Hadrian's Wall Path, finally W to the car park. Please avoid the Wall Path in wet weather.

78 HARTER FELL

Distance:	8 miles (13km)
Start/finish:	Middleton-in-Teesdale, DL12 0QA
Terrain:	Track, trail, short road section
Toughness:	Moderate
Ascent:	266 metres
Navigation:	Moderate
Good for:	Ascents, national trails, history
Route info:	wildrunning.net/78

This run celebrates the wonderful and varied scenery of the area. It starts along the classic long-distance trail and scene of past distance-running rivalry, the Pennine Way. From start head S along Bridge Street, crossing the Tees to reach B6277. The Pennine Way is signed straight over this road and can be seen looping its way up to Harter Fell. The prominent peak to the left of Harter Fell as you approach is Kirkcarrion, a strange and remote fell reputed to house the tomb of Brigantean prince, Caryn. After a fast, exhilarating descent into the Lune Valley, follow 'Grassholme Reservoir', leaving the Pennine Way at Grassholme Bridge, before taking to easy running on a section of old railway and returning to Middleton.

Above Ullswater

The Northern Lake District

The Lake District is so vast an area and with such endless scope for wild running routes that we were hard pushed to choose our favourites. It is our hope that those included act as a tempting introduction to the spectacular landscapes of the Lakes, and inspire you to explore further and seek out your own adventures. We have included some slightly more surprising routes in the lesser-known areas of the National Park, as well as some of the great fell classics. For simplicity, we have split the Lakes into north and south, with the Northern Lakes being the area north of Dunmail Raise.

We ran in the Northern Lakes in midsummer, camping in the Dovedale Valley in the shadow of the great fells of Dove Crag, Hart Crag and Fairfield. Waking early and eager to explore, we tackled the Kirkstone Pass pre-dawn and spent an hour or so running in the picturesque hills at its southern end. Contemplating the walk back down to the tent for breakfast we knew there was only one thing to do. Standing at the top of the road we surveyed our flight path: the long, pale ribbon of the Kirkstone Pass, glowing almost luminous silver in the early light. A brief moment – we exchanged a glance, an unspoken "get set" – and then launched, aeroplaning, helterskeltering, bodies wildly out of control, rapid-fire feet slapping the smooth tarmac as our speed blurred the views all around, unable to slow, to speak, to think until we had come to a stop in the valley below.

Run 81 traverses the picturesque eastern shore of Ullswater, giving wonderful views across the silver expanse of the lake. It follows the rough mountain tracks which lead along this less-visited shore from Patterdale in the south to Pooley Bridge in the north.

81

81

79

High Street's summit is a natural plateau with a wide, wonderfully inviting and, as long as the wind allows you to stay upright, fantastically runnable path along the length of its ridge (Run 80). The fell has a fascinating history; once the site of a Roman road that ran from Brougham near Penrith to Ambleside, it was used in the 18th and 19th centuries as a venue for summer fairs. The flat summit of High Street was used for horse racing and is still often referred to as Racecourse Hill. On a calm, sunny day it is a wonderful run, and even poor weather can add to the atmosphere and challenge of the route, however it can become quite extreme on the summits. During the 2005 Karrimor International Mountain Marathon, I found myself on High Street in atrocious weather, barely able to stand against the wind, my running partner and I fighting with the map in an attempt to locate the next checkpoint. In the end we spotted a long, low wall and made our way to it, hoping to take shelter on the other side, out of the wind. Climbing over, we found another dozen or so pairs had had the same idea and we all huddled together for a while, taking the opportunity to eat and drink and check our maps before eventually forcing ourselves to leave our sanctuary to head back into the storm.

The Fairfield Horseshoe is a classic walking route that is also a challenging and spectacular run (Run 79). There is an annual fell race held in May on the route of the Horseshoe, drawing the best fell runners to tackle this classic Lakeland challenge. First organised by the Lake District Mountain Trial Association in 1966, the race is 9 miles long with over 900 metres of ascent. At the time of writing the course records are held by Mark Roberts (1 hour 15 minutes in 2000) and Janet McIver (1 hour 28 minutes in 2008). Fell racing is hugely popular in this part of the country, with races, including many classics, being held throughout the year. There are also many great trail races in Cumbria, with the Cartmel 18k and Great Grizedale Forest 10 in March, the Hawkshead trail races in April, Borrowdale and Kentmere trail races in May, Grasmere, Keswick and Great Langdale in June and Coniston in October. The Lakeland Trails Series runs throughout the year, with well-organised races in some incredibly scenic places.

Cofa Pike

The Northern Lake District

79 FAIRFIELD HORSESHOE

Distance: 11 miles (18km)
Start/finish: Bridge House (NT), Rydal Road, Ambleside, LA22 9AN
Terrain: Footpath, road, fell
Toughness: Challenging
Ascent: 974 metres
Navigation: Moderate to challenging (weather)
Good for: Classic routes, ascents
Route info: wildrunning.net/79

The Fairfield Horseshoe is a classic walking route, traversing eight Wainwrights, and its challenging terrain lends itself perfectly to running. Head NW out of Ambleside, following Scandale Beck before ascending through Rydal Park with its stunning house and gardens. A road and then footpath make a zig-zag ascent up to Nab Scar, from where there are wonderful views across to Loughrigg Fells. Follow route N, over Heron Pike and Great Rigg, to summit of Fairfield with its cairns and shelters. From the summit head E, crossing Link Hause, Hart Crag and Dove Crag before turning S to High Pike summit and then descending steeply to Low Pike. Finally traverse High Brock and Low Brock before descending to Ambleside.

80 HARTSOP & THE BEACON

Distance: 6½ miles (11km)
Start/finish: Hartsop, CA11 0NZ
Terrain: Trail, track, path, open fell
Toughness: Challenging
Ascent: 632 metres
Navigation: Moderate to challenging (weather)
Good for: Ascents, really wild
Route info: wildrunning.net/80

This spectacular run starts and finishes in pretty Hartsop village, near the northern end of the Kirkstone Pass. From the stunning U-shaped valley with Gray Crag to L and Hartsop Dodd to R, the run path lies clearly ahead, climbing into the high fells. The path ascends steeply to Threshthwaite, heading L to the summit plateau of Thornthwaite Beacon with cairn and panoramic views. From here let clear path draw you along the ridge of High Street to summit, before descending along the Straights of Riggindale. A steep, fairly technical descent leads to footbridge at N end of Hayeswater – a wonderful place for a circular run taking in Angle Tarn – before descending a track past waterfalls at Hayeswater Gill and back to Hartsop.

81 AROUND ULLSWATER

Distance: 10 miles (16km)
Start: Side Farm campsite, Patterdale, CA11 0NP
Finish: Pooley Bridge
Terrain: Trail, track, road
Toughness: Moderate
Ascent: 391 metres
Navigation: Easy
Good for: Wild swimming, wildlife, families
Route info: wildrunning.net/81

This picturesque run traverses the E side of Ullswater. From Side Farm the bridleway along the lake is accessed L off the farm track. This can be undertaken as an out-and-back, or return on the paved western shore, running parallel to the main road for an 18-mile (29km) loop. The relaxing alternative is to jump on the Ullswater steamer and enjoy the fantastic scenery from a different perspective. A wonderful 3-mile (5km) loop of Hallin Fell, approximately halfway along the southern shore of Ullswater, run from either end of the lake, also makes for a great route. The tranquil woodland walks and spectacular waterfalls at Aira Force are worth a visit and great for families.

Wasdale

The Southern Lake District

The southern Lake District is an area of contrasts, from the busier tourist areas of Windermere and Kendal to England's highest peak, Scafell Pike at 978 metres, and the beautiful, remote areas around Wasdale and Wast Water. This is a superb and classic area for wild running and a destination every runner should visit at least once.

Stumbling into Bilbo's Café in Ambleside dressed in full winter running kit with muddy shoes, rucksacks and other bits and pieces of run-route reconnaissance paraphernalia, we could not have felt more at home. Photos of legendary Lakeland climber Dave Birkett, taken by his dad Bill, also a great Lakeland climber and walker, hung on the walls; running and climbing pictures and magazines were liberally distributed about and there was information on local clubs and fell races pinned to the wall. Bilbo's website claims their breakfasts have fuelled "Fell Runners, Climbers, Hill Walkers, Mountain Bikers, Triathletes, Orienteers, Swimmers and Adventure race teams in their search for adventure" and the cheery greeting we received did much to put our minds at rest that we were not an unusual sight in these parts.

Wasdale (Run 84), jewelled with the shining length of Wastwater and crowned with Scafell Pike, is the home and training ground of Joss Naylor, subject of the 2009 book *Joss: The Life and Times of the Legendary Lake District Fell Runner and Shepherd Joss Naylor* by Keith Richardson and Val Corbett. Over the span of his running career Iron Joss has racked up some truly impressive achievements, including the Welsh 3,000 metre peaks in 4 hours 46 minutes in 1973, the Pennine Way in 3 days and 4 hours in 1974, 72 Lakeland peaks

83

82

84

in under 24 hours in 1975 and, more recently, 70 Lakeland Peaks at the age of 70 in 2006.

Across the UK there are several recognised long-distance 'rounds', set as a challenge to runners to complete within a specified time limit. The main three are the Bob Graham in Cumbria, the Paddy Buckley in North Wales and the Ramsay Round in Scotland. Of these, the Bob Graham is probably the most famous, in part due to Richard Askwith's book *Feet in the Clouds* which explores so much of the history and culture of fell running, alongside the author's personal journey to conquer the Round itself. Starting and finishing at the Moot Hall in Keswick, the 66 miles over 42 Lakeland fells, with almost 8,230 metres of ascent, was first run by local hotelier Bob Graham in 1932 to celebrate his 42nd birthday. Rounds have been undertaken in various ways to make the already hard challenge even harder: supported and unsupported, in summer and winter, extended over additional peaks and even run two in succession. Those who complete a minimum of 42 peaks in under 24 hours are eligible to become members of the hallowed Bob Graham Club. At the time of writing, the records for the fastest classic 42-peak rounds are 13 hours 53 minutes for men (Billy Bland in 1982) and 18 hours 12 minutes for women (Nicky Spinks in 2012). The highest number of peaks run in 24 hours is 77 for men (Mark Hartell in 1997) and 64 for women (Nicky Spinks in 2011).

For a gentler introduction to Lakeland running, try The Cumbria Way, a waymarked 70 mile long distance route which traverses the Lake District National Park at a fairly low level, following tracks and paths through wonderful landscapes and scenery. The trail starts in Ulverston and passes Coniston Water (see Run 83), Tarn Hows and Dungeon Ghyll, crossing the Stake Pass to Borrowdale, Derwent Water and Keswick. It continues to Caldbeck either via Dash Falls or over High Pike, finally following the Caldew valley to Carlisle. There are several circular runs using the Cumbria Way, such as the Loughrigg Tarn run (Run 82), or take a few days and run it as a whole, immersing yourself in the magnificent scenery and fantastic running.

The Southern Lake District

82 LOUGHRIGG TARN - ELTER WATER

Distance:	4½ miles (7km)
Start/finish:	Elter Water car park, LA22 9HR
Terrain:	Grass path, track, quiet lane
Toughness:	Moderate
Ascent:	162 metres
Navigation:	Easy
Good for:	Wildlife, woodland
Route info:	wildrunning.net/82

A lovely quiet run through the Great Langdale valley, starting and finishing by Langdale Beck or, if flooded, the well-signed Cumbria Way. From start, follow Langdale Beck downstream. Run beside tranquil Elter Water, Lake of the Swans: often the birds can be seen in residence, with the Langdale Pikes as their stunning backdrop. Follow River Brathay upstream from Elter Water to Windermere. At Kirkstone Gallery, head N, taking in an anticlockwise loop around Loughrigg Tarn, a favourite place of William Wordsworth. Cross on paths through Little Loughrigg before a fantastic, long descent which steepens as it leads back down to Elter Water, turning R on reaching lake to follow Langdale Beck and the Cumbria Way back to the start.

83 AROUND CONISTON

Distance:	8 miles (13km)
Start/finish:	Walna Scar Road car park, LA21 8HD
Terrain:	Trail, path, ridge
Toughness:	Challenging
Ascent:	714 metres
Navigation:	Moderate (if weather good)
Good for:	Ascents, descents
Route info:	wildrunning.net/83

A stunning run around Coniston Fells, with its thrilling ridge path between The Old Man of Coniston and Swirl How, and the lone trail linking Swirl How with Wetherlam, the Prison Band. This classic loop takes in the summits of Wetherlam, The Old Man, Great How (Swirl Band), and Brim Fell. From the car park, head N towards Crowberry Haws and Stubthwaite Crag. A steep climb W brings you to tranquil Low Water before gaining the summit ridge. Follow the clear path of Prison Band, then drop down to Levers Water over some technically challenging terrain. Pass Kennel Crag, Grey Crag and Low Water Beck before returning over a footbridge to the start. ⚠ Navigation can be extremely challenging in poor weather.

84 WASDALE TO HONISTER

Distance:	10½ miles (17km)
Start:	Brackenclose car park (NT), Wasdale Head, CA20 1EX
Finish:	Honister Pass
Terrain:	Trail, fell, grass ridge, bog
Toughness:	Challenging
Ascent:	1707 metres
Navigation:	Moderate (if weather good)
Good for:	Ascents, descents, wildlife
Route info:	wildrunning.net/84

A challenging run, taking in nine beautiful and peaceful western fells. Except for Great Gable, these are some of the least visited and most tranquil Lakeland areas. Hardest climbs at the start; plenty of fine running over varied terrain throughout. From the start, turn L onto road and through gate, cross Lingmel Beck, head NW steeply up to Yewbarrow summit. Along ridge N towards Stirrup Crag, detour L at Dore Head to avoid rocky terrain. Continue over Red Pike (Wasdale), Steeple, Pillar, Kirk Fell, Great Gable, Green Gable, Brandreth, Grey Knotts. From here bear L to descend on grassy track along beck to quarry track and YHA. ⚠ Navigation v. challenging in poor weather.

Malham

Yorkshire Dales

Within the borders of the historic county of Yorkshire are areas widely considered among the greenest in England, with vast stretches of unspoiled countryside in the Yorkshire Dales and North York Moors inspiring running routes of outstanding quality. The county has a fine sporting pedigree to match: athletes from Yorkshire won seven gold medals, two silver and three bronzes in the 2012 Olympics which, were it a separate country, would have placed it twelfth in the world medals table. From the wide-open countryside of the North York moors to the peat bogs and tussocky hillsides of the South Pennine moors, Yorkshire is a perfect playground for the wild runner.

The Yorkshire Dales lie mostly within the Yorkshire Dales National Park, with Nidderdale just outside the Park on its eastern edge. The area is formed by a collection of valleys scored by the tumbling becks that make their way through the limestone geology, giving the Dales their characteristic green hilltops and boulder-strewn scree slopes reaching down to deep ravines below. The great scoop of limestone forming Malham Cove was, some 50,000 years ago, a huge, glacier-fed waterfall which sent meltwater crashing down to the valley floor. The limestone pavement, whose flat, water-sculpted boulders tile the roof of the Cove, is a strange and fascinating place and fun for boulder-hopping, although somewhat extreme when wet!

It's always exciting running on a new fell, following a new path, discovering new places; especially when the dense, grey mist shrouds the hilltops, adding extra excitement to navigation. The advice on the run at Malham Tarn (Fountains Fell, Run 87) warns that it is a strenuous route, only to be attempted in good weather. It was a grey day when I packed a map, compass and other essentials, looking forward to the challenge but only too aware of the consequences of getting lost as dusk fell. Part of this route follows the Pennine Way – a path I'd wanted to run since reading *Wild Trails to Far Horizons* many years ago. As

85

86

87

I ran I tried to imagine what it would feel like to have already completed over 100 miles at this point, how it's possible to keep running over such rough terrain for days and nights in succession. I headed off up the Way, well-marked and good underfoot, climbing Fountains Fell to the summit cairn which emerged unexpectedly out of the mist as I approached. I'm told the views from here are spectacular on a clear day. A left turn and I was traversing the boggy, peaty ridge – the character of the run changes here, following minimally waymarked paths, navigating using the tumbled-down drystone wall as a hand rail and trying to find the fastest, most runnable path. Another left turn and a sprint down one of the best descents I'd ever run. No set path and my fell running mantra of "strong knees, strong ankles, sure feet" repeating in my head, I hurled myself downhill. Relying on the fact that my feet hardly touch the ground so no holes or stones have time to snag them, I fell down the hill, skimming the grass and heather that zipped below me. I will definitely run this again, hopefully next time with a view from the top.

The 3 Peaks Race is a classic annual fell race which takes in the Yorkshire peaks of Pen-y-Ghent, Ingleborough and Whernside, and claims to be one of the oldest, most famous fell races in Britain. First run in 1954, it is a navigational challenge with strict cut-off points, covering 24 miles of the most rugged and spectacular countryside in the Yorkshire Dales National Park. Run 86, in Upper Wharfedale, gives a great view of these three peaks, the highest in the county.

The Howgill fells (Run 85) lie on the western edge of the Yorkshire Dales, in Cumbria. Separated from the Lake District by the River Lune and the M6 motorway, they have remained peaceful and relatively untouched by tourism. Elite mountain runner Heather Dawe, in her wonderful and inspiring book *Adventures in Mind*, suggests that the Howgills' grassy fells, high ridges and steep valleys provide some of the best running in England. They have also made their mark on mountain marathon history, with the 1998 Original Mountain Marathon (then the KIMM) being branded the 'Howling Howgills' on account of its famously atrocious weather.

Malham Cove

Yorkshire Dales

85 THE HOWGILLS

Distance:	6 miles (9km)
Start/finish:	Low Haygarth, LA10 5NE
Terrain:	Track, trail, fell
Toughness:	Challenging
Ascent:	526 metres
Navigation:	Moderate
Good for:	Really wild, ascents
Route info:	wildrunning.net/85

A wonderful run through the less-visited and much-underrated Howgill fells which, despite being in the county of Cumbria, are actually part of the Yorkshire Dales National Park. The run starts with a climb up onto the fells past the Cautley Spout waterfall, a spectacular sight as you approach the spout from the starting point at Low Haygarth. Taking the path on the side of Cautley Spout Tongue, the route follows Swere Gill to the Calf, the highest point in the Howgills at 676 metres. A brilliant section of running over the rolling fells follows before you drop down to Bowderdale. Despite being a wonderful place with many miles of fantastic walking and running trails, it's unusual to see anyone else on this part of the fells, making for a wonderfully solitary adventure.

86 UPPER WHARFEDALE

Distance:	6 miles (10km)
Start/finish:	Yockenthwaite, 300m NW of BD23 5JQ
Terrain:	Trail, moorland path, track
Toughness:	Challenging
Ascent:	346 metres
Navigation:	Moderate
Good for:	Histor, ascents
Route info:	wildrunning.net/86

A spectacular route, starting with a steep climb to Horse Head Pass before taking to fine running along a remote moorland ridge with wonderful views of the surrounding countryside. An exciting descent on the Dales Way brings you to the River Wharfe, which winds its way through the peaceful valley of Deepdale, meeting Dentdale above the village of Dent. There are great views of the Yorkshire Three Peaks from the top of the Pass. The run returns to Yockenthwaite passing limekilns and a stone circle, thought to be a Bronze Age burial site. This route has purple waymarkers at intervals; however, map navigation is still required, particularly when visibility is poor.

87 FOUNTAINS FELL, PENNINE WAY

Distance:	8½ miles (14km)
Start/finish:	Malham Tarn Field Centre, BD24 9PU
Terrain:	Track, trail, rough moorland
Toughness:	Challenging
Ascent:	395 metres
Navigation:	Moderate – sparsely waymarked
Good for:	Ascents, national trail, families
Route info:	wildrunning.net/87

A hugely enjoyable, varied run starting at the great silver expanse of Malham Tarn, and breathtaking views from the ridge. From start follow track SE towards Malham Tarn. Turn L onto Pennine Way and continue for 4 miles, ascending to Fountains Fell ridge. At cairn turn L leaving Pennine Way and follow waymarks along ridge. At third wall turn L following waymarks and wall SE on exhilarating descent to valley. Run through three gates to Yockenthwaite. At road turn R to return to start. Nearby Malham Cove and fascinating limestone pavement are within easy and enjoyable running distance, or great to take the family exploring. In August, there is a NT campsite at the Tarn, providing a perfect base for running here.

Cleveland Way

North York Moors

The North York Moors National Park is one of the largest expanses of heather moorland in the United Kingdom, covering an area of 554 square miles. The running here is fantastic and varied, from open moorland to woodland trails and windswept coastal paths. To the east the area is edged by the impressive cliffs of the North Sea coast, providing classic and enjoyable technically challenging coast path running along the Cleveland Way at Robin Hood's Bay (Run 89). The northern and western boundaries are defined by the steep scarp slopes of the Cleveland Hills edging the Tees lowlands and the Hambleton Hills above the Vale of Mowbray. Our Run 88 over Commondale, in the Esk Valley, travels the ancient paved pannierway of the Quakers' Causeway. To the south lies the broken line of the Tabular Hills and the Vale of Pickering. On a summer run, the song of skylarks fills the air and the heather blazes a spectacular purple against wide blue skies as your feet crunch contentedly along miles of pale limestone trails, winding their way invitingly across the landscape.

So great is the wonderful expanse of these moors that the Lyke Wake Walk was devised by local farmer Bill Cowley in 1955. He claimed that, with the exception of one or two road crossings, it was possible to walk 40 miles across the North York Moors on heather all the way. So the challenge was set: to walk the 40 mile route in less than 24 hours, from the standing stone at Osmotherley to the trig point at Ravenscar. The name comes from the Lyke Wake Dirge, an old Yorkshire dialect verse telling of the soul's passage through the afterlife. The route is traditionally walked from west to east to travel with the prevailing wind, which would also lay the heather

88

90

89

away from the walker. Those who complete the full distance in under 24 hours are eligible for membership of the Club. There is an annual ultramarathon held over the course in July, with a 12-hour time limit, but this is an anytime challenge. Please note that there is no officially recognised route and it is recommended that the route be undertaken only in dry weather and with care to avoid unnecessary damage to the sensitive natural environment.

For those living in or visiting York and seeking an urban escape, the York Millennium Way (Run 90) and the Harrogate Ringway provide waymarked, circular tours of these two historic areas at distances of 23 miles and 20 miles respectively. The York Millennium Way is a fascinating tour of the many unusual and interesting green spaces around the city, truly interspersing the wild and the metropolitan, with interludes into the city punctuated by visits to marshes and open moors.

Other well-marked long distance trails include The Cleveland Way (featured in Run 89): 106 miles of fabulous trails starting at Sutton Bank and following the western edge of the high moors to Osmotherley. Traversing the moor, the Way reaches the coast at Saltburn-by-the-Sea where it follows a varied and undulating coastal path. The Cinder Track, following the old railway line from Scarborough to Whitby, is also great for some peaceful, off-road training on hard-packed surfaces. It is part of the National Cycle Network so is also suitable for a day out on the bike or for a family outing.

There is a thriving race scene in this area, with a summer and winter fell race series and the National Trust's Tom's Bransdale Fell Race. There are trail races including the Dalby Dash in November and the Ravenscar Half Marathon in April and many road and multi-terrain events too. For those seeking a longer challenge, the Hardmoors Series tackles routes within the North York Moors of varying distance from the 15-mile New Year's Day race to the classic Hardmoors 110 along the Cleveland Way and the ultra hard Ring of Steel race where competitors have 48 hours to complete 160 miles, including nearly 7,000 metres of ascent.

88

North York Moors

88 COMMONDALE

Distance:	5½ miles (9km)
Start/finish:	Roadside parking west of Commondale, YO21 2HG
Terrain:	Moorland track, field
Toughness:	Easy to moderate
Ascent:	136 metres
Navigation:	Moderate to challenging
Good for:	History, really wild
Route info:	wildrunning.net/88

A varied and interesting run with plenty of navigational challenges, taking in much of the history of the area and a huge variety of landscape. You will experience wild, open moorland with far views, great expanses of heather, picturesque woodland paths and old mine workings frozen in time. From start, run through Commondale Village. Take footpath L and run N to join the Quakers' Causeway, a fine example of exposed stone pannierway, for a mile over the moor. At track junction bear L, leaving the Causeway, and run across open moorland to cross the tiny stream of Tidkinhow Slack to reach a line of boundary stones. Head generally S on indistinct paths to reach Whiteley Beck. Cross footbridge and follow track to start.

89 ROBIN HOOD'S BAY

Distance:	7 miles (11km)
Start/finish:	Bank Top car park, Robin Hood's Bay, YO22 4RL
Terrain:	Beach, coast path, woodland trail
Toughness:	Moderate
Ascent:	406 metres
Navigation:	Moderate
Good for:	Coast, woodland, national trail
Route info:	wildrunning.net/89

A fantastic run, first on the sand and pebble beach along Robin Hood's Bay, running at the sea's edge and with great coast views. A contrasting return leg takes in beautiful countryside and scenery, joining the Cleveland Way. From the start, head S and bear L on path down to sea level. ⚠ May not be passable at high tide. Run along the beach, passing Boggle Hole and Stoupe Beck Sands before climbing onto rocky platform. Continue as far as Old Peak before ascending steeply up to Ravenscar. From there join the waymarked Cleveland Way N back to Robin Hood's Bay on perfect running trails across grassy meadows and through tranquil woodland.

90 YORK MILLENNIUM WAY

Distance:	25 miles (40km)
Start/finish:	Lendal Bridge, York, YO1 6FZ
Terrain:	Road, field path, track
Toughness:	Easy
Ascent:	167 metres
Navigation:	Easy (waymarked)
Good for:	History, urban escape
Route info:	wildrunning.net/90

An intriguing tour over easy terrain looping in and out of historic areas of York city and with open moorland, the rivers Ouse and Foss, and picturesque countryside. The run crosses the ancient common of Hob Moor and visits the marshlands of Knavesmire, Fulford Ings, the Strays (Walmgate Stray, Monk Stray and Bootham Stray) – 800 acres of open land within the bounds of the city and the conservation area of Clifton Ings. The route is fully waymarked from Lendal Bridge, and can be undertaken as the full distance or in sections from the city. The run is mainly on converted railway tracks, quiet roads and field paths, making for enjoyable and interesting running, often feeling a long way from the busy city with the hedgerows laden with blackberries in late summer.

Bamburgh Castle

Northumberland

Early on a June morning, woken by the distant roar of waves breaking on the shore, I emerged sleepily from my tent and followed tracks across farmland towards the sea. Warmed by the sun, already gaining height in a deep blue sky, I dropped down onto a deserted beach which lay gleaming and newly wave-washed before me. Abandoning my socks and shoes high up on a rock I ran barefoot, right at the water's edge, joyfully finding perfect running on the firm, white sand which stretched into the distance as far as the eye could see. On the horizon, brooding on its rocky, volcanic pedestal and marking the turning point of my run, sat the dark bulk of Bamburgh castle. This is Run 91.

The vast Northumberland skies arch over an ever-changing landscape, each area having its own distinct character: the peaceful, sandy expanses of the beaches at Bamburgh; the rugged, sea-bird-filled Farne islands; the remote northern moorlands; the Cheviots and the rolling, forested hills of the picturesque National Park and finally the windswept wilds surrounding Hadrian's Wall. The county appears relatively untouched by tourism, and the landscape feels ancient and preserved, inviting exploration. In early summer, the hills and hedges are ablaze with purple as the rhododendrons which adorn this part of the country come into glorious bloom. The beaches are vast and quiet, bordered by dunes which may provide pain or pleasure, depending upon whether they are run laboriously up or bounded down.

Around 70 percent of Northumberland National Park is moorland, some of which is heather-covered, but most is open grassland. There are many areas that feel truly wild: on an hour's run here, I saw no other person or building, a rarity indeed in Britain. The coast path which edges Northumberland provides spectacular scenery and enjoyable, interesting running. Part of the North Sea Trail, it runs for 64 miles from Cresswell to Bamburgh before heading inland. The quiet lanes

93

91

92

which criss-cross Northumberland provide some wonderful road running over many well-signposted miles through spectacular landscapes. Even at the height of summer, there are large stretches rarely used by cars. The route at the National Trust's Cragside Estate is, unusually for a wild run, all on road as it follows the one-way 6-mile loop around the estate's astoundingly beautiful parklands, past rocky crags, lakes and the occasional adventure playground (Run 92). There is also plenty to explore off the road, with over 40 miles of waymarked woodland trails. One of our favourites is the 4½ mile Armstrong Trail which takes in the rocky climb up to the Cockrow Stone and Nelly's Moss North and South Lakes.

The Lakeside Way beside beautiful Kielder Water (Run 93) takes in a 26 mile loop of the lake, the same route taken by the annual marathon here. A surfaced trail suitable for bikes, this is also perfect for a family day out.

For a greater challenge or multi-day excursion, Northumberland has some well-signed long distance paths including St Oswald's Way, a 97-mile waymarked route from the coast at Lindisfarne in the north to Hadrian's Wall in the south. Lindisfarne, famous for its castle and varied history, is also a beautiful and tranquil place and can be accessed on foot at low tide, a 3-mile run along the Pilgrim's Way, a tide-washed sandy path following a line of tall marker poles.

Aside from the wonderful running and land-based adventures, the great expanses of the North Sea here should also be explored. The rocky outcrops which make up the Farne Islands are home to puffins, guillemots, razorbills and fat grey seals who observe the tourist boats lazily from their wave-washed beds. These trips provide a fantastic family day out, with the option to land on the islands and see the birds close up.

There are some incredible races in Northumberland which showcase the beauty and diversity of the area. The Northumberland Coast Marathon in August, Kielder Marathon in October and the Northumberland stage of the Endurancelife Coastal Trail Series are all brilliantly organised events taking in some of the region's most picturesque areas.

Northumberland

91 BAMBURGH CASTLE BEACH RUN

Distance:	6½ miles (10km)
Start/finish:	St Aidan's beach car park, Seahouses, NE68 7JH
Terrain:	Sand beach
Toughness:	Easy, totally flat!
Ascent:	12 metres
Navigation:	Easy (along beach and back)
Good for:	Families, wildlife, beach, history
Route info:	wildrunning.net/91

A stunning out-and-back run on perfect, runnable sand, which can be linked to St Oswald's Way and the Northumberland Coast Path. Best run at mid- to low-tide to reveal the firm sand and to expose the full expanses of the beach and wonderful feelings of freedom this brings. Early morning is a fantastic time to experience the full glory of the sun rising over the sea. As you run, take in the views out to the Farne Islands and their 70,000 strong puffin colony and, further north, the holy island of Lindisfarne. From start, scale dunes and drop down on to the beach at its S end. Head N and run the length of the sandy section of beach until reaching the rocks below the castle at Bamburgh. Return the same way.

92 CRAGSIDE ESTATE

Distance:	5½ miles (9km)
Start/finish	Cragside Visitor Centre (NT), Rothbury, NE65 7PX
Terrain:	Surfaced road
Toughness:	Easy
Ascent:	210 metres
Navigation:	Easy
Good for:	Families, history, wildlife
Route info:	wildrunning.net/ 92

An unusual candidate for a wild running book, this route is entirely on road and hidden within the National Trust's Cragside Estate (entry payment or membership required). However, it is worth the slight discomfort of the hard surface underfoot and the occasional car passing (at a maximum speed of 15mph) for the wonders within. The estate is built on a rocky platform, high above the Debdon Burn, and was sculpted by the inventor Lord Armstrong. The vast grounds enclose rock gardens, lakes, red squirrels and fantastic other-worldly trees. From the Visitor Centre, follow the well-marked tarmac Estate Drive as it passes the grand house, formal gardens, vast lakes and much more.

93 KIELDER LAKESIDE WAY

Distance:	26½ miles (42.5km)
Start/finish:	Hawkhope car park, NE48 1BB
Terrain:	Trail
Toughness:	Easy to moderate
Ascent:	671 metres
Navigation:	Easy (waymarked)
Good for:	Families, woodland, wildlife
Route info:	wildrunning.net/93

This wonderful run on the surfaced, multi-user, waymarked Lakeside Way follows the full route of the Kielder Marathon, a classic on the race calendar. Starting at Hawkhope, the route takes a gently undulating loop of the lake taking in the spectacular scenery. There are switchback sections which climb upwards from the lake, encompassing crags and pine forests with beautiful views out across the water, a spectacular bridge over the burn and the famous Kielder viaduct to cross. The south shore has visitor centres and the Leaplish Water Park, whereas the north shore is more remote. There are options to return to the start on the Osprey ferry – please check timetables prior to setting out. The centre has plenty for families to do too.

South Pennines

The Pennines, often described as the backbone of England, stretch from the Peak District in Derbyshire northwards through Lancashire, Greater Manchester, the Yorkshire Dales and past the Cumbrian Fells to the Cheviot Hills on the Anglo-Scottish border. North of the Aire Gap, the Pennines' western spur into North Lancashire forms the Bowland Fells, and south of the gap is a spur into east Lancashire, comprising the Rossendale Fells and West Pennine Moors. The highest point of the Pennines is Cross Fell in eastern Cumbria at 893 metres.

The South Pennines lie hidden between the better-known Yorkshire Dales to the north and the Peak District to the south, with the city sprawl of Greater Manchester to the west. This is a unique landscape which has inspired many great writers and poets, including the Brontës and Ted Hughes. It is a vast, open area of sweeping, high moorland intersected by steep-sided narrow valleys, including the strangely named Forest of Rossendale, a predominantly treeless moorland despite its name. Many of these valleys contain settlements built from the local gritstone. The hillsides and drystone-wall-enclosed pastures bear the scars of a long history of industry and human use, from Mesolithic, Bronze Age and Iron Age findings to Roman roads and forts, and the mills and factories of the industrial revolution, powered by the area's fast-flowing streams. The peaceful expanses of gritstone moorland, dotted with historical remains and networked with fine, runnable trails, are the venues for our wonderful runs on Silsden and Skipton moors (Run 94) and Ilkley Moor (Run 95), part of the larger expanse of Rombalds Moor which lies between Ilkley and Keighley in West Yorkshire. We spent several days exploring this area and fell in love with its tranquility and seemingly endless fantastic running trails.

169

96

95

94

In their jointly-conceived book, *Elmet*, the beautiful marriage of Ted Hughes' poems with Fay Godwin's haunting black and white photographs truly distills the essence of the South Pennines. Hughes' poem Pennines in April captures perfectly the remoteness elevation of this immense, boulder-strewn landscape:

"If this county were a sea (that is solid rock
Deeper than any sea) these hills heaving
Out of the east, mass behind mass, at this height
Hoisting heather and stones to the sky."

The South Pennines have extensive open-access areas and are connected by a dense network of footpaths and packhorse trails, providing easy access to wild places and great running. The South Pennines Walk and Ride Festival is held in September each year, with plenty of events and activities for runners. The Dales Way runs for 78 miles from Ilkley in West Yorkshire to Bowness-on-Windermere in Cumbria, traversing many beautiful fells and dales along the way. There are several excellent circular runs which take in parts of the Dales Way, including our Run 96 which also takes in the landmark of the Otley Chevin, an imposing Millstone Grit ridge which overlooks the Wharfe Valley. The Chevin itself lies within the Chevin Forest Park, a wonderful place to explore on foot, bike or horse. A fantastic network of trails winds its way around the hills and wooded valleys here. The highest point, Surprise View at 282 metres, is recognised as one of the finest viewpoints in Yorkshire, with views of 60km around.

The South Pennines have a busy fell racing calendar, including the wonderfully named 7.5 mile Reservoir Bogs race in June. There's also a great selection of trail races, including the Baildon Boundary Way half marathon and the popular Guiseley Gallop 10k in April. Ilkley Trail Race and the Marsden 10 Mile Challenge are held in June and the Idle Trail Race in July. The Chevin Chase is a hugely popular 7-mile multi-terrain race organised by the Airecentre Pacers. It is held on Boxing Day and takes in a loop of the famous Otley Chevin ridge from Guiseley.

South Pennines

94 SILSDEN & SKIPTON MOOR

Distance:	11½ miles (18km)
Start/finish:	Parson's Lane, Addingham, near LS29 0LE
Terrain:	Moorland path /trail, quiet road
Toughness:	Moderate
Ascent:	322 metres
Navigation:	Moderate
Good for:	Wildlife, views
Route info:	wildrunning.net/94

This wonderful run takes in the moors of Silsden and Skipton, with beautiful views, fine running and plenty of variety and interest along the way. To start follow the Millennium Way up to High Marchup on a gently inclining lane. The track leads onto Silsden Moor before following Cowburn Beck. Climb over moor to High Bracken Hill, through Jenkin to Peel's Laithe, from where breathtaking views open up across the moorland and the valleys below. The run descends on bridleways to Low Bradley before climbing up onto Skipton Moor for the second half of the run. Rocky outcrops, spectacular views and perfect running trails lead across to Draughton Moor before descending back to Parson's Lane.

95 TOUR OF ILKLEY MOOR

Distance:	7 miles (11km)
Start/finish:	Wells Road car park, Ilkley, about 200m SW of LS29 9JG
Terrain:	Path, open moorland
Toughness:	Moderate
Ascent:	286 metres
Navigation:	Easy to moderate
Good for:	Wildlife, history
Route info:	wildrunning.net/95

This wonderful run tours the length and breadth of the wild and windswept Ilkley Moor on fine, runnable and easy-to-follow trails. The moor is part of the larger Rombalds Moor and has many fascinating features, from the craggy outcrop, the Cow and Calf, to the prehistoric rock carvings to be found about the moor. Starting in Ilkley itself the run follows the Millennium Way west to Piper's Crag before taking an obvious path south towards Shepherd's Hill. On reaching Shepherd's Hill, fork left, and on reaching West Buck Stones run along a good path to White Crag. At White Crag the route heads north to join up with the Dales Way link back to Ilkley.

96 OTLEY CHEVIN

Distance:	4½ miles (7km)
Start/finish:	Beacon House car park, York Gate, Otley, LS21 3DG
Terrain:	Path, forest trail
Toughness:	Easy
Ascent:	174 metres
Navigation:	Easy
Good for:	Ascents, urban escape
Route info:	wildrunning.net/96

This route is a short but classic run up to the summit of the Chevin and back. This ancient gritstone ridge, covered in old woodland and heathland, overlooks the town of Otley and is only a mile from Leeds Bradford airport, however the feeling of escape and tranquillity here is wonderful. The highest point of the Chevin is Surprise View at 282 metres and is the site of a beacon. The forest trails provide great running and the views from the top over Otley and Lower Wharfedale are spectacular. Head N from Beacon House car park to meet the Dales Way, continuing E to the summit of the Chevin. Or simply explore the many footpaths and bridlepaths which loop the hill.

Snaefell

Isle of Man

Summertime on the Isle of Man is a glorious picture of rolling hillsides covered with yellow gorse and purple heather, leafy woodland and peaceful glens, bright green against a backdrop of sparkling blue sea. On a clear day, the scene is framed by mountain views across to southern Scotland, Snowdonia, the Lake District and the Mournes in Northern Ireland. Walking here is something of a national pastime, and there are two annual festivals celebrating the wealth of well-maintained trails and paths that explore the island. A perfect place, then, to explore at a run. Lying in the middle of the northern Irish Sea, the Isle of Man is 32 miles long and at most 14 miles wide, surrounded by smaller islands, some of which are seasonally inhabited. The far north of the island is a flat, glacial plain, whilst rolling hills across the rest of the island are separated into northern and southern halves by a central valley. The highest point on the island is Snaefell at 621 metres, from where it is said that it is possible to see seven kingdoms: those of the Mann, Scotland, England, Ireland, Wales, Heaven and the Sea. Snaefell is visited on the route of the 22-mile Millennium Way (see Run 99), one of several excellent long-distance trails here. The 10-mile Heritage Trail follows the old railway line across the island from Douglas to Peel, providing enjoyable, level running, and the Herring Way takes a more road-based route, passing through several plantations on its way from Peel to Castletown. The 95-mile Isle of Man coast path is known locally as the Raad ny Foillan or Way of the Gull. This great trail was recommended to us many times in our research on runs in the area. It uses public roads as little as possible and takes in some of the island's best, hilliest and most exciting running.

99

99

98

The scenery and landscapes vary widely, from the shingle beaches of the Ayres in the north to the precipitous cliffs and stacks in the west. It would be a great route to run over the course of a few days, as it passes through many settlements and has excellent public transport links. The section of the Coast Path between Peel and Port Erin (Run 98) was some of the best and most scenic running we found anywhere, with three challenging climbs, including one up and over the heather-clad moorland slopes of Cronk ny Arrey Laa, which rises to a breathtaking 437 metres. Away from the waymarked trails there is an abundance of countryside to explore, providing absorbing running, from the peaceful lanes and forestry tracks of the lower reaches to the tussocky, remote hillsides and fine ridges higher up. Ballaugh Mountain (Run 97) encompasses much of what the island's wilder inland landscape has to offer.

There is a vibrant running scene on the Isle of Man, with an annual Easter Festival of Running organised by Manx Harriers offering 5km and 10km road races and the Peel Hill Climb with a traditional 11-mile jog/pub crawl back to Douglas after the race. The Manx marathon and half marathon are held in August. Off-road, there is the tough Isle of Man Mountain Ultra, a 50k fell race with a shorter 28k option. There's also a full calendar of local races throughout the year, including the Manx Fell Running Series and a great 10-mile trail run from Peel to Douglas along the old steam railway line. Aside from running, the Isle of Man offers much in the way of activities and entertainment. Mountain and road biking are hugely popular here, particularly in recent years following the success of multiple Tour de France stage-winning Manxman Mark Cavendish. It's a perfect place to take the family cycling, with many trails and quiet roads awaiting exploration. The TT is a massively popular annual event, worth attending if you're a fan of motorbikes; if not, it's best to avoid the island altogether during the May/June event.

Isle of Man

97 BALLAUGH MOUNTAIN

Distance:	6 miles (10km)
Start/finish:	Ballaugh Plantation car park, 1 mile S of A3 at Ballaugh
Terrain:	Trail
Toughness:	Moderate
Ascent:	293 metres
Navigation:	Easy to moderate
Good for:	Woodland, ascents, really wild
Route info:	wildrunning.net/97

This remote and varied run starts with an enjoyable climb through leafy Ballaugh Plantation, emerging onto the heather-clad slopes of Ballaugh Mountain. A relatively level run around this picturesque plateau returns to the plantation, finishing with a long, enjoyable descent along a forest road. The very minor roads are fantastic to run on, with almost no traffic. From plantation entrance, follow forest path E, gradually climbing to reach Druidale Rd. Turn R on road then L onto track across open moorland. Head to L of Ballaugh Mountain, contouring around it in a clockwise direction to meet Greenway Rd. Turn R and follow Greenway and Druidale Rds back to plantation. Enter and follow road then forest track to start.

98 PEEL TO PORT ERIN

Distance	13½ miles (22km)
Start:	Peel Castle car park
Finish:	Port Erin
Terrain:	Path, trail
Toughness:	Easy to moderate
Ascent:	1324 metres
Navigation:	Easy to moderate
Good for:	Coast, national trail, ascents
Route info:	wildrunning.net/98

Taking in three great climbs, including the highest point in this part of the island, Cronk ny Arrey Laa, this is the best section of the island's stunning coast path. From the castle, head S, climbing over Peel Hill, venue of the infamous annual Hill Race. Continue over Corrins Hills before descending to coast path. Follow coast path S, passing Glen Maye, where a waterfall and a short section on the beach await. Cross Glion Mooar and climb over Cronk ny Arrey Laa, continuing over Lhiattee ny Beinnee before descending to Fleshwick Bay. The final climb over Bradda Hill rewards with an enjoyable descent into Port Erin. There are regular buses back to Peel.

99 MILLENNIUM WAY

Distance:	22½ miles (36km)
Start:	Sky Hill, A3 1 mile W of Ramsey
Finish:	Castletown
Terrain:	Moorland, path, road
Toughness:	Challenging
Ascent:	812 metres
Navigation:	Easy (waymarked)
Good for:	National Trail, ascents, descents
Route info:	wildrunning.net/99

Starting at the foot of Sky Hill, this fully waymarked trail ascends its heather-covered slopes before making its way through open moorland and along mountain roads, passing the highest point on the island, Snaefell at 621 metres. Skirting the NW slopes of Snaefell, the route reaches the road at Cleigh yn Arragh before crossing the valley to cross the saddle between Beinn-y-Phott and Carraghan. From West Baldwin, it passes through Crosby village before a short section of surfaced road. Scenic tours through Ballamodha, and gentle, wooded hills bring you to Silverburn River at Mullen ny Carty and café at Silverdale. Join Old Royal Way along the Silverburn to finish at Castletown. ⚠ Road crossings.

Wales

With its amazing diversity of landscapes and wild places, from the rolling grassy valleys and spectacular sandy beaches of the south, through the remote tranquillity of the Black Mountains to the rugged peaks of Snowdonia and rocky coastal path, Wales is a fantastic place to run.

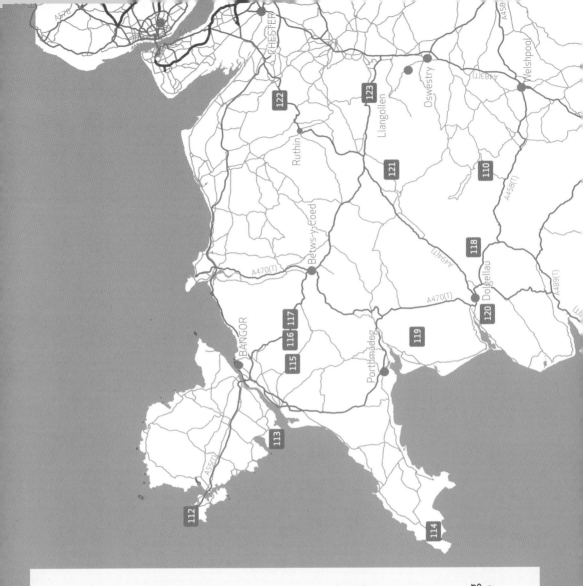

Highlights
Wales

Our favourite runs include:

101 Run barefoot along the sandy expanse of Rhossili Beach and out to the tidal islands at Worms Head

120 Seek out the giant's chair on the rocky summit of the spectacular mountain of Cadair Idris

106-108 Explore caves, coves and beaches, with exciting and varied running along the rugged Wales Coast Path

115-117 Tackle Snowdonia's highest mountains, from the long climb to the summit of Snowdon to an exhilarating run across the Glyder ridge

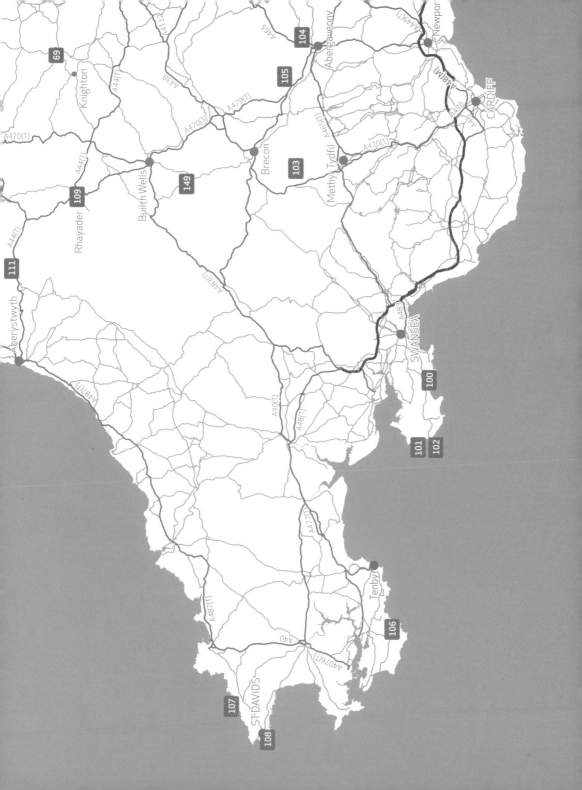

Rhossili

Gower

From Mumbles, south-west of Swansea, the Gower Peninsula stretches westwards for 19 miles out into the Bristol Channel. The UK's first designated Area of Outstanding Natural Beauty, this part of the country is packed with nature reserves, ancient ruins and fossil-filled caves: the petrified bones of woolly rhino, mammoth, reindeer, bear and wolf have all been found here. Many travel here for sport, whether climbing on perfect slabs of limestone (known locally as Sutton Stone), swimming, surfing, triathlon or simply to enjoy some of the best coastal running to be found anywhere in Britain. Being at once challenging and spectacular, the trails here are also very runnable, with many fast sections over easy grassy slopes and paths. Although there are some excellent steep climbs and descents, there isn't the incessant up and down that you find in some coastal areas – this is high quality and immensely enjoyable running, with non-stop views to boot. Run 100 takes in the Coast Path around beautiful Three Cliffs Bay, just south-west of Swansea, a chance to experience some of the best of Gower.

The beaches in this area deserve a particular mention, immaculate sandy expanses which can be linked together at low tide. The sand is often soft and fairly hard-going, particularly in the dunes, making for a good workout. Although many of the larger beaches see thousands of visitors each year, their expanses seem to swallow them up, maintaining their wild and remote nature. Early mornings or windy winter days are my favourite times to run on Rhossili beach, when its vast, empty expanse stretches out before you as you descend the path down to the sand. Run 101 returns on this beach after a panoramic run along Rhossili Down.

101

102

102

I remember a run here in early summer when gentle breezes ruffled the grasses on a winding path over Gower's sunny green-grey hills. Wildflowers nodded serenely in meadows along the tops of limestone cliffs. It was a calm evening, breaking waves making mirrors of the sand, the setting sun a deep red orb melting into the silver water. The sandy expanse of the bay stretched out before me. For that moment, I had it all to myself, a peaceful world of wave-washed solitude, a beach just for running. The receding tide revealed the temporary passage that linked my beach with the next. I wove my way between the rocks and round an edge to find another empty crescent arching before me. I made my first print on the newly sea-rollered sand and, once again, claimed the beach as mine.

The Gower section of the Wales Coast Path stretches for 38 miles from Mumbles to Crofty, providing fantastic and varying running, with the only steep, scrambly sections being those around Rhossili (Run 102). There are also several long-distance paths, including the Gower Way, a 35-mile waymarked route which bisects the Gower Peninsula, running from Rhossili inland to Penlle'r Castell. It explores many of the lesser-known parts of Gower, from the coast to rolling green hills and tranquil forests and passing many historical sites on the way.

There are many road and off-road races around Gower taking in the wonderful variety of scenery and terrain which both challenges and delights runners. The Endurancelife Coastal Trail Series Gower stage, held in November each year, is certainly one of the toughest and most scenic races in the series, with distances from 10km up to ultramarathon. It is a fantastic place for multi-sport racing too, with its fine mix of trails, quiet roads and accessible sea for swimming or surfing. The Gower Triathlon, organised by Activity Wales Events, who also stage the tough annual Wales Marathon in Tenby, is a classic on the triathlon calendar and a great way to finish off the season, being held in September at Port Eynon. The 0.9 mile swim in the bay at the blue flag beach of Port Eynon is a particular highlight.

Gower

100 THREE CLIFFS BAY

Distance:	9½ miles (15km)
Start/finish:	East Cliff car park (NT), Pennard, SA3 2DJ
Terrain:	Cliff path, woodland trail, road
Toughness:	Moderate
Ascent:	337 metres
Navigation:	Easy to moderate
Good for:	Coast, beach, history
Route info:	wildrunning.net/100

Facing the coast, head L along the cliff top coast path. In 500m find the tricky scramble down to Minchin Hole bone cave, once home of many fascinating artefacts now housed in the Swansea Museum. The route outlines the Pwlldu Head; there is an option to detour down onto the beach at Pwlldu Bay before heading inland. Follow the river upstream along farm tracks, fields and through woodland, passing the villages of Kittle and Ilston. Run through the wooded limestone Ilston valley, dry in the summer but with a flowing river after heavy rain. Pass the golf course and enjoy spectacular views out across Three Cliffs Bay and towards 12th century Pennard Castle. Follow headland above the bay back to car park.

101 RHOSSILI BEACH / WORMS HEAD

Distance:	6½ miles (10km)
Start/finish:	NT visitor centre, Rhossili, SA3 1PR
Terrain:	Trail, beach, quiet road section
Toughness:	Easy to moderate
Ascent:	231 metres
Navigation:	Easy
Good for:	Coast, beach, wildlife
Route info:	wildrunning.net/101

This wonderful run has a north and a south loop, including some of the area's most stunning landmarks. From start, head N over Rhossili Down, following the obvious and inviting path. Breathtaking panoramic views from The Beacon summit. On reaching Hillend, descend to beach and follow the great, golden crescent all the way back to path which ascends to the visitor centre, passing the famous wreck of the Helvetia. The second half of the run heads straight out along the peninsula to Worms Head. For a short window at low tide, you can drop down to sea level and run to the island. ⚠ Check tide times before crossing. Return on the inland path directly back to the start.

102 RHOSSILI TO OXWICH

Distance:	11 miles (17km)
Start:	NT centre, Rhossili, SA3 1PR
Finish:	Oxwich, SA3 1LS
Terrain:	Coast Path, track
Toughness:	Moderate
Ascent:	361 metres
Navigation:	Easy
Good for:	Coast, wildlife
Route info:	wildrunning.net/102

This is a magnificent run along the Wales Coast Path as it winds its way around the peninsula, passing rolling grassy sections, peaceful woodland, sandy beaches and wonderful cliff-top trails. This is the most remote of the sections of the as-yet unofficial Gower Coast Path, with fine views across spectacular beaches throughout. From the NT visitor centre, head S on paths to reach the coast path at Fall Bay, turning L to head SE along coast path towards Oxwich. The route briefly passes through Oxwich Nature Reserve, a haven for the wildlife that visits this rich coastal habitat and a great place for further exploration. Finish at Oxwich Bay. ⚠ Easy scrambles may become very slippery when wet.

Brecon Beacons & Black Mountains

Stretching northwards over 500 square miles from south to mid Wales, the Brecon Beacons National Park contains some of the most spectacular and distinctive upland formations in southern Britain. The Central Beacons dominate the skyline to the south of Brecon and rise to 886 metres at Pen y Fan, the highest point in south Wales. Further west lies the sandstone massif of Fforest Fawr, with its steep river valleys and spectacular waterfalls, and Y Mynydd Du, The Black Mountain. Here the summit of Fan Brycheiniog is the site of the two enchanting glacial lakes of Llyn y Fan Fach and Llyn y Fan Fawr.

Much of the National Park is formed from Old Red Sandstone, resulting in the smooth, rolling outlines of the hills with brick-coloured paths that wind invitingly through bright green bracken, giving tough but straightforward running. The geology, and therefore the terrain, changes along the southern edge of the range, where outcrops of limestone and millstone grit predominate. The limestone landscape provides technical mountain running with many ridges and screes. In some areas the land is pockmarked with the deep hollows called shakeholes or swallow holes, where the land has sunk into the cave network below. These magnificent caves and passages which lie hidden below the surface are adorned with stalagmites and stalactites. The millstone grit, pristine and sparkling on a sunny day but sombre and reflective of a grey sky, forms many of the spectacular waterfalls in this area of the Park. Wales' first International Dark Sky Reserve, the Brecon Beacons National Park, is perfect for a night run or some wild camping and stargazing as part of a multi-day jaunt. To the east of the Park and forming the Wales/England border with Herefordshire lie the Black Mountains, where the wedge-

104

105

103

shaped Skirrid Fawr rises up sharply from the surrounding fields.

We ran over Skirrid Fawr (Run 104) on a freezing winter's day, hats pulled down over our ears, the tips of our fingers and toes tingling with cold. We started in Llanvihangel Crucorney and found our way through fields around to the steep, northern end of the mountain. Its distinctive shape was created by an Ice Age landslip; local legend, however, has several more colourful explanations, from the shape carved by the keel of Noah's Ark to the footsteps of a giant. Motivated by a need to get warm, we headed straight for the top, scrambling as fast as we could, grasping tufts of grass in gloved hands, moving on all fours, although almost upright because of the gradient. The run off the top, down the gentle incline on soft turf along the well-worn path of the Beacons Way was wonderful and almost relaxing after the exertions of our ascent. We followed the Way to Abergavenny and dived into the first café we saw.

There are several long distance trails providing access and challenges within the Brecon Beacons. The Beacons Way is a 95-mile, partially waymarked route that runs from The Skirrid in Abergavenny to Bethlehem, Carmarthenshire. The route involves remote and rugged terrain and some 2,590 metres of ascent, with waymarking being sporadic and mainly limited to farmland areas. This is therefore a serious challenge requiring a good level of navigational ability. (Run 105 covers part of the Beacons Way, but with easier route-finding.) In addition to climbing many of the area's major peaks, including Fan y Big and Pen y Fan (both included in Run 103), the route passes glistening glacial lakes, ancient standing stones and solitary churches, and offers fine mountain views throughout.

There are several notable races in this area, including the Cribyn Fell Race in April, the weekend double of the Pen y Fan and Fan y Big horseshoe races in July, and the 19½ mile Brecon Beacons Fell Race in August. Wales-based endurance events company Might Contain Nuts hold a trail marathon and ultramarathon series in the Brecon Beacons and Black Mountains area. The Three Peaks Trial is held in March each year, with distances ranging from 10 to 20 miles.

Brecon Beacons & Black Mountains

103 PEN Y FAN

Distance:	8 miles (13km)
Start/finish:	Forest car park, 1½ miles NW Pentwyn Reservoir CF48 2UT
Terrain:	Track, mountain path
Toughness:	Moderate to challenging
Ascent:	516 metres
Navigation:	Easy to moderate
Good for:	Ascents, descents
Route info:	wildrunning.net/103

A wonderful run starting up Corn Du and then heading straight for the summit of Pen-y-Fan along a breathtaking and wonderfully runnable U-shaped ridge. To find start, head N through Pontsticill, keeping L for Neuadd Reservoir. From the second parking area head N along access road. Head W across the valley just before the reservoir and climb up to head N along ridge, bearing L at junction to reach summit of Corn Du, continuing to summit of Pen y Fan. Continue from Pen y Fan up a steep climb to Fan y Big for a breather and a wealth of views to admire. A clear track from Fan y Big takes you on a wonderfully exhilarating descent back to the car park.

104 SKIRRID FAWR

Distance:	3 miles (5km)
Start/finish:	Car park on B4521, 300m W of NP7 8AP
Terrain:	Track, path, some rocky terrain
Toughness:	Moderate
Ascent:	323 metres
Navigation:	Easy
Good for:	Ascents, descents
Route info:	wildrunning.net/104

This relatively short but varied run takes you from the car park, N through peaceful woodland along the bottom L of the hill for 2 miles before turning R to the start of the steep climb to the trig point/summit. The route descends gently S along the ridge, following the Beacons Way. At the waymarker, descend back into the woodland and back to the finish. The Beacons Way continues for a further 98 miles from here to Llangadog on the far western edge of the Brecon Beacons. An optional longer route, following the original route of the Three Peaks Trial, can be run over the summits of The Skirrid, The Sugar Loaf and The Blorenge, totalling 20 miles, with 1,524 metres of ascent.

105 WAUN FACH HORSESHOE

Distance:	17½ miles (28km)
Start/finish:	Red Lion pub, Llanbedr, Crickhowell, NP8 1SR
Terrain:	Mountain path, bog
Toughness:	Moderate to challenging
Ascent:	985 metres
Navigation:	Easy to moderate
Good for:	Ascents, descents
Route info:	wildrunning.net/105

A wonderful clockwise loop taking in six summits of the Black Mountains. Head E from pub, crossing the river, taking road N for ½ mile before joining the Beacons Way L to the summit of Pen Cerrig-calch. It's then an easy-to-follow fun run along the ridge, arriving at a col just beyond Mynydd Llysiau, for incredible views. From here, head N to the rounded subtle summit of Waun Fach, the highest point in the Black Mountains. Leaving the summit, aim SE to run around the head of the valley, following the ridgeline over Pen y Gadair Fawr and Pen Twyn Mawr. Run along the edge of a forest until reaching an obvious trail junction, shortly after the end of the plantation. Take the path R and descend back to Llanbedr.

Blue Lagoon, Abereiddy

Pembrokeshire

The Welsh weather was blustery, intense and changeable. I returned from a morning run feeling as though I had just been through the wash: drenched and wrung out, drenched and wrung out, spin-cycle as I descended the final hairpinned path, then finally hung out to dry, dancing in the wind and sun. The following evening I took to the Coast Path again as the sun began to drop towards the sea, first tinging the world with gold, then red-orange and finally painting the whole sky and sea a spectacular display of deep red, pink and blue. The path underfoot was firm and easy to run, and I sped along, listening to the waves breaking on the rocks below. I could see my way clearly ahead as the Coast Path wound its way around headland after headland, each one reaching out into the sea. Tiny coves and sandy beaches appeared and disappeared below. Gorse and brambles caught at my legs as I passed. Gulls mewed high above and somewhere, far away on the horizon, a boat sounded its horn. I spotted several as I ran, massive ships carrying huge cargoes, their lights twinkling in the failing light. I ran out onto the headland and made my way carefully down to the rocky platform right at the sea's edge. Taking off my shoes and socks I spent a few moments feeling the waves wash over my feet, icy cold on my warm skin. Finally, I headed back; the land was almost dark, yet the sea and sky still luminous from the fast-vanishing sun.

Bordered by the sea on three sides, Pembrokeshire is home to the UK's only coastal National Park. The 186 miles of the Pembrokeshire Coast Path scale dramatic cliffs, drop into peaceful coves and traverse wide, sandy beaches on their undulating journey from Amroth in the south to St Dogmaels in the north. Runs 107 and 108 explore gorgeous sections of the Coast Path north and west of St David's. Inland, the landscape is equally beautiful. Wooded estuarine valleys lead through rolling farmland, vast open heathland is sprinkled with wildflowers in summer, and gentle waterways meander

108

108

108

through oak and ash woodland. Stackpole (explored in Run 106) covers several miles of spectacular coast, with vast sandy beaches, dunes, rugged cliffs, peaceful wooded valleys and a fantastic network of trails to discover. The area is a National Nature Reserve, with the Bosherton Lakes being an important habitat for wildlife and a strange and intriguing place to run.

The islands off the Pembrokeshire coast are a wonderful place to explore, abundant with wildlife from puffins and Manx shearwaters to seals, dolphins and porpoises. Self-catering accommodation is available on Skomer Island for much of the year, providing the opportunity to experience its unique environment at all times of the day and night. Access is restricted to the paths which make a figure-of-eight around the island, but exploration is encouraged. Although Skomer is only 2 miles long by 1½ miles wide, a gentle, early morning run here, before the day-trippers have arrived, is a truly magical experience. The whole island loop is approximately 4 miles in length.

There are many excellent races in Pembrokeshire, often making full use of the spectacular and challenging landscape of the coast path itself. Endurancelife hold the Pembrokeshire stage of their Coastal Trail Series at Little Haven, with distances from 10km to ultramarathon. The VO2 Pembrokeshire Coast Challenge is also staged here in October, covering a marathon a day for three consecutive days, or the full distance in one. The Wales Marathon, a hilly road loop between Tenby and Pembroke, is staged annually as part of the Long Course Weekend in June, which also includes swimming and cycling events. Held over the same course, the Wales Ironman triathlon, a 2.4-mile swim, 112-mile cycle and 26.2-mile run, takes place in September. Tenby is also home to Rosie Swale Pope, runner of many epic challenges including crossings of Cuba, Albania, Nepal, Iceland and Romania. Leaving her home on her 57th birthday, 2 October 2003, Rosie ran around the world, completing the 19,900 miles in five years, raising funds and awareness for charity. Her book, *Just a Little Run Around the World: 5 Years, 3 Packs of Wolves and 53 Pairs of Shoes* describes her incredible journey.

Pembrokeshire

106 STACKPOLE NATURE RESERVE

Distance:	6 miles (10km)
Start/finish:	Stackpole Quay car park, 200m SW of SA71 5LS
Terrain:	Beach, trail, path
Toughness:	Easy
Ascent:	160 metres
Navigation:	Easy
Good for:	Wildlife, beaches
Route info:	wildrunning.net/106

A wonderful loop around the Stackpole Nature Reserve. From the start, run S along spectacular coast path to Barafundle Bay before descending to beach to run across the sands. Ascending into woodland and back onto the Coast Path it reaches Stackpole Head with its magnificent limestone arches. Pass Stackpole Warren, with open grassland filled with summer wildflowers. Head NW to Bosherton lily ponds. At Bosherton, cross 18th-century Eight Arch Bridge before heading SE, crossing footbridge and then N for ¾ mile before crossing final bridge and back to Stackpole Quay. Beautiful Stackpole Estate has eco-award-winning accommodation and miles of trails to explore.

107 PORTHGAIN TO WHITESANDS

Distance:	9½ miles (15km)
Start:	Porthgain car park, SA62 5BN
Finish:	Whitesands Bay car park
Terrain:	Coast Path, steps, paved section
Toughness:	Moderate
Ascent:	576 metres
Navigation:	Easy (waymarked)
Good for:	Wildlife, beaches, ascents
Route info:	wildrunning.net/107

This particularly wild and remote section of the Pembrokeshire Coast Path takes you along an exhilarating and sometimes rugged cliff-top path beneath the dramatic volcanic outcrops of Penberry, Carnedd-lleithr and Carn Llidi. From the harbour, head W up to the Coast Path, enjoying expansive views and some technical terrain over volcanic cliff. Some scrambles over rocky sections, one taking you to the pretty cove at Aber-pwll. The run rounds the rocky peninsular of St David's Head, where gannets, seals and porpoises sport in the sea below. The route passes the flooded Blue Lagoon above Abereiddy on a section of surfaced path. A final, fast and fun descent to Whitesands, a wonderful stretch of sand and surf.

108 THE TREGINNIS PENINSULA

Distance:	6½ miles (10km)
Start/finish:	Porthclais Harbour (NT) car park, SA62 6RR
Terrain:	Coast path, some quiet road
Toughness:	Moderate
Ascent:	217 metres
Navigation:	Easy to moderate
Good for:	Ascents, wildlife, beaches
Route info:	wildrunning.net/108

This fantastic run loops around the stunning Treginnis Peninsula, across some of the oldest rock to be found in Wales. Leaving the car park, take the quiet road R heading inland then L at crossroads. At road end follow tracks and paths N past the great rocky outcrop of Carn Trefeiddan before heading seaward on road to St Justinian's. Here join the coast path S, where there are truly spectacular views out to Ramsey Island. There is excellent running along the coast path here, with technical ascents and descents to keep it interesting. Final section winds through fine coastal heathland and down to the rocky and secluded cove of Porthlysgi. Continue on coast path to Porthclais Harbour and back to the car park.

Plynlimon

Mid-Wales & the Cambrian Mountains

The area of Mid-Wales is loosely defined as the counties of Ceredigion and Powys, along with part of the county of Gwynedd. It is dominated by the rolling Cambrian Mountains, a peaceful range which lies between the Brecon Beacons in the south and Snowdonia in the north.

The summit of Plynlimon (Welsh: Pumlumon) is the highest point in Mid-Wales and the source of the rivers Wye and Severn. Its name means 'five peaks', of which Pen Pumlumon Fawr is the highest at 752 metres (Run 111). The other primary peaks are Pen Pumlumon Arwystli, Y Garn, Pen Pumlumon Llygad-bychan and Pumlumon Fach, a massif which together covers much of the county of Ceredigion. The Cambrians have been called 'the green desert of Wales' for their remote and desolate nature; however, these are the very features that lend them so well to some really wild running adventures.

There are several excellent long-distance routes that cross this region. The Cambrian Way is a tough, high-level, unmarked route, traversing 274 miles across upland Wales from Cardiff to Conway and involving some 18,757 metres of ascent. The challenge is enhanced by difficult navigation and rapidly changing weather. The Glŷndwr's Way National Trail is a waymarked route that runs for 135 miles from Knighton to Welshpool, linking with Offa's Dyke National Trail at both ends. It also links with the fantastic 7-mile Ann Griffiths Walk, which is included as Run 110.

The Elan Valley, with its many lakes and reservoirs, is a river valley situated to the west of Rhayader and the setting for Run 109. The area covers 70 square miles of lake and

111

110

111

countryside, with over 80 percent being designated as Sites of Specific Scientific Interest. The running terrain here is hugely varied, from wonderfully runnable grassy slopes to steep-sided valleys and tortuous boggy, tussocky areas, well worth avoiding whenever possible. The 2009 Original Mountain Marathon was held in the Elan Valley. The weather, for once, was mild and generally dry. We headed out at our allotted start time, feeling fresh and looking forward to two days out on these beautiful fells. The running was fine underfoot, with beautiful scenery all around and red kites wheeling overhead. We took the first day fairly steadily, both of us having paid the price in a previous year, on day two, for an over-zealous first day. Some good navigational decisions meant that we missed out much of the slower-going terrain, sticking higher up in the river valleys on faster, easier surfaces. We arrived at the overnight camp in 57th place, much earlier in the day than we had anticipated and a little disappointed, as we both felt we could have gone more quickly. Day two took us over some wonderful higher terrain where we were able to push the pace much harder. A fast, zig-zagging descent into the finish completed two fantastic days of running and saw us gain some 20 places on the previous day.

There are many great races in Mid-Wales, each taking full advantage of the fantastic fells and trails the region offers. The Red Kite Challenge Weekend in May has trail races of a half marathon on the Saturday and a 17½-mile race on the Sunday, starting from the Bwlch Nant yr Arian Visitor Centre in Ponterwyd, Aberystwyth. This race was also the Welsh Trail Championships in 2013. The Trail Marathon Wales is held in Dolgellau in June and the classic August multi-terrain race, Race the Train, sees runners tackling a muddy, 14-mile course in an attempt to beat the steam train which puffs its way out along the Talyllyn railway and back, carrying dozens of waving spectators. The train usually completes the course in around 1 hour and 48 minutes, with around a quarter of runners beating it back to Tywyn.

Race the Train

Mid-Wales & the Cambrian Mountains

109 ELAN VALLEY TRAIL

Distance:	8½ miles (14km)
Start:	Car park off B4518, Rhayader, LD6 5EU
Finish:	Craig Goch Dam car park
Terrain:	Surfaced path
Toughness:	Easy
Ascent:	307 metres
Navigation:	Easy
Good for:	Families, wildlife
Route info:	wildrunning.net/109

The Elan Valley Trail follows the heart of this beautiful valley, hugging the shores of the River Elan and several reservoirs along its way. As a surfaced, multi-user route it is a great trail for family days out on bicycles, as well as being an enjoyable run in its own right. The visitor centre with its café and shop, about half way, creates the perfect stop-off point. To start, cross the road and join signed Elan Valley Trail, heading S. The Trail also provides an easy way of accessing many of the wilder parts of the valley and surrounding hills from a well-marked starting point. Maps and information on other excellent self-navigating routes can be found at the visitor centre.

110 ANN GRIFFITHS WALK (RUN!)

Distance:	7 miles (11km)
Start:	Forestry Commission car park, Pont Llogel
Finish:	Pontrobert, SY22 6JS
Terrain:	Trail, track, path
Toughness:	Easy
Ascent:	225 metres
Navigation:	Easy (waymarked)
Good for:	National trail, woodland
Route info:	wildrunning.net/110

Named after a local, prolific hymn writer, the Ann Griffiths Walk is a beautiful route which lends itself incredibly well to running, winding its way through contrasting Powys landscapes with stunning views of the Berwyn mountains. This route follows the River Vrynwy SE from Pont Llogel, along fantastic running trails through river gorges, woodland, valleys, meadows and open hilltops. From the lower end of the car park the first waymarkers for this run and Glyndŵr's Way can be found. These are easy to follow along the length of the route. Take care as the route detours from the river at a short section N to the B4382 before returning to the river path.

111 PLYNLIMON / PUMLUMON

Distance:	11 miles (18km)
Start/finish:	Eisteddfa Gurig car park (on A44) SY23 3LE
Terrain:	Footpath, trail, track, road
Toughness:	Challenging
Ascent:	661 metres
Navigation:	Challenging
Good for:	Ascents, really wild
Route info:	wildrunning.net/111

This is a truly wild run, through remote landscapes of the high plateaux around Pumlumon, but it is a serious navigational challenge due to indistinct paths. ⚠ Do not undertake in poor visibility. For all this, it offers a wonderful run with spectacular views. From Eisteddfa Gurig, follow occasional waymarks and reasonable tracks N to the panoramic summit of Pumlumon Fawr. Then head E, then NW before descending steeply to the N tip of Llyn Llygad Rheidol reservoir. Follow Nant y Llyn river N before crossing to contour around Pumlumon Fach to reach Nant y Moch reservoir and its dam. Follow paths S, then turning E through Dyll Faen wood, back to start.

Llanddwyn Island

Anglesey & the Llŷn Peninsula

The Isle of Anglesey Coast Path runs for 121 miles through a designated Area of Outstanding Natural Beauty that covers 95 percent of the coast in this area. It passes through an ancient and historic landscape that includes a wonderful mixture of rolling, green farmland, coastal heath, dunes, salt-marsh, foreshore, cliffs and a few pockets of woodland. It is worth making the most of any opportunities to stop for breath and admire the fine views of the coast and surrounding mountains. Although undeniably technical and challenging at times, the terrain along this part of the coast path is, in general, flatter and more runnable than other coastal terrain, for example that in the south west of England. This makes for many miles of fantastic, flowing running accompanied by wonderful Welsh coastal scenery.

Holyhead Mountain is the highest point in Anglesey, at 220 metres. The holy mountain's rugged terrain and inviting trails make it a great place to run, exhilarating in places as your feet skim along narrow, twisting paths above the steep slopes straight down into the Irish Sea (Run 112). In fact the running all around Anglesey is enjoyable and fantastically varied, from precipitous cliff-top paths to gentle, runnable trails, from rocky scrambles to muddy, boggy tracks. The views from the summit of Holyhead Mountain are spectacular on a clear day, with a 360-degree vista of the surrounding landscape from the mountains of Snowdonia out across the glittering sea to Ireland and the Wicklow Mountains. Llanddwyn Island, off the

113

114

112

west coast of Anglesey, is a magical and remote place of sand dunes, rocky outcrops and rolling seas, calm and soothing in fine weather yet exciting and elemental in a storm (Run 113). Not quite an island, as it can be reached on foot via a fine, sandy beach at all but the highest of tides, Llanddwyn is rich in legend and history, from its associations with Dwynwen, the Welsh patron saint of lovers, to the filming of Demi Moore's thriller *Half Light*. There are 10 miles of trails to explore on the island, running on fine surfaces with stunning coastal views all around.

The lost world of the Llŷn Peninsula lies to the south west of Anglesey, jutting out on a long, narrow finger 30 miles into the Irish Sea, in a shape often likened to a dragon's tail. Surrounded on three sides by water, and therefore able to remain quite separate from the mainland, it is a place where Welsh traditions and culture stand preserved. Remote and beautiful, the peninsula feels vast despite its size, with big skies arching over verdant grassland, immaculate beaches and clear blue seas, all set against a rugged, mountainous backdrop. Much of the area is managed by the National Trust, preserving its status as a haven for wildlife. There are many fine routes to be run, from trails through the picturesque countryside and woodland of the Plas yn Rhiw estate, to the coast with its secluded coves and pristine beaches. Running around its rugged perimeter, the Llŷn Peninsula stretch of the Wales Coast Path (Run 114), covers many coastal areas but also regularly tours inland to showcase the wonderful variety of landscape on offer.

There are some excellent and, should you choose to participate in such things, truly epic races held on Anglesey. The Endurancelife Coastal Trail Series has a stage here, with terrain ranging from fast-and-furious to muddy, boggy quagmire, and distances from 10km up to ultra. VO2 organise an Anglesey Coastal Challenge: choose between three marathons in three days or the full distance non-stop. The Ring O' Fire ultra is a 135-mile coastal ultramarathon held over the bank holiday weekend in August. There is also a hugely popular road half marathon, the Island Race, held in March each year, and the Island Trail Race in September, with courses of half marathon or 10km taking in some of the area's beautiful trails.

Anglesey & the Llŷn Peninsula

112 HOLYHEAD MOUNTAIN

Distance:	5 miles (8km)
Start/finish:	Breakwater Country Park, Holyhead, LL65 1YG
Terrain:	Coast path, track
Toughness:	Easy to moderate
Ascent:	392 metres
Navigation:	Easy to moderate
Good for:	Coast, history, national trail
Route info:	wildrunning.net/112

This run tours the North and South Stacks either side of the rugged summit of Holyhead Mountain which, at 220 metres is the highest point in Anglesey. The run starts by heading NW directly onto the Coast Path and then passes the North Stack fog signal station, from where there are wonderful coastal views across to the rugged cliffs of South Stack. The path now winds its way southwards before the run detours the path, climbing to the summit of Holyhead Mountain with its fantastic views and Iron Age hill fort. Descending back to the coast path, the route loops around South Stack to the Seabird Centre. Here the route turns inland, heading NE around base of Holyhead Mountain and back to Country Park.

113 LLANDDWYN ISLAND

Distance:	3½ miles (6km)
Start/finish:	Newborough Beach car park, 1½ miles SW of LL61 6SG
Terrain:	Beach, coast path
Toughness:	Easy
Ascent:	53 metres
Navigation:	Easy
Good for:	Coast, beach
Route info:	wildrunning.net/113

A lovely, gentle run out onto atmospheric Llanddwyn Island, perfect for a wild run. From the car park head straight out onto the beach, turning R and running along the sandy shore towards the rocky outcrops of the island, visible in the distance. At Llanddwyn follow the clear path that heads SW – one of two main paths that traverse its length. Follow this wonderfully runnable trail, drinking in the sights and sounds all around you until you reach the path's end, stopping to enjoy the views. Head back, following the alternative path to the mainland. Back on the main beach, either take the path inland after 300m and then R back to the car park or return via the beach. ⚠ Access to island is limited during very high tides.

114 LLŶN PENINSULA

Distance:	20 miles (32km)
Start:	Aberdaron car park, LL53 8BE
Finish:	Abersoch car park, LL53 7EA
Terrain:	Coast path, quiet lane, farm track
Toughness:	Moderate
Ascent:	767 metres
Navigation:	Easy to moderate
Good for:	Coast, history, national trail
Route info:	wildrunning.net/114

A fantastic, varied and often challenging route follows the newly opened Wales Coast Path around the Llŷn Peninsula, from the sleepy village of Aberdaron to the chic surfer town of Abersoch; two more contrasting places it would be hard to imagine. From start follow path along the stream first NE then continuing as it winds its way through picturesque Welsh countryside, passing disused mines, rolling farmland and wooded areas. You will pass spectacular pieces of coast, where wonderful sea views open out before you. The coast path is waymarked, however the way is not always obvious and signs are easy to miss, so bring navigation equipment. Buses run, changing at Coed y Fron, between Aberdaron and Abersoch.

Northern Snowdonia

It was the start of the Snowdonia Marathon, a race that circles the rugged peaks of Snowdon range. Our running was mostly on roads but with some short sections of trail, most notably within the final miles, when rough terrain and steep inclines combined with fatigued bodies to create some truly painful experiences. This was, however, my first attempt at the race and I was blissfully unaware of what was to come. The early morning sun peered weakly through the chilly mist as I and a thousand or so other runners tried to keep warm, jumping on the spot, huddling together, the sound of nervous chatter all around. Eventually the gun went off. For the first mile out of Nant Peris I could not feel my feet. This was an odd sensation as I was aware of them hitting the ground but had no feeling beyond that. As the route climbed the long, winding Llanberis Pass I started to warm up and was grateful to reach the summit where a big crowd waited to cheer us on. The next miles were a break from the climbs, but it's all too easy to push too hard. I ran fast, probably too fast, on the long downhills, passing half-way, feeling like I was flying. My elation was short-lived, however, and as I slowed on the final, unmetalled climb, cramp seized my thigh muscles, forcibly straightening both legs and making walking, let alone running, almost impossible. I finally hobbled my way to the top and began the long, painful descent into Llanberis with gritted teeth and tears running down my cheeks, finally crossing line to collapse with exhaustion and relief.

Snowdonia has a heritage rich in mountain sports, with runners, walkers and climbers frequently testing their limits. There is huge scope for exploration and adventure here. Our Wild Runs 115 to 117, take in some of the best and most iconic landscapes in the area, following spectacular routes to the

summit of Snowdon and out across the Glyder range and the Carneddau ridge.

The legendary Dragon's Back Race follows the mountainous spine of Wales from northern Snowdonia to the Brecon Beacons. It is an epic, five-day journey of approximately 186 miles with 17,000 metres of ascent, seeing runners navigate their way across wild, trackless, remote and mountainous terrain. The original Dragon's Back took place in 1992 and was won by Helene Diamantides and Martin Stone. Despite looking certain to become a classic endurance challenge, there was no repeat of the race for two decades. Then, under the direction of élite mountain runner Shane Ohly, the second Dragon's Back Race finally took place in September 2012. Half of the competitors who started the race failed to finish. Of the those who completed the challenge, Steve Birkenshaw and Helene Diamantides (now Whittaker) claimed victory, 20 years after Helene's first success at the race. The Dragon's Back Race is considered to be one of the hardest mountain races in the world, and is set to be held again in June 2015. The multi-award winning film of the 2012 race is a fantastic watch for anyone interested in the world of extreme endurance.

The Welsh 3000s have long stood as a great endurance challenge, and the record has been fiercely fought over by many of the fell racing greats. Also known as the 14 Peaks (there are actually at least 15!) the traditional challenge is to complete all of the Welsh mountains above 914 metres in under 24 hours. At the time of writing, the record for running the route is held by Colin Donnelly, whose incredible time of 4 hours and 19 minutes was set in 1988. Angela Carson set the women's record time of 5 hours and 28 minutes in 1989. In 1978 John Wagstaff completed a triple crossing in 22 hours and 49 minutes. *The Welsh Three Thousand Foot Challenges: A Guide for Walkers and Hill Runners* by Roy Clayton and Ronald Turnbull is a great handbook for the Welsh 3000s and other great challenges in this area. Wales aso has its own long-distance Round: the Paddy Buckley, a 47-summit, 100km challenge. The current record is held by Tim Higginbottom, who completed in 17 hours and 42 minutes in 2009.

115

Northern Snowdonia

115 SNOWDON, LLANBERIS PATH

Distance:	9 miles (15km)
Start/finish:	Car park, Llanberis, LL55 4TU
Terrain:	Path, trail
Toughness:	Moderate to challenging
Ascent:	956 metres
Navigation:	Easy
Good for:	Ascents, classic routes
Route info:	wildrunning.net/115

The classic route up the main path of Snowdon from Llanberis to the summit, this run is iconic as it follows the same route as the Snowdon International Mountain Race. There are many other routes, of course, which vary in length and technicality, and then there's the train which can be taken up or down. Out of season is, without doubt, the best time to run here, as during the summer it does get busy with leisure and charity walkers. However, do not underestimate Snowdon. It is a high and exposed mountain with changeable and extreme weather further up and, should you get into difficulty or stray from the path in poor visibility, consequences can be serious. From A4086 through Llanberis run up Victoria Terrace to follow Llanberis Path to summit and back.

116 THE GLYDER RIDGE

Distance:	5½ miles (8km)
Start/finish:	Ogwen car park, Llyn Ogwen, S of Bethesda, LL57 3LZ
Terrain:	Mountain track, trail
Toughness:	Challenging
Ascent:	731 metres
Navigation:	Moderate to challenging
Good for:	Ascents, views, really wild
Route info:	wildrunning.net/116

This run is a spectacular and exhilarating tour of the highest summits of the Glyder range, as well as the iconic landmarks of the Devil's Kitchen and the Idwal Slabs. Leave Ogwen Cottage SE on the main track for 400 metres before branching off, continuing SE, climbing to the shores of Lake Bochlwyd. Ascend to Bwlch Tryfan, passing to the S of Bristly Ridge and ascend to the rocky moonscape of the summit plateau of Glyder Fach (994 metres) and Glyder Fawr (1001 metres) with its wonderful views. Descend a technical path NW to Llyn y C n and the Devil's Kitchen, finally passing Llyn Idwal (on your L) and beneath the Idwal slabs before returning to start. Including the summit of Tryfan will extend the run by 2 miles.

117 HIGH CARNEDDAU, OGWEN

Distance:	9 miles (14km)
Start/finish:	Gwern Gof Isaf Farm, LL24 0EU
Terrain:	Trail, path, open mountain
Toughness:	Challenging
Ascent:	900 metres
Navigation:	Moderate (if weather good)
Good for:	Ascents, views, hard-as-nails
Route info:	wildrunning.net/117

This tough run up to and along the wonderful Carneddau ridge affords breathtaking views throughout, journeying over some of the quieter peaks in Snowdonia. From the farm and campsite, cross the A5 following the surfaced access road N to Ffynnon Llugwy reservoir. Scramble up a steep path to the main ridge, passing Pen yr Helgi Du and Craig yr Ysfa on your right. Follow the path NW to Carneddau's highest summit, Carnedd Llewelyn at 1064 metres. Continue SW along the ridgeline to Carnedd Dafydd, then on past the cairn of Cardedd Fach to the flat summit plateau of Pen yr Ole Wen. Descend E from the ridge, flying past Ffynnon Lloer and then descending S and returning to the A5. Cross the road at Gwern Gof Uchaf and follow the clear bridleway path back to start.

Cadair Idris

Southern Snowdonia

Many giants of Welsh folklore are said to have dwelt upon its mountains and within its ancient castles. One such giant was Idris, who appears in many guises: as giant, prince, philosopher and astronomer. It is said that the great mountain summit of Cadair Idris was his rock-hewn chair, where he would spend clear nights sitting and gazing at the stars in the vast skies which sweep over Snowdonia. The chair, forming the mountain's summit plateau, is said to inflict madness, poetic inspiration or death on those who sleep upon it. On one run here, on a freezing, misty day when damp cloud swirled around the summit, we stopped at the little hut just short of the top for a moment's shelter from the buffeting wind and driving rain. Entering the hut, we found a cheerful couple enjoying a roast dinner, complete with china plates and cutlery. Of the many extraordinary things we thought we might encounter on the mountain, this was certainly not one.

Whenever I start running up Cadair I'm always envious of whoever lives in the little walled cottage by the start of the track: what an amazing place to live, to be able to do this run every day! As soon as I push through the gate and start the steep climb up past the stream, my every-day cares are forgotten and my focus is concentrated on breathing and trying to maintain some speed up the steps. I love the feeling of this early part of the run; there's no warm up, just straight uphill until it starts to flatten out as you emerge from the woodland and leave the path of the stream.

From here, there is a scramble uphill to climb onto the rocky hump just before the lake. I always climb up here and run along the huge striation that has scarred the rocks; I imagine the force that the ice must have had to drag a boulder big enough to scratch the rock like this. On this occasion I jumped off the tail of the rock and skipped across the stepping stones to

120

119

118

the right of the lake. To the left is the easier path that follows the ridge, but today I wanted the challenge and the steepness of heading straight up the scree. I peered up, looking for the best path, trying to decide if it was best to follow the water-cut channels or run/crawl up the stepped grassy banks that eventually lead to the steep scramble over the top to the ridge. I love popping up onto the main path; looking back down it seems improbable that you can actually run up from the lake to here. Reaching the summit, I always give the trig point a kiss; I don't really believe that the mountain knows of my existence or of my struggle and appreciation, but at that moment it feels right.

Across the grassy summit plain and down the far side I ran fast, trying not to miss the path that starts to form somewhere on my right and quickly becomes a giant swoop across peat and scree to the stile and then the exhilarating descent to the stream at the top of the woodland. As I reached the stream I found the little bridge had flooded, soaking my feet for the final descent.

Cadair Idris lies on the southern edge of Snowdonia, away from the main tourist areas. It is a peaceful place, and a picture-perfect mountain. The three main paths, of which the Pony Track is the most straightforward (Run 120), lend themselves well to fantastic and enjoyable mountain running. The mountain's natural bowl-shaped depression was formed by a glacier and, along with the *roches moutonnées* (sheep-back rocks), the tear-drop shaped hills above the edge of Llyn Cau, were created by the abrasive action of the ice. Lying in lush green surrounds to the east of Cadair Idris, the Aran range is a peaceful discovery. Aran Fawddwy (Run 118) is a beautiful mountain with superb scenery and wonderful running terrain.

East of Harlech sits the Rhinogydd mountain range. The terrain in these mountains is generally rocky and technical and well suited to the fleet of foot, predominantly fell runners and walkers seeking a quieter corner of Snowdonia, along with the local population of wild goats (Run 119). The landscape is rugged and wild, with rocky outcrops topping the many peaks, whilst in the valleys lie ancient woodlands of stunted, gnarled oaks and gushing rivers feeding flat, silver tarns.

120

Southern Snowdonia

118 ARAN FAWDDWY

Distance:	7½ miles (12km)
Start/finish:	Cwm Cywarch road-end, NW of SY20 9JG
Terrain:	Quiet lane, path, track, moorland
Toughness:	Moderate to challenging
Ascent:	749 metres
Navigation:	Moderate to challenging
Good for:	Ascents, really wild
Route info:	wildrunning.net/118

Aran Fawddwy, at 905 metres, is a beautiful mountain with superb scenery and wonderful running terrain and a far cry from the crowds of Snowdon. Starting in the beautiful valley of Cwm Cywarch, park and follow the road to its end and join the footpath N, climbing up through a spectacular rocky, craggy landscape to reach a col below Glasgwm. Great running NW across open moorland takes you to the rocky summit of Aran Fawddwy and the gleaming water of Creiglyn Dyfi a thousand feet below. Turning back run SE, passing a memorial cairn and the summit of Drysgol. Here the route heads S and descends SW down a clear path giving fast, easy running all the way back to the start.

119 RHINOG ROMAN STEPS

Distance:	5 miles (8km)
Start/finish:	Cwm Bychan car park, 1¼ miles NE of LL45 2PH
Terrain:	Mountain track, path
Toughness:	Challenging
Ascent:	576 metres
Navigation:	Moderate to challenging
Good for:	Swimming, ascents, history
Route info:	wildrunning.net/119

A run in the peaceful Rhinogydd, starting with a climb of the Roman Steps. These are the well-preserved remains of a medieval packhorse trail leading from Chester to Harlech Castle. From start and campsite head S on the footpath through woodland. The steps provide great running as they ascend towards the visible summit of Rhinog Fawr in the south. Follow the N shore of Llyn Du, boulder-hopping to reach a clear path. An enjoyable scramble up a gully takes you to the summit of Rhinog Fawr. At this point, either retrace your steps or continue onwards down vague paths to the western shores of breathtaking Gloyw Llyn, the 'gleaming lake', a perfect pool for soothing weary muscles. Rejoin path N to car park.

120 CADAIR IDRIS PONY PATH

Distance:	5½ miles (9km)
Start/finish:	Car park Tynyceunant, ½ mile SW of LL40 1TL
Terrain:	Mountain trail
Toughness:	Challenging
Ascent:	691 metres
Navigation:	Easy to moderate (weather)
Good for:	Ascents, history
Route info:	wildrunning.net/120

A spectacular and rewarding run from the Ty Nant car park, following the obvious Pony Path to the top of one of the most beautiful, picture-perfect mountains in Wales. Route starts by winding its way S over a babbling stream and through mixed woodland. The path zig-zags up the hillside, emerging onto open mountainside with views left to the Cyfrwy ridge. The route then climbs steeply, zig-zagging up Rhiw Gwredydd, before levelling out onto a grassy path. Heading E climb again to Bwlch y Gwynt ('Windy Pass'), as views open out over the shining lakes of Llyn y Gadair and Llyn Gafr below. Finally make your way to the summit cairn, with its nearby shelter. Descent is by the same route, back to the start.

Moel Famau

The Clwydians & the Dee Valley

The Clwydian Range stretches for around 20 miles down the eastern side of Wales, from Prestatyn, near the north coast, to the remote Berwyn Mountains in the south. These purple heather-clad mountains, topped with ancient hill forts overlooking the beautiful Dee Valley, provide some wonderful, exciting and varied running. In contrast to their open moorland summits, the surrounding valleys are lush and green. To the east, the foothills of the Dee Estuary and the Clwydian Range are the gateway to the wonderful and little-explored Llandegla Moors, Ruabon Mountains, the high pastures of Esclusham Mountain, the World Heritage site of Pontcysyllte Aqueduct and Canal, and the National Trust's Chirk Castle. There are excellent country parks at Moel Famau and Loggerheads, both with a network of waymarked trails and many other interesting features to explore. The geology in this area is fascinating and determines the shapes of the landscape and the nature of the trails here. Loggerheads Country Park is nestled beneath dramatic limestone cliffs and there are limestone pavements at Bryn Alyn and Aber Sychnant. Some of the most impressive scree slopes in Britain can be found at Eglwyseg Rocks. Moel Famau (meaning 'Mother Mountain' in Welsh) is the highest point of the Clwydians at 554 metres (Run 122).

The Berwyn Range, tucked away in Wales' less visited and sparsely populated north-eastern corner, is a fantastic place to visit for wild running adventures. Lower and often more runnable than many of Snowdonia's rugged mountains, they are for the most part heather-clad with inviting, winding tracks. Cadair Berwyn, the highest in the range, provides outstanding ridge running, with views to match (Run 121).

121

121

123

There are several long-distance paths running along or through the Clwydian Range. The 177 miles of the Offa's Dyke Path follow the Range and the 122-mile Clwydian Way passes through it. The 60-mile North Wales Path follows the foot of the scarp between Prestatyn and Dyserth. The challenging North Berwyn Way and the easier Dee Valley Way are each 15-mile linear routes that can be joined to make a 30-mile loop between Corwen and Llangollen (Run 123). We ran this loop on an overcast weekend in June, the recent heavy rainfall having swollen the rivers and made the already verdant landscape almost luminous in its green-ness. We started our run in Corwen, heading through the town and out along an old railway line through pastureland, following the banks of the River Dee. Despite the rain, the path was firm underfoot and great to run on, winding into the distance and drawing us on through the tranquil countryside. After a short section on a quiet lane, we found ourselves running uphill through a conifer forest, peaceful and pine-scented all around. Emerging from the woods we climbed through open moorland to the summit of Moel Fferna, the distant mountains springing into view all around as we reached our high point. A fantastic descent into a valley and then a climb again, brought us back onto the main ridge and up to the rounded summit of Vivod Mountain, from where we could see across to Llantysilio Mountain in the distance and back along the ridge to Moel Fferna, now a long way behind us. More wonderful running across high remote moorland on fine trails followed, before a fast, fun descent on a bridleway through fields and farmland, gradually steepening until it reached the end of the trail at Llangollen. We returned on the more gentle but equally beautiful Dee Valley Way the following day.

The Clwydian Fell Race is an annual event organised by North East Wales Search and Rescue in November. It involves a tough, 10-mile course over 945 metres of ascent, including running over the summit of Moel Famau. The Clwydians are also fantastic for cycling, with the highly acclaimed Etape Cymru taking place on the roads around these mountains, including the infamous climb up the Horseshoe Pass.

The Clwydians & the Dee Valley

121 CADAIR BERWYN

Distance:	9½ miles (15km)
Start/finish:	Llandrillo car park, LL21 0TG
Terrain:	Road, track, path, moorland, bog
Toughness:	Challenging
Ascent:	625 metres
Navigation:	Challenging
Good for:	Wildlife, ascents
Route info:	wildrunning.net/121

The Berwyns are one of the largest areas of upland heath in Wales, carpeted in heather and bilberry. The views from the summit ridge and across U-shaped valleys carved by ancient glaciers are fantastic. Start from pretty Llandrillo, looking L, take the R fork and then second R, following the quiet road to the farm at its end. Continue on the path S through woodland then SE across open moorland, climbing steadily onto the main ridge. Reaching the ridge, turn right and continue to climb, eventually reaching the trig point at the summit of Cadair Berwyn. Head N along Craig Berwyn before turning L where clear paths descend to a stream and crossing before following tracks back down to Llandrillo. ⚠ Stream crossing may be difficult after heavy rain.

122 FOEL FENLI & MOEL FAMAU

Distance:	10 miles (16km)
Start/finish:	Loggerheads Country Park car park, CH7 5LH
Terrain:	Trail, quiet lane, path, green lane
Toughness:	Moderate
Ascent:	608 metres
Navigation:	Easy to moderate
Good for:	National trail, ascents, families
Route info:	wildrunning.net/122

A lovely scenic run enjoying magnificent mountain views. Cross the road, joining the quiet lane S before joining the Clwydian Way S. On entering Maeshafn take path SW along a mixture of field paths and tracks, passing Llanferres and briefly joining Offa's Dyke Path. Climb to Bwlch Crug-glas and then steeply upwards to the summit of Foel Fenli, where you are rewarded with spectacular views and remains of an ancient fortification. A fast descent to Bwlch Penbarras is followed by a great run along the obvious Offa's Dyke Path to the summit of Moel Famau, the highest point of the Clwydian Range. Descend E on green lanes and tracks to footbridge crossing the river, following the river path back to the start.

123 THE DEE VALLEY WAY

Distance:	16½ miles (27km)
Start:	Llangollen car park, LL20 8PW
Finish:	Corwen car park, LL21 0DD
Terrain:	Trail, track, quiet lane, towpath
Toughness:	Easy to challenging
Ascent:	883 metres
Navigation:	Easy (waymarked)
Good for:	History, wildlife
Route info:	wildrunning.net/123

The gentle Dee Valley Way is a fantastic opportunity to experience the full length of a waymarked long-distance trail in only a few hours and while passing through wonderful countryside with fascinating history, wildlife and great running Start along the towpath in Llangollen following the river upstream. At Horseshoe Falls, the Way winds its way inland, along quiet country lanes, across the gorse and bilberry-covered slopes of the Llantysilio Mountains and through woodland paths carpeted with green and heady wild garlic in summer. From Corwen, take the bus or maybe steam train back, or combine the Dee Valley Way with the more challenging North Berwyn Way, forming a 30-mile round trip, to make the perfect running weekend.

Scotland

Scotland's remote and rugged terrain, from its bleak lowland moors and extensive forests, across windswept and beautiful islands to the summits of the highest mountains in Britain, provides a wonderful playground for wild running.

Highlights
Scotland

Our favourite runs include:

137 Conquer the bleak summit of Ben Nevis, following much of the route of the iconic Ben Nevis Fell Race, before letting gravity take you on a speedy descent back to the valley below

124-126 Explore the little-visited Scottish Borders on winding trails through pine-scented forest, alongside babbling burns and over gently rolling hills

142-147 Go island-hopping, savouring the unique character and varying running challenges of Scotland's many islands

130-132 Escape from Edinburgh and Glasgow's buzzing streets to find wild and peaceful places just a short distance from the city

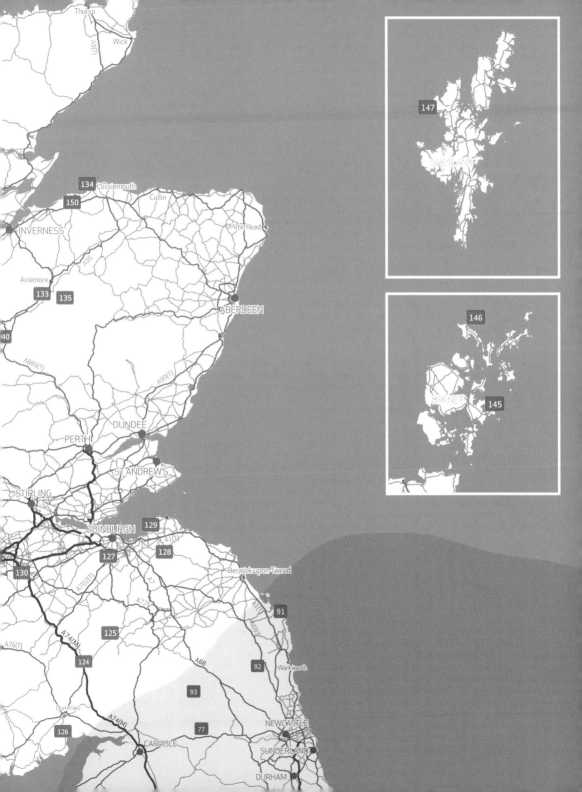

Blake Muir

The Borders & the South

Dumfries and Galloway, in the western Southern Uplands of Scotland, is a lush mix of vast forest, scenic coastline, rolling hills and rugged countryside. Galloway Forest Park is the UK's first Dark Sky Park and is a haven both for trail runners and for the rich diversity of wildlife that is found in this area. The Lowther Hills, venue for the 2007 Original Mountain Marathon, are great to explore, with their steep, tussocky hillsides and wonderfully runnable tops. The rolling, grassy hillscapes of the Moffat Hills rise from the borders to a height of 821 metres at the summit of White Coomb, and their steep scree-covered slopes make for some exciting and adventurous running. The beautiful Annandale Way is a waymarked, 55-mile route, following the valley of the river Annan from its source to the sea. This new route starts high above the Annan's source, taking in the dramatic hollow of the Devil's Beef Tub, home of the fast and furious 2-mile Devil's Beef Tub Hill Race, held in September, before descending its eastern side and following the river along the valley bottom into the pretty market town of Moffat (Run 124). From here, it follows the Annan river valley to its glorious end in the Solway Firth.

For the perfect early morning barefoot run, family days out building sandcastles or an evening sunset walk, head for the hundreds of miles of golden sandy beaches of the Solway Coast that gild the edge of Dumfries and Galloway. North of Newton Stewart lies the 5,000-year-old Wood of Cree, the largest ancient oak woodland in southern Scotland, covered with bluebells in spring and a magical place to run. Tumbling waterfalls cascade down mossy, tree-lined gullies, the calls of tawny owls fill the evening air and otters can be spotted playing in the pools and babbling streams.

124

126

124

Peebles, in the Scottish Borders, lies at the heart of Upper Tweeddale, a picturesque landscape of gently rolling hills and heather moorland sweeping into valleys through which flow crystal-clear rivers full of leaping salmon. Both the 537-mile Scottish National Trail and the 212-mile Southern Upland Way pass through this beautiful area. We ran a fantastic horseshoe, looping out from Peebles and around Dun Rig, taking in unmarked country over the four peaks surrounding Glensax. The run took us far longer than we had expected as we found ourselves wading through deep mud, bog-hopping over tussocky grasslands and making frequent detours to try to find the most runnable surface. In the end, much of the run turned into an exercise in balance and explosive power, followed by a lengthy soak for us and our kit on returning to Peebles. The next day we headed out onto the contrasting Southern Upland Way, following well-signed, runnable trails around tranquil lochs and through stunning moorland landscapes. This run combined the wild and scenic nature of the previous day's excursion with perfect running terrain. Our favourite section was that between St Mary's Loch and Traquair (Run 125).

Southern Scotland has a solid tradition of running and racing, with the popular Dumfries half marathon having been held for over 30 years. The Jedburgh Festival of Running is an autumn highlight, with varying race distances including the 38-mile Three Peaks Ultra. The Criffel Fell Race, held annually in March, is a 6½-mile run that sees runners take to the tracks and paths from the village of New Abbey, south of Dumfries, to the summit of Criffel Hill. The hill itself is invariably a muddy quagmire, and the summit often snow-covered, making for a tough but memorable race. The record holders are Mark Croasdale (47 minutes 34 seconds) and the legendary Angela Mudge (56 minutes 47 seconds). Such was the enthusiasm with which we were told about the race, and our enjoyment when we ran here, that it had to be included as a Wild Run (Run 126). One of the strangest races of all has to be the notorious Mighty Deerstalker which takes place in Innerleithen in March, and sees runners tackle a varied and adventurous course in descending darkness, with the wearing of tweed strongly encouraged.

125

The Borders & the South

124 DEVIL'S BEEF TUB

Distance:	14 miles (23km)
Start/finish:	Moffatt, station car park, DG10 9EP
Terrain:	Footpath, trail, quiet road, bog
Toughness:	Moderate
Ascent:	515 metres
Navigation:	Easy to moderate (waymarked)
Good for:	Ascents, views, really wild
Route info:	wildrunning.net/124

This run takes in the first and most exciting stage of the waymarked Annandale Way. From the car park, follow the signs N along the Annan river path before continuing N along a minor road and farm tracks for 1 mile. Fork L onto the moorland hills that wall Annandale to the north. After fording the Larie Linn, begin the steep climb NW over Eric Stane Hill. A splendid run along the ridge follows, skirting the Devil's Beef Tub to Annanhead Hill and along the Chalk Ridge Edge, before turning S for the exhilarating descent back down to the minor road at Ericstane and back to Moffat. The marker stone for the official start of the Annandale Way lies at the head of the River Annan, to be discovered along the way.

125 ST MARY'S LOCH TO TRAQUAIR

Distance:	12 miles (19km)
Start:	Tibbie Shiels Inn, St Marys Loch, Selkirk, TD7 5LH
Finish:	Traquair parking area, EH44 6PJ
Terrain:	Path, tracks
Toughness:	Easy to moderate
Ascent:	384 metres
Navigation:	Easy (waymarked)
Good for:	National trail, ascents
Route info:	wildrunning.net/125

This wonderful run along the well signed, well maintained Southern Upland Way starts by following the eastern edge of St Mary's Loch N, winding in and out of woodland and through the sailing club before reaching Bowerhope Farm. Cross the bridge over Yarrow Water and then ⚠ the A708 before following the Way passing South Hawkshaw Rig and North Hawkshaw Rig. Continuing NE, the route passes through forest and emerges onto open moorland, climbing to the summit of Blake Muir with breath-taking views all around. A fantastic, fast descent along its north ridge takes you over Fethan Hill and down to Traquair. No facilities in Traquair, but Innerleithen is nearby.

126 CRIFFEL HILL

Distance:	7½ miles (12km)
Start/finish:	Sweetheart Abbey car park, New Abbey Bridge, DG2 8BU
Terrain:	Path, bog
Toughness:	Challenging
Ascent:	560 metres
Navigation:	Easy to moderate
Good for:	Ascents
Route info:	wildrunning.net/126

The outward section of this run follows the route of the Criffel Hill fell race to the summit of Criffel Hill, with breath-taking views out across Loch Kindar and the Nith Estuary. From start turn R following quiet lane SW to end. Cross bridge following path SE to the W shores of Loch Kindar before following the path up and S. Ascend W up Craigrockall Burn and S to Criffel. From the sizeable summit cairn there are magnificent views over the Solway Firth Taking the path L at the top, the run descends the hill N and loops to rejoin the outward path before returning to New Abbey. Most of the route is on well-made paths; however, the hill itself is a challenging, boggy fell run, hugely enjoyable. Take a change of outfit for the car!

Aberlady Bay

Edinburgh & the East

Easily escapable on foot, Edinburgh could be a city designed with runners in mind. From the city's centre rises the inviting challenge of Arthur's Seat, the main peak of the hills of Holyrood Park, perfect for an early morning excursion, often in the company of other runners. There are some wonderful trails around Holyrood, taking in Salisbury Crags and the summit of the Seat itself, all with fantastic views out across the city and beyond.

Looking out from the city, the hills of Corstorphine, Blackford and the Braids that form the skyline all around stand waiting to be conquered. To the east lies East Lothian, with its beautiful coastline, sandy beaches, dunes and nature reserves. Aberlady Bay, Britain's first local nature reserve, has a stunning beach that can be relatively busy in summer but out of season becomes a vast, runnable expanse (part of our Run 129). For the most peaceful running and the best chance of spotting wildlife, visit during the morning or evening. The conservationist and father of National Parks, John Muir, was born in Dunbar on this coast in 1838; the fully waymarked John Muir Way runs for 45 miles from Musselburgh, east of Edinburgh, to the East Lothian border near Cocksburnpath. The Country Park in Dunbar, which also bears his name, is a great place for exploring trails and the local wildlife, either running or walking with the family.

The Pentland Hills dominate to the south of Edinburgh, stretching in a south-westerly direction for around 20 miles from the city's outskirts towards Biggar and the Upper Clydesdale. The northern hills are a designated Regional Park

129

127

127

and have over 62 miles of waymarked trails that are perfect for running and exploring (Run 127). Local running club Carnethy Hill Runners organises the classic Carnethy 5 Hill Race in February, which commemorates the Battle of Roslin, and the tough, 16-mile Pentland Skyline Hill Race in October.

Between Lothian and the Borders, the great, rolling, green and mauve patchwork of the Lammermuir Hills forms a natural boundary. Although not high relative to many of the Scottish ranges, the steep gradients and lack of natural passes mean that only the A68 crosses the hills and is frequently closed in winter, adding to the area's remote wildness. The highest points of the Lammermuirs are Meikle Says Law at 535 metres and its more famous and picturesque neighbour Lammer Law at 528 metres.

We ran Lammer Law on one of the hottest days of the year, the path below our feet dry and dusty, baked by a rare fortnight of warm, dry weather. We made our way from the car park up the main path, climbing steadily on pale trails that wound their way, snake-like, across the hills ahead of us, seeming to climb forever into the distance. Wonderful views of the empty moorland all around and, further away, the Firth of Forth coming into view, took our minds off the sweltering heat and relentlessness of the climb. Finally, after a stretch of rough ground, amazingly still boggy underfoot, we reached the summit cairn and trig point and stopped to enjoy the light breeze cooling our bodies. The great views were worth the climb and we spotted Arthur's Seat, the venue for the previous day's run, far away in the distance. A fantastic, long but not too steep descent on good tracks took us flying down towards Hopes Reservoir, gleaming invitingly from its peaceful spot, nestled within hills and trees. Just before the reservoir, we ran through Hopes Burn at a ford, splashing our legs and feeling the icy cold water seeping through our shoes and cooling our tired, hot feet. Finally, we jogged back along a stretch of tarmac road, chatting excitedly about the route and the runs to come. This is our Wild Run 128.

129

Edinburgh & the East

127 CARNETHY HILL

Distance:	7½ miles (12km)
Start/finish:	Flotterstone Ranger Centre, Penicuik, EH26 0PR
Terrain:	Track, path
Toughness:	Moderate
Ascent:	520 metres
Navigation:	Easy to moderate
Good for:	Ascents, urban escape
Route info:	wildrunning.net/127

This scenic route takes in the highest point of the Pentlands, Scald Law, and the picturesque summit of Carnethy Hill. The main route provides wonderful running on clear paths that switchback enticingly up the hillside. From the car park, head L of the Ranger Centre, joining the path and avoiding the road. Follow signs for Scald Law, climbing up to the summit of Turnhouse Hill before taking to the ridge, passing cairn after cairn. Continue running SW, climbing up and down Carnethy Hill and ascending to the summit of Scald Law. A fun, fast descent L leads down to the road and house at the head of Loganlea Reservoir. Follow the quiet burn track 3 miles back to Flotterstone.

128 LAMMER LAW

Distance:	9 miles (15km)
Start/finish:	Longyester, near EH41 4PL
Terrain:	Track, trail, grass path, bog, lane
Toughness:	Moderate
Ascent:	307 metres
Navigation:	Moderate
Good for:	Ascents, urban escape
Route info:	wildrunning.net/128

This is a great circuit, taking in two of the iconic landmarks of this region: Lammer Law and Hopes Reservoir. Much of the running is fast and firm underfoot, gravelly at times, and along pale, winding trails that draw you along through the picturesque hills and valleys. The out-and-back to the summit itself can be very boggy and can be omitted; however, the views from the cairn are spectacular. From Longyester, climb S on tarmac, past Blinkbonny Wood, then on a trail. Continue on tracks, climbing to the summit of Lammer Law on indistinct paths across boggy terrain. Return to the track looping SE then NE to the ford at Hopes Burn and the south side of Hopes Reservoir. Continue N and join the lane at East Hopes back to start.

129 ABERLADY BAY

Distance:	7 miles (11km)
Start/finish:	Aberlady Bay car park EH32 0QB, ½ mile E of Aberlady on A198
Terrain:	Sandy beach, grass path, track
Toughness:	Easy
Ascent:	110 metres
Navigation:	Easy to moderate
Good for:	Coast, families
Route info:	wildrunning.net/129

This is a great, circular run on inviting trails through the open grasslands of East Lothian, with fine coastal views. From the Nature Reserve at Aberlady Bay, head out NW passing Marl Loch on L and follow waymarkers around the edge of a golf course. Continue on past tank defences to Gullane Bents. On reaching the beginning of the wood at Jamie's Neuk, head W to reach the sea and run back hugging the coastline. At Gullane Point, drop down onto the beach and run along the firm sand to continue back around the bay. At high tide, take the footpath sign leading back up to the golf course. The nearby John Muir Country Park is perfect for a family day out.

Glasgow & the West

It was early – very early – on a Saturday morning in July. A group of weary-looking people stood huddled around a small shelter behind a café in an obscure field which borders the West Highland Way not far from Loch Lomond. Dressed the same: waterproofs against the driving rain, hats with nets which secured with drawcords around our necks against the itchy, biting clouds of midges, and expectant looks, gazing down the West Highland Way, awaiting our runners.

The West Highland Way, crossing the Scottish Highlands from Milngavie, on the outskirts of Glasgow, to Fort William, was officially opened in 1980 and has become a popular route for walkers and runners. In 1985 two runners, Duncan Watson and Bobby Shields, set off from Milngavie railway station for a head-to-head race along the Way, to Fort William. As the official race website retells it "neither man gave an inch in this titanic struggle. As they started to cross Rannoch Moor after 60 miles they realised that, with this mindset, mutual destruction was the most likely outcome. So they pooled resources, and continued on to finish together in the fine time of 17 hours 48 minutes." And so the West Highland Way (WHW) Race was born. The 1989 race played host to a mighty duel between multi-record holding Mike Hartley and Dave Wallace, the previous year's winner. Finally overtaking Hartley on the last 7-mile stretch at Lundavra, Wallace triumphed, retaining his title and beating Hartley by 6 minutes in a time of 15 hours and 26 minutes. After a dwindling number of participants during the 1990s, the event was in danger of being discontinued, until two former WHW race competitors, Dario Melaragni and Stan Milne, decided the event was just "too much of a classic to die out and go away". With their input and the increasing popularity of ultradistance running, the race has since gone from strength to strength and is now a key race on the ultramarathon calendar. The current race

130

130

131

record holders are Paul Giblin of Paisley with a time of 15 hours 7 minutes, in June 2013, and Lucy Colquhoun of Aviemore with a time of 17 hours 16 minutes, set in 2007.

There are many great places to run within a short distance from Glasgow, from rolling hills to fantastic woodland trails. Chatelherault Country Park, only 20 minutes by train from central Glasgow, is one of our more gentle Wild Runs (Run 130). The Clyde Walkway is a 40-mile route taking you from the city centre out through Strathclyde to the spectacular gorge and waterfalls at Clyde. This route can also be linked with the West Highland Way, using the Kelvin Walkway to Milngavie. The 40 mile Clyde Stride Race is held on the Walkway in July, one of the 16 races in the Scottish Ultramarathon Series.

Lying across the Highland Boundary Fault, and often considered to be the boundary between the lowlands and highlands of Scotland, the great, glassy expanse of Loch Lomond seems to accompany you for an eternity as you travel the busy, winding A82 north. Loch Lomond is the largest area of inland water in Britain, its 27 square miles dotted with wooded islands, yachts and kayaks. The West Highland Way takes in a different view of the Loch, following its eastern shores, winding through forest and often dipping right down to the water's edge. It is a glorious place to be in early spring, but can be a war with the midges during the summer months. The Trossachs lie to the east of Ben Lomond, the landscape gentler than that of the highlands, scattered with quiet lochs and forested glens. Escape to nearby Leannach Forest (Run 131) for a tranquil view of West Scotland's peaks and lochs.

The peaceful islands of Jura, Islay and Colonsay lie just off this western coast: magical and remote lands less than three hours by car or bus from Glasgow. The islands form part of the Inner Hebrides, which also includes Mull, Rum and Skye. Islay is home to glorious landscapes and scenery, and with its vast white-sand beaches, coastal cliffs and a rugged interior demands to be run (see Run 132). On Jura, the infamous Jura Fell Race, held every year in May, starts in Craighouse and covers 16 miles including a total ascent of 2,286 metres over seven mountain summits, including all three of the iconic Paps of Jura.

Glasgow & the West

130 CHATELHERAULT

Distance:	4½ miles (7km)
Start/finish:	Chatelherault Visitor Centre (near Hamilton), ML3 7UE
Terrain:	Woodland path, trail
Toughness:	Easy
Ascent:	135 metres
Navigation:	Easy (waymarked)
Good for:	Woodland, families, urban escape
Route info:	wildrunning.net/130

This wonderful route passes high above the picturesque Avon Gorge in the Clyde Valley Woodlands National Nature Reserve. It's a gentle run on perfect, waymarked, woodland trails carpeted with pine needles. From the Visitor Centre (10 minutes walk from Chatelherault station), follow signs for Green Bridge until the path drops steeply into gorge bottom and Avon Water. Cross Green Bridge, with accessible Avon Water babbling invitingly below, and continue NW down into the wonderfully named Divoty Glen. Pass Cadzow Oaks and the remains of Cadzow Castle. Finally cross Dukes Bridge, high above Avon Water with splendid views of the gorge, before returning to the start.

131 LEANNACH FOREST

Distance:	5 miles (8km)
Start/finish:	Leannach forestry car park, 2 miles SE of Loch Katrine ferry, FK17 8JA
Terrain:	Woodland path, path
Toughness:	Easy
Ascent:	220 metres
Navigation:	Easy (waymarked)
Good for:	Woodland, families
Route info:	wildrunning.net/131

A wonderful, peaceful run on firm, waymarked trails through tranquil forest in the glorious Queen Elizabeth Forest Park. Follow red waymarkers throughout; enjoy the run and the simple pleasure of running through trees and enjoying fantastic glimpses of mountains and lochs without having to worry about navigation. Gentle climbs reward you with great views of the beautiful Trossachs, including the fine peaks of Ben A'an and Ben Venue. From the car park, follow the signed track towards the forest, heading directly towards Ben Venue and crossing bridge. Bear right at Ben Venue sign, re-cross stream and continue to follow red waymarkers uphill to rejoin outward track back to car park.

132 KILLINALLAN POINT, ISLAY

Distance:	6½ miles (10km)
Start/finish:	Killinallan, 3 miles N of PA44 7PN
Terrain:	Sandy beach, farm track
Toughness:	Easy
Ascent:	44 metres
Navigation:	Easy
Good for:	Coast, views, wildlife
Route info:	wildrunning.net/132

This stunning run takes in the beautiful beaches and coastline around Loch Gruinart, in the north of Islay. The colours here are remarkable: blue skies, turquoise water and pale sands. From the parking area, a grassy verge on the minor road off the B8017 (SP Killinallan 3), a white arrow points you towards the sea. Turn L, at low tide along the sands, at high tide along the shoreline. Head NW past basking seals to Killinallan Point, continuing to Traigh Baile Aonghais. This may require some paddling at high tide. Continue along the beach to the Gortantaoid River. Just before the river a faint path leads up through the dunes to a clear track, and the remains of Gortantaoid Farm. Follow this great, runnable track SW back to the start.

The Cairngorms & the North East

The Cairngorm massif is Britain's highest and largest mountain range. It is home to five of the six highest mountains in Scotland, with the highest in the range, Ben Macdui, standing at 1,309 metres. Rugged and remote, the Cairngorms are a serious undertaking, particularly in the colder months when they become a snowy, icy arena, popular as a venue for winter climbing, mountaineering and snow sports. Cairn Gorm itself lies within a vast plateau that is the snowiest place in Britain. A wild place, exposed to the most extreme elements, this was the site of the greatest wind speed ever officially recorded in Britain, at 173 miles per hour, in March 1986. The lower slopes of these mountains are forested and tranquil, and within the valleys are sparkling lochs and gushing, tumbling, clear rivers. The mountains themselves form only part of the Cairngorms National Park, the biggest National Park in Britain, covering some 1,748 square miles.

There are some fantastic waymarked long-distance trails in this part of the country: the East Highland Way runs for 83 miles from Fort William, and the Speyside Way is 66½ miles from Buckie on the Moray coastline, both ending in Aviemore on the western edge of the Cairngorms. Many sections of these routes make great out-and-back or linear runs, generally on excellent paths. Multisport racing is popular here, with several duathlons, triathlons, biathlons (shooting and skiing) and adventure races. The Rigby Round, devised by Mark Rigby who completed it in July 1988, takes in all of the Cairngorm Munros in approximately 75 miles of running with 19,000 feet of ascent in under 24 hours. This is something of an alternative challenge, as detailed on the official website: "The spirit of this

133

134

135

wild landscape appears to have cast its own magic spell by inspiring a tradition of true adventure running. In contrast with most other runs it is suggested that the route is completed solo and unsupported and, ideally, there should be no prior reconnoitre!". Since the inaugural run, Angel Peak has been elevated to Munro status and the challenge now stands at 18 Munros. Wild Run 135 climbs only one of the Cairngorm Munros (twice) – Beinn Mheadhoin – but this is no mean feat!

We ran up Glen Feshie on a perfect autumn morning. This breathtaking route along a perfect Scottish glen would certainly have made it into this book were it not for the fact that Carnachuin Bridge, an important crossing point for the preferable circular route, was washed away in 2009 and had not, at the time of writing, been replaced. It is still well worth a trip for the out-and-back run from the house at Achlean up the rough, stony paths on the eastern shore of the river to Ruigh Aiteachain, an open bothy maintained by the volunteers of the Mountain Bothy Association. We followed the path as it climbed steadily, a delightful, sensory journey taking us through dense, heavily-scented Scots pinewoods, the musical babbling of the river accompanying us the whole way. Our alternative, the equally fantastic Run 133, follows the River Spey through this beautiful area.

The Moray coastline has superb sandy beaches interspersed with cliffs, rocky arches and sea stacks. Moray Firth dolphins can be spotted playing in the sea, and there is abundant birdlife here. Inland, the peaceful fields and farmland rise to open moors and the foothills of the Cairngorms. The Moray Way, the Dava Way, the Moray Coast Trail and the Speyside Way together form a circular route of around 95 miles. The section along the coast, the Moray Coast Trail, links the coastline and settlements of Moray in a waymarked route of 50 miles from Findhorn, south of the Moray Firth, eastwards along the spectacular North Sea coast to Cullen, near to Buckie. We ran the length of the trail in a leisurely three days, however it can be run as an ultradistance challenge (Run 150) or in sections, of which our favourite was from Burghead to Lossiemouth (Run 134).

135

The Cairngorms & the North East

133 BADENOCH WAY

Distance:	11 miles (17km)
Start:	Dalraddy Caravan P'k, PH22 1QB
Finish:	900m E of Ruthven Barracks, PH21 1NR
Terrain:	Paths, tracks, quiet roads
Toughness:	Easy
Ascent:	270 metres
Navigation:	Easy (waymarked)
Good for:	Woodland, wildlife
Route info:	wildrunning.net/133

This peaceful run follows the winding River Spey through moorland, forest and farmland. Well waymarked, the run takes in many runnable trails through a wide variety of stunning landscapes. Follow waymarkers from start, heading SW across Dalraddy Moor, before diving into lush woodland on perfect grassy trails. Follow the River Spey, eventually reaching the road at Kincraig. Wind your way through the town, cross the river, pass Insh Church and follow waymarkers, skirting Insh Loch's SE shore until you again escape into tranquil woodland. Pass RSPB Insh Marshes, before and continuing to Drumguish. Follow the Insh Marshes Invertromie Trail to the finish.

134 BURGHEAD TO LOSSIEMOUTH

Distance:	8 miles (13km)
Start:	Burghead village centre
Finish:	Lossiemouth
Terrain:	Trail, sandy beach, paths, road
Toughness:	Easy
Ascent:	107 metres
Navigation:	Easy (waymarked)
Good for:	National trail, coast, swimming
Route info:	wildrunning.net/134

Our favourite section of the 53-mile, fully waymarked Moray Coastal Trail, this run takes in spectacular, rugged coastline, sandy beaches, sparklingly clean seas and its contrasting settlements. The running is varied and interesting and the views are glorious, accompanying you for the entire journey, out across the many coves and beaches and over to the skerries. Leave Burghead following waymarkers E of village. Follow track to Hopeman, passing through village to the car park. Continue along trail from there towards Covesea along the length of the Hopeman Ridge. Pass the lighthouse, drop down onto the beach and follow the trail through the sand dunes to Lossiemouth.

135 BEINN MHEADHOIN

Distance:	11½ miles (18km)
Start/finish:	Cairngorm Ski Centre car park, Aviemore, PH22 1RB
Terrain:	Open moor, mountain track, path
Toughness:	Challenging
Ascent:	1268 metres
Navigation:	Challenging
Good for:	Ascents, really wild, hard-as-nails
Route info:	wildrunning.net/135

A hard, mountain run in a remote and testing part of the Cairngorms. It is an exhilarating and hugely rewarding adventure, especially when travelling fast and light, requiring high levels of fitness, mountain and navigation skills and experience. ⚠ Route described is for fine summer conditions. Start by following the funicular railway to the halfway station, leaving the path here to climb the west side of Coire Cas. Follow the ridge of Fiacaill a' Choire Chais to its summit. Descend into Coire Raibert, and S to Loch Avon, continuing SW to the head of the loch. Follow a narrow path passing the huge block of the Shelter Stone to the summit ridge-plateau of Beinn Mheadhoin with its range of granite tors. Retrace your steps to the start.

West Highland Way, Glencoe

Fort William & Lochaber

The Lochaber region, diverse and spectacular in landscape and scenery, reaches from Rannoch Moor and Glencoe in the south to the Great Glen in the north, and from Fort William along the west coast to Mallaig, including the small Isles of Eigg, Rum and Muck. Westwards it extends out into the Atlantic to Ardnamurchan Point, the most westerly part of the UK mainland. Lochaber also includes the Glen Spean area, and Loch Laggan and part of Argyll in the south-west.

Fort William is something of a hub for outdoor enthusiasts. Runners, climbers, walkers and mountain bikers flock here to explore the wonders of the surrounding landscapes. The Great Glen Way and the West Highland Way (Run 136) both start or end here. The Nevis Range is startlingly beautiful, from the brooding form of Ben Nevis (Run 137), its summit often obscured by swirling cloud, to the peaceful, golden valley of Glen Nevis with its cascading waterfalls, woodland trails and bracken-covered hillsides. Run 138 takes in remote and serene Loch Ossian, inaccessible by road but a great run from Corrour Railway Station, as a picturesque alternative with less ascent.

On a recent trip to the area, we stayed in a tiny cabin, huddled in the relative shelter of Glen Nevis. Our view of the mountains was spectacular: the softer, greener slopes of Aonach Mor lay to one side whilst the dark, jagged edges of the north face of the Ben rose sharply to the other, its summit shrouded in a veil of cloud for our entire stay. Of an early morning, from the comfort of our valley, I could make out the distinct, diagonally rising edge of Tower Ridge, highlighted against the darker, murkier crags behind. Steel-grey clouds swept fast over the tops, and I knew how it would feel to be up there, barely able to stand, fighting for breath and balance against the elements. The great challenges of the mountains called to us and heightened our building frustration with the weather.

137

137

138

Several days later, a weather window provided the briefest of opportunities, and we found ourselves jogging along the familiar path to the North Face car park. Pushing up the steep track through the woods, we continued up the valley to the hut and eventually reached the foot of the Douglas Gibson boulder. Here we stopped to change from fell shoes to rock boots, enjoying the feeling of lightness as we took the weight of the gear we would use for the ascent off our backs. The climb up Tower Ridge was easy but absorbing, the positions exposed and exhilarating, perched high above the valley below. The rock was cold and slightly damp beneath our hands but the route was unusually empty, and we saw no one else on our ascent. Finally we pulled up over the top and onto the summit plateau, walking a few steps from the edge into the mist that hadn't left the top for days. It was windy and cold, the heat generated by our climb quickly leaving our bodies, and we packed up as fast as we could, digging out the map and compass to take the all-important bearing to the zig-zags at the top of the Mountain Track. Many have taken this bearing too soon, in poor visibility, and followed it straight over the precipitous edge of Five Finger Gully. Only once we had found the path and descended out of the mist could we relax and enjoy the emerging views and winding run down the iconic track to Glen Nevis.

The Ben Nevis Race is an infamous run to the top of the Ben and back, and a classic fixture on the fell racing calendar. Starting and finishing at Claggan Park in Fort William, runners take to the road before following the Mountain Track to the top, with some straight-lining up and down grass and scree slopes at the switchback sections. Each September, some 600 runners take up the challenge, which has been held every year since 1951 with the exception of 1980, when it was cancelled due to poor weather. The records for the race are held by Kenny and Pauline Stuart who, in 1984, posted times of 1 hour 25 minutes, and 1 hour 43 minutes respectively. The Aonach Mor uphill race, held brutally on New Year's Day, sees runners starting at the Nevis Range Ski Centre and heading uphill for nearly 2½ miles to the finish. Records are held by Robbie Simpson in 22 minutes, and Nicola Meekin in 26 minutes.

Fort William & Lochaber

136 INVERORAN TO KINLOCHLEVEN

Distance:	17 miles (28km)
Start:	½ mile NW of Inveroran Hotel, PA36 4AQ
Finish:	Ice Factor, Kinlochleven
Terrain:	Path, track, short road section
Toughness:	Moderate
Ascent:	744 metres
Navigation:	Easy to moderate (waymarked)
Good for:	National trail, really wild
Route info:	wildrunning.net/136

The first half of this run, across the vast wilderness of Rannoch Moor, is one of the classic stages of the West Highland Way. From Victoria Bridge at the start, it follows the clear path of Telford's Parliamentary Road SW through a sea of heather and bog, surrounded by towering mountains on either side. In fine weather, this is a place of wild and peaceful beauty, turning to an exposed and foreboding arena on the arrival of a storm. Underfoot conditions are generally easy and runnable. The second half of the run is the most dramatic section of the Way, as it climbs to the highest point on the route. The final long descent, with excellent views, to Kinlochleven is an enjoyable finish.

137 BEN NEVIS MOUNTAIN TRACK

Distance:	10½ miles (17km)
Start/finish:	Glen Nevis Visitor Centre car park, PH33 6ST
Terrain:	Path
Toughness:	Moderate to challenging
Ascent:	1279 metres
Navigation:	Easy (if weather good)
Good for:	Classic route, ascents
Route info:	wildrunning.net/137

This run follows the main route up Ben Nevis on runnable but steep trails. Crossing the river R, follow the obvious, wide path, zig-zagging as it climbs higher. Take care not to miss a sharp left turn at the head of the Valley of the Red Burn. The going becomes rougher and then levels out at the summit plateau. From the summit, the views are spectacular, covering much of the Highlands, and the sheer north face with its classic rock climbs that vanishes below. The return is made by the same route. In misty conditions and/or with snow covering the path, very careful navigation can be required to steer a course between Gardyloo Gully and Five Finger Gully. ⚠ Adhere to safety warnings.

138 LOCH OSSIAN LOOP

Distance:	9 miles (14km)
Start/finish:	Corrour Station, PH30 4AA
Terrain:	Gravel path, track
Toughness:	Easy
Ascent:	122 metres
Navigation:	Easy
Good for:	Really wild, wild swimming
Route info:	wildrunning.net/138

A wonderful, gentle run on good paths around a stunning loch in a remote and spectacular location. From Corrour railway station, run along a dirt track following signposts east towards Tulloch, aiming for the Youth Hostel on the shores of the loch. From here, follow the path that loops the loch in either direction. The path provides great running on firm ground with some rougher, muddier terrain on the southern shore. This route is accessible only by a scenic train ride to Corrour Station. Accommodation is available at the SYHA Loch Ossian Hostel, from where there are many miles of trails and hills to explore. Much of the surrounding terrain is wet and boggy, but nonetheless this is enjoyable running in a fantastic location.

Old Man of Stoer

Central & Northern Highlands

Tucked into the far north-west corner of Scotland, the landscape around Assynt and neighbouring Coigach is truly extraordinary. From a vast, undulating, loch-studded moorland, rise a series of steep mountains, their individual shapes standing out incongruously, completely separate from one another. The coastline around Assynt is equally beautiful, with rugged cliffs, stunning white sand beaches and impressive sea stacks. One such stack is the immense Old Man of Stoer (Run 139): a classic rock climb, the Old Man is also a nesting ground for fulmars, wheeling on the thermals. The seas here are fantastic for whale and dolphin spotting.

The landscapes of north-west Sutherland are remote and hauntingly beautiful. Empty, sandy beaches line the coast; inland there are vast moorlands and shimmering lochs edged by bare, rocky mountains. The wonderful Cape Wrath Trail runs for 200 miles from Fort William to the dramatic cliffs of Cape Wrath.

Further south, Ben Alder is the highest mountain in the remote central highlands. Rare visitors to the mountain's summit may find themselves alone, with only deer and wheeling birds of prey for company. Journalist Jean Rafferty writes of the place, "up here, near the rounded plateau of the summit, the weather is worse than anywhere else in the surrounding area, colder, and with a ferocious wind that can pull the rucksack off a climber's back. Snow veils the mountain for up to nine months of the year, and locals say you can find as many as 120 beasties lying dead up there at the end of winter". The Munro's vast summit plateau is home of one of Britain's highest bodies of standing water, Lochan a' Garbh Coire, a slender mirror reflecting the oft-changing mood of the sky. There are two

141

139

141

bothies in the area: Culra Bothy (see Run 140) and Ben Alder Cottage, in which shelter can be found.

Our first experience of Ben Alder was on a cold winter's day. We struggled through the deepening snow – knee-deep, then waist-deep – for eight hours until we finally reached the small loch below the summit, where we pitched our tent to escape the freezing wind that found its way through even the tiniest gap in our clothing. Early next morning, still exhausted, we slowly climbed the last slopes to the summit, to be rewarded with a blanket of cloud instead of the fine view we hoped for, and a pelting by freezing, sharp hailstones. Cold, tired and hungry, we retreated back to Rannoch as quickly as we could, awakened to the real challenges of these winter mountains. Our second attempt was on a warm day in summer, and we were fitter, more experienced and keen to try to enjoy the mountain more. Our memories from last time were of struggle, survival, cold and pain, but also of the satisfaction of having pushed our mental and physical limits. We wanted to test ourselves again. We started early, running up the track from the small hamlet, rucksacks full of essential kit for a couple of days on the fells. The distance up to Ben Alder, past Loch Ericht, isn't huge and, although it took eight hours last time, the mountain felt like a different place today. We ran easily along the track, taking in the sun-bathed scenery all around, quickly reaching the loch, and then the hut. It all looked much more welcoming than last time but we were still acutely aware of the remoteness of our position. We climbed the hill and pitched our tent with a breathatking view out across the valley before setting out with lighter steps to explore. An early start the following morning and we climbed to the summit, rewarded at last with a stunning view across Rannoch Moor and back the way we had run towards Loch Rannoch. We ran fast all the way back, wanting to push ourselves and reach civilisation before darkness fell. We long to return in both summer and winter. Ben Alder's remoteness and contrasts draws us back.

Our final run, 141, takes in the rocky slopes of Ben Hope, the most northerly of the Scottish munros, a wonderfully tranquil place in summer, when pretty alpine flowers line the trails.

Central & Northern Highlands

139 THE OLD MAN OF STOER

Distance:	4½ miles (7km)
Start/finish:	Stoer Head lighthouse car park, 1 mile W of IV27 4JH
Terrain:	Rough coastal terrain, grass
Toughness:	Moderate
Ascent:	275 metres
Navigation:	Moderate
Good for:	Coast, classic routes, wildlife
Route info:	wildrunning.net/139

This wonderful run follows the edge of Assynt in remote far north-west Scotland. It visits the Old Man of Stoer, a towering 60-metre sea stack of Torridonian sandstone, once a rocky arch over to the mainland, but now an island. Popular with climbers, the high-quality routes on the stack require a Tyrolean traverse to reach. From lighthouse, follow signed path to the Old Man of Stoer, climbing on good, runnable tracks alongside rugged coast as spectacular views emerge all around. Continue NE along coast to reach the Point of Stoer. Return S over summit of Sidhean Mòr, with fine views of the Sutherland coast and mountains of Assynt. Follow paths past a ruined WWII radar station back to start.

140 DALWHINNIE TO CULRA BOTHY

Distance:	9½ miles (15km) (each way)
Start/finish:	Dalwhinnie Railway Station, PH19 1AD
Terrain:	Path, track
Toughness:	Easy to moderate
Ascent:	203 metres
Navigation:	Easy to moderate
Good for:	Views, really wild
Route info:	wildrunning.net/140

This enjoyable run through wonderful highland scenery takes you to the remote Culra Bothy, a perfect base for exploring Ben Alder and the other great mountains in this area. The bothy sleeps 22 and can get busy but you can also camp nearby. From Dalwhinnie Station, follow road SW to Loch Ericht, continuing along loch-side track into forestry. Take track forking R and then L as it climbs behind Ben Alder Lodge, emerging into wilder and more remote country as the mountains come into view. Follow well-made path S of Loch Pattack, following river upstream towards Culra Bothy, which soon comes into view. Cross newly-built signposted bridge and turn left onto a track which leads to the bothy itself.

141 BEN HOPE

Distance:	9 miles (14.5km)
Start/finish:	Roadside car park, 8 miles S of A838/Altnaharra Road junction
Terrain:	Mountain track, path, rock
Toughness:	Moderate to challenging
Ascent:	836 metres
Navigation:	Easy (challenging if visibility poor)
Good for:	Ascents, views, really wild
Route info:	wildrunning.net/141

This is a fantastic, hard-as-nails, rocky and scrambly out-and-back run up the most northerly of the Munros, Ben Hope at 927 metres. From the car park beside the minor road that follows the river Strathmore, follow the signs for 'Ben Hope Path' uphill on the SE bank of the burn, Allt a' Mhuiseil. The route winds its way up, dodging crags and waterfalls, climbing steeply until it reaches the mountain's W ridge. Follow the ridge N on a clear path, finally reaching the trig point on the rocky summit plateau, to be rewarded by astonishing panorama. Descent is by the same path. A short extension can be added by continuing along the escarpment of Leitir Mheuiseil, and the waterfall above Alltnacaillich before descending to the road.

Black Cuillin

Lewis, Harris & Skye

The Outer Hebrides – the Western Isles, or Long Island as they are sometimes known – include Lewis and Harris, North Uist, Benbecula, South Uist, and Barra. This cluster of islands is a magical place, with a huge diversity of landscapes creating vast scope for on-foot exploration. The delicate pink rock is ancient Lewisian gneiss which forms the bedrock of the islands. It is amongst the oldest in Europe, formed by bubbling Precambrian volcanoes some three billion years ago. The diversity and abundance of wildlife on the islands is breathtaking – the calls of dunlins, lapwings and ringed plovers fill the air, puffins and razorbills huddle noisily on the rocks and surf on the waves. Inland, the rasping cries of the corncrake, a rare summer visitor, can often be heard, but these are shy and elusive birds; the poet John Clare wrote of the corncrake in his comic verse *The Landrail* about the difficulty of seeing these shy creatures " 'Tis like a fancy everywhere / A sort of living doubt". Fulmars scythe their way around the sea cliffs, and hen harriers and golden eagles arch majestically over the rugged landscape. There are 7,500 lochs in the Outer Hebrides alone; salmon and trout swim in the crystal-clear water, and otters can be spotted playing in the shallows. The seas are home to basking sharks, whales and dolphins. It is upon these islands, perhaps, that it is possible to get the closest to true wildness anywhere in Britain. Our two Outer Hebridean runs (Run 143 and Run 144) explore sea lochs and rugged highland sections.

Although part of the same landmass, Lewis and Harris have their own distinct characters, from the mountainous northern reaches that provide wonderful, peaceful running through spectacular, rolling landscapes, to the rugged coastline, beautiful beaches and tiny villages of the south. The Harris

144

142

143

Walkway has some excellent running (with some boggy sections), and is formed from the linking up of a series of old paths to make a waymarked route of over 20 miles from the northern end of Harris to the machair at Seilebost. There are many waymarked routes on the Islands, frequently crossing areas of beauty and historical interest. Much of the ground is boggy and pathless between waymarkings, so a map is essential, particularly in poor weather.

Skye (Run 142), lies between the Outer Hebrides and the mainland. It is the largest of the Inner Hebrides and upon its remote landscape tower the mountain ranges of the Red and Black Cuillin. The traverse of the great ridge of the Black Cuillin on Skye is one of the great fell walking and running challenges in Britain. It is a serious and committing undertaking, and the 7-mile ridge (the actual distance to be crossed, including ascents and descents, is nearer to 9 miles and includes some 3,048 metres of ascent) has a recommended time for walking of 15–20 hours. In 2007, Es Tresidder set a time of 3 hours 17 minutes 28 seconds for running the ridge, which was beaten in 2013 by climber, international mountain runner and GP Finlay Wild who completed it in 3 hours 14 minutes 58 seconds. Typically, approaching the ridge from Glenbrittle, walkers take five hours to reach the TD Gap, the first technically challenging part of the route. There follow around eight hours of technical walking, climbing and scrambling to reach the final summit of Sgurr nan Gillean. A two-hour walk to Sligachan completes the classic route. Although runners may be considerably faster in many places, some sections of the traverse itself require specialist equipment, navigational and technical skills and knowledge. The weather here is also notoriously fickle, "a defier of all forecasts" according to Cuillin authority and author of the definitive book on the range, Gordon Stainforth. He likens climbing the ridge well to "playing a long and difficult piece of music: it's like trying to follow a beautiful melodic line through space – sometimes simple, sometimes very intricate – accomplishing all the technical difficulties and obstacles as smoothly as possible. It's about flow and pace and rhythm."

Lewis, Harris & Skye

142 COIRE LAGÀN, SKYE

Distance:	5½ miles (9km)
Start/finish:	Glenbrittle campsite, IV47 8TA
Terrain:	Path, trail, scramble sections
Toughness:	Moderate
Ascent:	563 metres
Navigation:	Easy
Good for:	Wild swimming
Route info:	wildrunning.net/142

This fantastic run, on fine paved paths through stunning scenery, takes you from the campsite at Glen Brittle right into the heart of Coire Làgan, a great, rocky amphitheatre bordered by towering gabbro crags, including the famous Inaccessible Pinnacle, part of the classic Cuillin Ridge traverse. From the campsite take the path as it climbs E into Coire Làgan. Continue ENE along the path, looping clockwise around the tiny loch that lies in the hollow at the base of Sgurr Mhic Choinnich. Return along the path W to the base of the Coire joining the equally spectacular NW path along the N side of Loch an Fhir-bhallaich to Glen Brittle. The wonderful, crystal clear Allt Coir' a' Mhadaidh pools and waterfalls are nearby, perfect for a post-run swim.

143 ALONG THE COAST OF LEWIS

Distance:	12 miles (19km)
Start:	Garenin Blackhouse Village car park, HS2 9AL
Finish:	Bragar village centre
Terrain:	Bog, path, short road section
Toughness:	Moderate
Ascent:	397 metres
Navigation:	Easy to moderate
Good for:	Coast, wildlife, really wild
Route info:	wildrunning.net/143

Lewis is the largest of the Outer Hebrides, at its centre a peat plateau, giving way to sandy beaches and rocky cliffs. This great point-to-point run follows the rugged north-western coast of Lewis across varying terrain from rocky, scrambly sections to boggy, pathless stretches between the occasional waymarkers. From Garenin / Na Gearrannan, follow the intermittent path along the coast N, then winding and zig-zagging in a general NE direction around its many coves, lochs and inlets and, often venturing slightly inland, to pass the villages of Dail Beag and Siabost. After running past Loch Ordais follow the footpath R to the finish at Bragar. Occasional buses back to Garenin.

144 URGHA & MÀRAIG, HARRIS

Distance:	12 miles (19km)
Start/finish:	Lochannan Lacasdail car park, 1¼ miles E of Tarbert, HS3 3BL
Terrain:	Trail, path, quiet road
Toughness:	Moderate
Ascent:	696 metres
Navigation:	Easy to moderate
Good for:	Coast, ascents, really wild
Route info:	wildrunning.net/144

A varied and exciting circular run that starts along the old footpath from Urgha to Rhenigidale, with stunning coastal views and some fantastic technical sections. From the car park, follow the path E and NE as it climbs and descends to the northern shores of Loch Trolamaraig. Before Reinigeadal, head NW, following the quiet minor road to the E of Todun. At the river at the head of Loch Mharaig leave the road returning along the old path over Bràigh an Ruisg and past Lochannan Lascadail. Some of the sections are boggy, but once higher ground is reached the paths are wonderfully runnable. An optional 2 mile extension detours down into the deserted, desolate village of Moilingeanais: steep climb back.

Deerness

Orkney & Shetland

Orkney lies only 10 miles off the north coast of Caithness, yet it feels like another world compared with almost anywhere in mainland Britain. It comprises around 70 islands, of which 20 are inhabited: the Mainland, the North Isles and the South Isles. The remote and uninhabited islets of Sule Skerry and Sule Stack lie nearly 40 miles away from the main island group. The climate here is mild, on account of the Gulf Stream, and the land is low-lying and fertile with pleasant green, rolling hills, heather-covered moors and a rich abundance of flora and fauna. Our grassy Run 145 takes in one of the many nature reserves here. There are magnificent red sandstone cliffs on the island of Hoy, where the towering sea stack of the Old Man of Hoy rises imposingly from the breaking waves below. These cliffs contrast starkly with the wide, white sand beaches of Papay, Sanday and Stronsay. Papay (Papa Westray) is a tiny island with a population of around 90. Although just 4 miles long by 1 mile wide it has a fascinating and diverse range of landscapes, places of archaeological interest and wildlife. A run around the coastline of the entire island is a lovely way to explore the variety it has to offer (Run 146). Access to the island is by ferry or the eight-seat Islander plane and, although it is possible to get to the island from mainland Orkney, spend a few hours soaking up its unique character and return to the mainland in a single day, a longer stay is recommended. There is a community-run shop and accommodation on Papay.

There are several races on Orkney, from the 10km races held in Kirkwall in April, Flotta in May, Stromness in July and Dounby in September, to the half marathons in Hoy in June and Kirkwall in August.

145

145

146

The hundred or so islands that make up Shetland lie 50 miles to the north-east of Orkney, and 110 miles north of mainland Scotland. Sixteen of the islands are inhabited, with a total population of about 23,000. Shetland has over 1,000 miles of coastline, from rugged and spectacular to peaceful and sandy. 'Mainland' Shetland is the third largest Scottish island and the fifth largest in Britain, with a network of 'core paths' allowing easy access for exploration. Shetland is home to 19 Marilyns, hills with a relative height over 150 metres; the highest is Ronas Hill, at 450 metres. In 2012, local runner Luke Holt ran end to end across Shetland, from Sumburgh Lighthouse on the southern tip to the cliffs of Hermaness at the most northerly point, a distance of some 77 miles. There are few waymarked routes on Shetland, but the landscape and terrain lends itself perfectly to exploration on foot. As a friend and resident of the islands once told me, "Well, it's not the sort of place that has marked routes for anything. You just go where you want!" Wild Run 147 finds a route around the stunning Esha Ness peninsula, on the extreme west of the main island.

The Out Skerries, often just referred to as 'Skerries', lie to the east of the main Shetland island group. A fantastic circular route around the very edge of the main islands, Bruray and Housay, takes in great scenery and enjoyable running terrain, a distance of around 6 miles. Another enjoyable route, on mainland Shetland, runs from the access road to the transmitter station, off the A970 near North Collafirth, to the summit of Ronas Hill. The route is pathless and occasionally boggy but in general on wonderful, runnable terrain. There are far-reaching views from the summit cairn over the landscape and sea all around, for a hundred miles.

There are a few races in Shetland, friendly, welcoming and invariably extremely scenic; however, they tend to be only locally advertised. The 'Simmer Dim' Shetland Half Marathon is held annually in July and the Hairst Marathon and Half Marathon in September.

Orkney & Shetland

145 DEERNESS, ORKNEY MAINLAND

Distance:	4 miles (6km)
Start/finish:	Mull Head car park, 1¼ miles N of KW17 2QJ
Terrain:	Grass, gravel path, steps, track
Toughness:	Easy
Ascent:	111 metres
Navigation:	Easy
Good for:	Coast, wildlife, beaches
Route info:	wildrunning.net/145

This enjoyable and gentle run around the Deerness peninsula in the east of mainland Orkney takes in the wonderful coastal scenery and fantastic wildlife abundant in this area. From the car park, follow a gravel path E to The Gloup, a dramatic collapsed sea-cave separated from the mainland by a rocky bridge. Follow the coast, hugging footpath N to the grassy Brough of Deerness, where the remnants of an early Celtic monastery are still just visible. Continue along the Brough, following the coast N to Mull Head, a local Nature Reserve. Continue around the edge of the peninsula until reaching a fence – from here head SE up through open moorland to East Denwick, finally following paths to start.

146 PAPA WESTRAY, ORKNEY

Distance:	9 miles (15km)
Start/finish:	Airfield, Papa Westray
Terrain:	Path, grass trail, quiet road, beach
Toughness:	Easy
Ascent:	142 metres
Navigation:	Easy
Good for:	Coast, wildlife
Route info:	wildrunning.net/146

This is a wonderful tour of the remote and scenic island of Papa Westray, also known as Papay, home to just 40 households. The run takes in the surprising diversity of this tiny island. From the airfield run N to the North Hill RSPB Nature Reserve - a wonderful place for some further exploration - and follow a grassy path E and N, turning R towards the clifftops at Fowl Craig. Seals can often be seen here, basking on the rocks below. Continue S along South Wick turning R at Mayback to St Boniface Kirk. Follow the coastline S to reach the Knap of Howar and then E on a track to the community shop at Beltane House. Head S along coast path to the head of the bay of Mocklett then head NW to pass ferry landing. From here follow lane N back to start.

147 ESHA NESS, SHETLAND

Distance:	4 miles (6km)
Start/finish:	Lighthouse car park, ¾ mile W off B9078 at West Heogaland
Terrain:	Coastal track, path, beach
Toughness:	Easy
Ascent:	54 metres
Navigation:	Easy to moderate
Good for:	Coast, wildlife, history
Route info:	wildrunning.net/147

Esha Ness's breathtaking scenery, diversity of landscape and historical interest makes it a great place to explore. Starting at the lighthouse (which can be rented), perched high on an outcrop of volcanic rocks, this fantastic run takes you along the dramatic coast to the head of Calder's Geo, a deep inlet gouged by the sea into the dark rocks. Continue NE along the coast towards the great, sea-carved hole of Grind of the Navir, with its bouldery beach and strange sea loch. Continue NE to The Burr, and after Croo Loch, head back SW reaching the Loch of Houlland following its W shore. Springy turf provides wonderful running past the twin inlets of Drid Geo and Calder's Geo on R and back to the lighthouse.

South West Coast Path

Ultradistance Routes

Ultramarathons are considered an ultimate challenge, often far beyond the marathon in terms of distance and duration. They push the mind and body beyond anything generally experienced in daily life, stripping us back to our basic elements of endurance and the moment-by-moment management of the mind and body. Many runners say they find peace and clarity, along with a deeper self-knowledge and self-reliance, amidst the pain of running beyond the marathon.

Britain has a strong history in ultradistance running, with the 1980s being something of a golden era, when many of the records that still stand today were set. The recent resurgence of interest in this area is perhaps fuelled by our increasingly sedentary lives, which lack the thrill of extreme challenges, or perhaps even by the increase in marathon participation, which has moved the definition of a challenge up a notch; it has led to a rapid rise in the number of ultramarathon races on the calendar. Adding to established classics such as the West Highland Way Race (95 miles), the Ridgeway Challenge (85 miles) and the Grand Union Canal Race (145 miles), several of the well-established trail running series have introduced an ultradistance category to their races; new race organisers are also emerging, whose focus is solely on ultra or extreme challenges. 2013 saw the running of the UK's first six-day race since 1990 at the British Ultra Fest in Oxfordshire, an event which also includes 24- and 48-hour races. This phenomenon is occurring worldwide. Iconic races such as the Ultra Trail du Mont Blanc in the Alps, the Comrades in South Africa, the Marathon des Sables in Morocco and Badwater in America's Death Valley attract worldwide publicity and entrants. International ultradistance runners are becoming well known through their extreme achievements, providing inspiration and motivation and bringing this once niche sport to the attention of the masses.

148

149

148

The logistics involved in running non-stop for many hours differ greatly from those for shorter runs, with considerations around kit, food and water and the effects of the weather being far more important. The successful planning and completion of an ultradistance run is generally a hugely rewarding experience.

The following routes can be run in one go or split up into sections for a more gentle multi-day challenge. We ran the East Devon Way (Run 148) west to east, before returning at a more leisurely pace on the South West Coast Path, stopping at beautiful Budleigh Salterton, Branscombe, Beer and finally Lyme Regis along the way. This is an area with so much to explore that it also lends itself well to a multi-day adventure or to linking up with other excellent running trails locally.

We next venture into Wales and to Mynydd Epynt, an area of rolling moorland and deep river valleys to the north of the Brecon Beacons. The Epynt Way (Run 149) is an unusual run that takes in the wild, and until recently inaccessible, strip of land that loops around the perimeter of Sennybridge military firing range and separates it from the fields and hills beyond. The Epynt Way website www.epyntway.org contains full details regarding access to the Way, including links to Ministry of Defence information on firing times and other activities which may affect path users.

For an incredible coastal challenge, the Moray Coast Trail (Run 150) runs along the North Sea coast from Forres in the west to Cullen in the east, taking in its spectacular, rugged coastline, sandy beaches, sparklingly clean seas and delightfully contrasting settlements along the way. The running is varied and interesting, including beach, coastal paths, quiet roads and former railways. The views are glorious and accompany you for the entire journey, out across the many coves and beaches, over to the skerries and finally the vastness of the Moray Firth and the North Sea. Dolphins can be spotted playing in the waves; ospreys circle overhead. We took three leisurely days to complete the Trail, but the route lends itself well to a single push, for those wishing for a more lengthy challenge.

Ultradistance Routes

148 EAST DEVON WAY

Distance:	39½ miles (63km)
Start:	Exmouth station car park, EX8 1BZ
Finish:	Lyme Regis
Terrain:	Track, trail, field, road
Toughness:	Moderate
Ascent:	1409 metres
Navigation:	Easy (waymarked)
Good for:	Coast, views, history
Route info:	wildrunning.net/148

Also known as the Foxglove Way, the East Devon Way is a waymarked route that follows the Exe estuary before heading over the rolling hills of the E Devon AONB. From the car park, head N along a cycleway to Lympstone before following waymarkers up to Woodbury Common. Continue across Aylesbeare Common, crossing the Rivers Otter and Sid, and dropping down into Sidbury. Travel up the Roncombe Valley to remote Farway. From Colyton, cross the Axe Valley, passing Uplyme, to Lyme Regis, with its breweries, bakeries and beaches. Can break at pretty Branscombe, half way; worth a detour for its wonderful pebble beach and pubs. Take bus back, changing in Exeter.

149 EPYNT WAY

Distance:	50 miles (80km)
Start/finish:	Epynt Visitor Centre, B4519, 2 miles NW of LD3 9RG
Terrain:	Trail, bridleway
Toughness:	Moderate
Ascent:	1904 metres
Navigation:	Easy (waymarked)
Good for:	Really wild, wildlife
Route info:	wildrunning.net/149

A wonderful and unusual run in the wild lands around the perimeter of the Sennybridge military training area, where red kites soar above a diverse and beautiful landscape. ⚠ Check MOD firing times, do not disturb military equipment or personnel. The Epynt Visitor Centre, beside the B4519 at the NE of the ranges, has facilities and information on the area. From here, follow green and white waymarkers E to join the main trail. At track junction turn L and follow trail anticlockwise around the perimeter. Carry food and water. Nearest station is Llangammarch Wells, from where there is a waymarked route taking you to the Epynt Way.

150 MORAY COAST TRAIL

Distance:	45 miles (72km)
Start:	Forres railway station, IV36 1EL
Finish:	Cullen, AB56 4AG
Terrain:	Trail, sandy beach, path, road
Toughness:	Easy
Ascent:	536 metres
Navigation:	Easy (waymarked)
Good for:	National trail, coast, wild swimming
Route info:	wildrunning.net/150

The Moray Coast Trail is a fully waymarked, scenic and enjoyable tour of the rugged cliffs, hidden coves and sandy beaches along this dramatic and beautiful coastline. The trail is on generally level running, with some short, steep climbs, and passes through several coastal settlements with plenty of refuelling options along its way, making it ideal for an ultradistance challenge. From the start at the station, turn L onto minor road, following signs to Kinloss and then Findhorn to reach the coast. At Findhorn follow waymarkers E along Burghead Bay. Continue E passing through Hopeman, Lossiemouth and Spey Bay, arriving at Cullen Bay to finish.

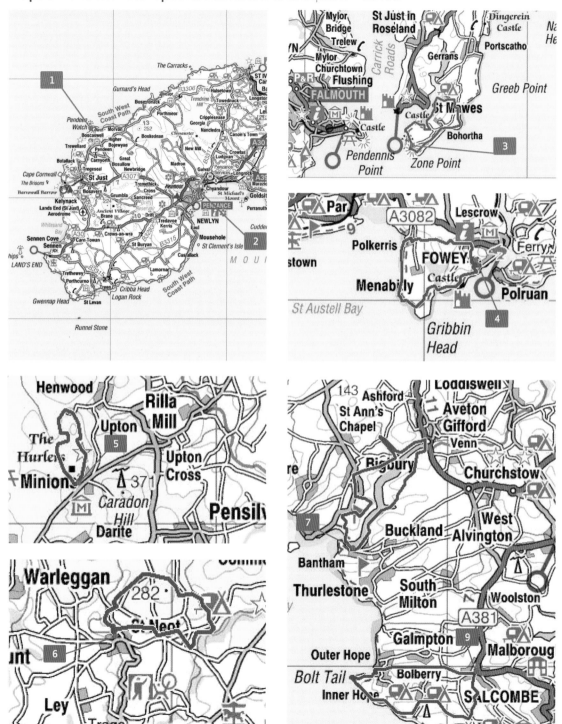

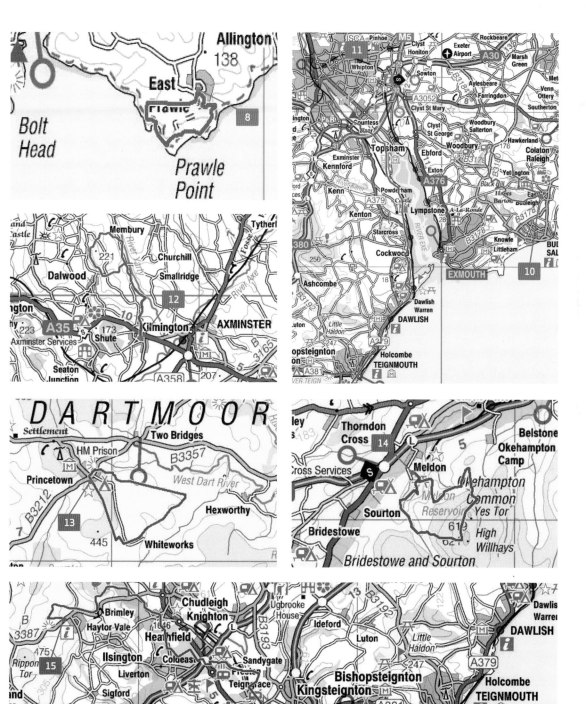

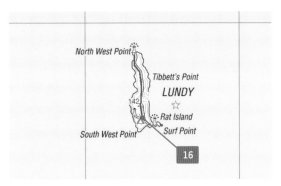

North West Point
Tibbett's Point
LUNDY
☆
142
Rat Island
South West Point
Surf Point

16

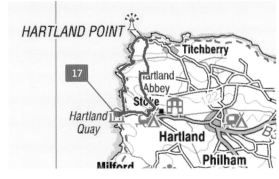

HARTLAND POINT
Titchberry
17
Hartland Abbey
Stoke
Hartland Quay
Hartland
Milford
Philham

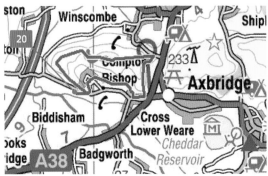

Woody Bay
Heddon's Mouth
Trentishoe
Martinh...
Toll
349
artin
Heale
Kemacott
A39
183
East
18
Parracombe

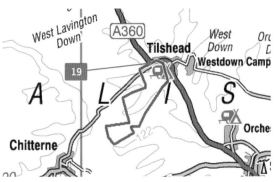

West Lavington Down
A360
West Down
Or...
D...
Tilshead
Westdown Camp
A   L   I   S
19
Chitterne
Orche...

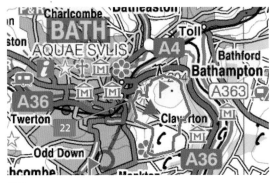

ston
Winscombe
Ship...
20
...n
Compton Bishop
233
Axbridge
Biddisham
Cross Lower Weare
Cheddar Reservoir
...oks
...dge
A38
Badgworth

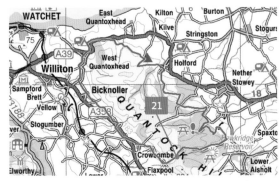

WATCHET
East Quantoxhead
Kilton
Burton
Kilve
Stringston
Stogurs...
75
A39
West Quantoxhead
Holford
Nether Stowey
Williton
Bicknoller
-18
Sampford Brett
Vellow
21
Stogumber
QUANTOCK H...
Spaxto...
...wkridge Reservoir
...lworthy
Crowcombe
Lower Aisholt
Flaxpool

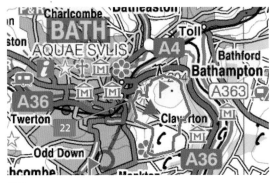

Charlcombe
Batheaston
BATH
Toll
AQUAE SVLIS
A4
Bathford
Bathampton
A36
A363
Twerton
Claverton
22
Odd Down
A36
...hcombe

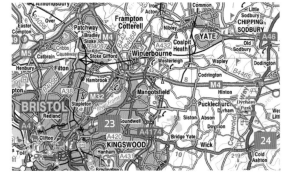

Almondsbury
Iron Acton
Common
Little Sodbury
CHIPPING SODBURY
A46
Over
Frampton Cotterell
Nibley
Easter Compton
Patchway
Bradley Stoke
M4
Coalpit Heath
YATE
Old Sodbury
Cribbs Causeway
Stoke Gifford
A432
Wapley
Dodington
M5
Catbrain
Winterbourne
Westerleigh
Codrington
Henbury
Filton
Hambrook
Mangotsfield
Hinton
M4
...pton
A38
M32
Stapleton
Pucklechurch
Dyrham Park
BRISTOL
Siston
Abson
Redland
Soundwell
A4174
Doynton
A4
Clifton
A420
Bridge Yate
Wick
KINGSWOOD
Hanham
A431
Toll
Brislington
Cold Ashton
23
24

254

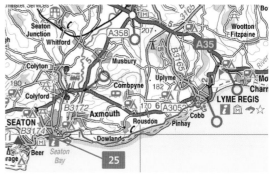

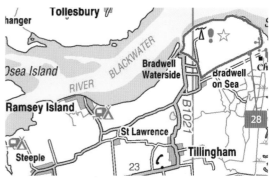

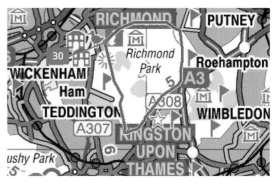

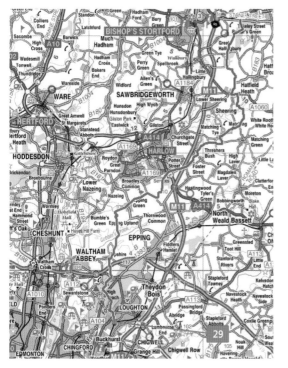

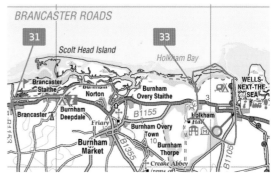

St Peter
Caston
Stow Bedon
Rocklan
Thompson
Lower Stow Bedon
All Sain
Breckles
32
Shropham
PEDDARS WAY
Great Hockham
14
B1111
Stonebridge
Pe

Abbey
A1120
Darsham
Dunwich
Sibton
Yoxford
Westleton
Middleton
45
A12
B1122
Theberton
Eastbridge
34
Kelsale
Carlton
Leiston Abbey
Power Station
Sizewell
ffling
SAXMUNDHAM
B1119
13
at
B1121
Knodishall
LEISTON
ham
Coldfair
Aldringham

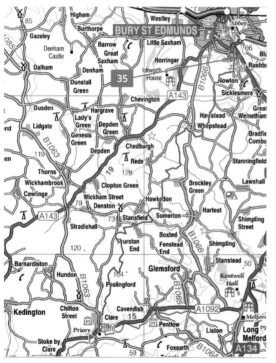

85
Higham
Westley
BURY ST EDMUNDS
Abbey
Gazeley
Burthorpe
Little Saxham
i
66
Bla
085
Denham Castle
Barrow
Great Saxham
Horringer
Rushb
Dalham
Denham
Ickworth House
B1066
Nowton
Sicklesmere
Dunstall Green
35
Chevington
Great Welnetham
Dusden
Hargrave
A143
Havstead
Lidgate
Lady's Green
Depden Green
Whepstead
Bradfie
Combu
B1063
Genesis Green
Depden
Chedburgh
119
Thorns
Rede
Stanningfield
Wickhambrook
19
128
Clopton Green
Brockley Green
Lawshall
Cowlinge
Wickham Street
Denston
Hawkedon
Hartest
A143
79
Shimpling Street
Stradishall
73
Stansfield
Somerton
Boxted
Thurston End
Fenstead End
Shimpling
Barnardiston
120
Stanstead
50
Hundon
B1063
164
Glemsford
Kentwell Hall
Kedington
Poslingford
B1065
Melfor
Chilton Street
Clare
15
Pentlow
Liston
Long Melford
Stoke by Clare
Priory
A1092
Cavendish
Foxearth
B1064
A134
59

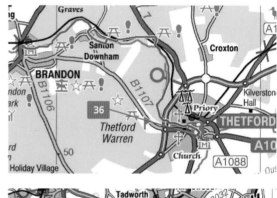

Graves
A1
Santon Downham
Croxton
BRANDON
ndon
rk
B1106
B1107
Kilverston Hall
36
Priory
THETFORD
Thetford Warren
A10
rd
50
Church
A1088
Holiday Village
Ous

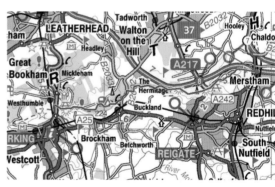

Tadworth
ham
LEATHERHEAD
Walton on the Hill
37
B2032
Hooley
Chaldo
Headley
A217
Great Bookham
Mickleham
B2033
Merstham
The Hermitage
Westhumble
A242
REDHI
RKING
A25
224
Buckland
Nutfiel
Vestcott
Brockham
Betchworth
REIGATE
South Nutfield

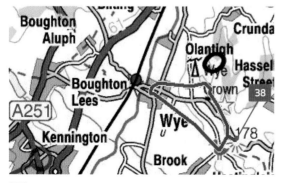

Billing
61
Crunda
Boughton Aluph
Olantigh
Hassel
Boughton Lees
ye
Street
rown
38
A251
Wye
178
Kennington
Brook

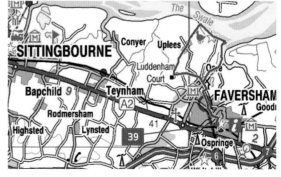

The Swale
Conyer
Uplees
SITTINGBOURNE
Luddenham Court
Bapchild
9
Teynham
FAVERSHAM
A2
Goodn
Rodmersham
i
Highsted
Lynsted
41
Ospringe
6
2

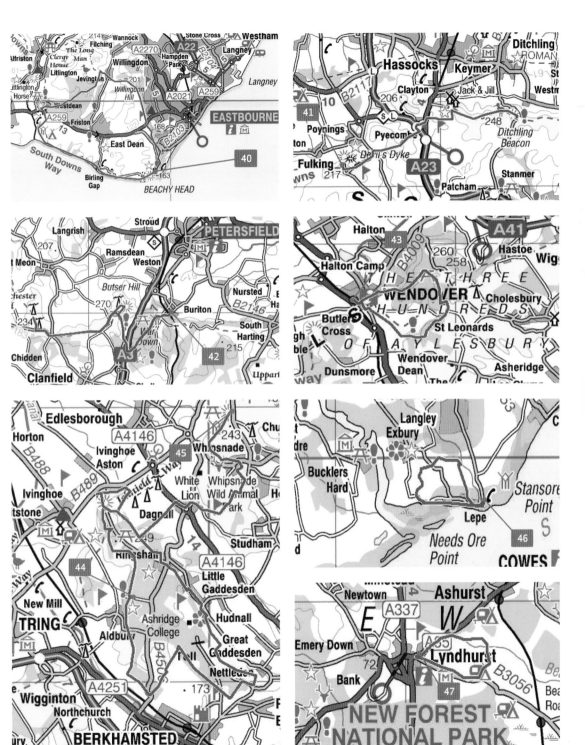

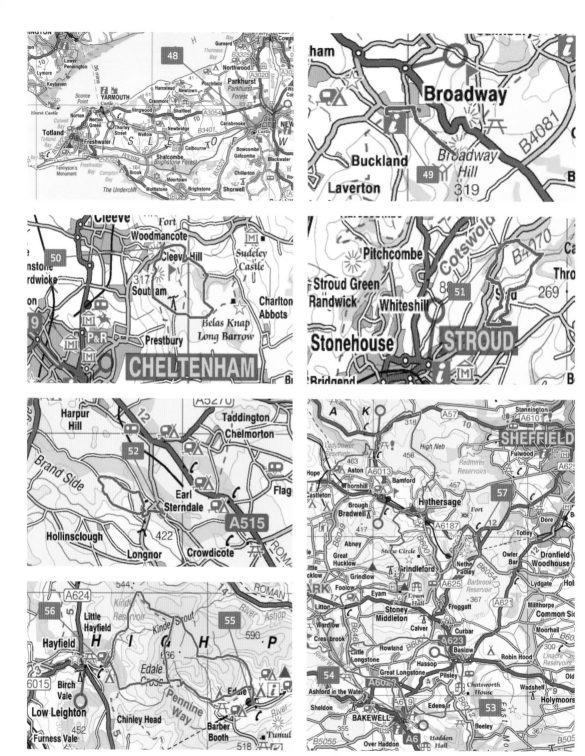

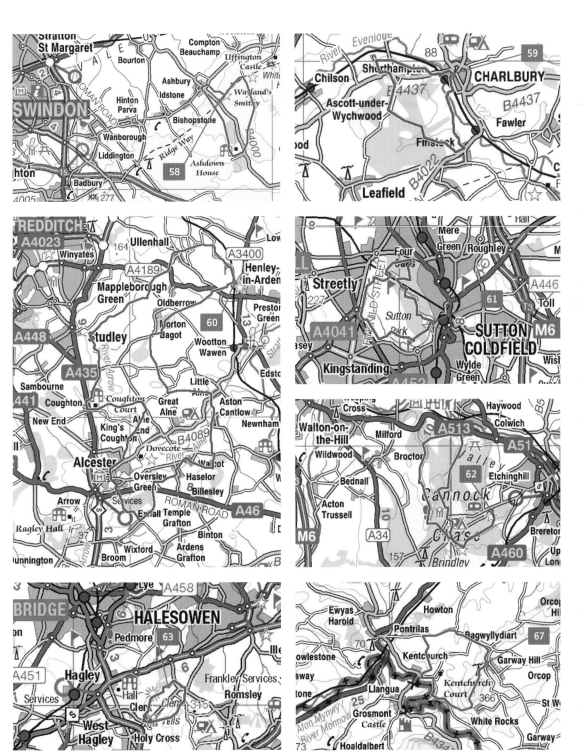

Map 58 (top left):
Stratton St Margaret
SWINDON
Compton Beauchamp
Bourton
Uffington Castle
White
Ashbury
Idstone
Wayland's Smithy
Hinton Parva
Bishopstone
Wanborough
Ridge Way
Liddington
Badbury
Ashdown House
VALE
ROMAN ROAD
B4000
58

Map 59 (top right):
River Evenlode
CHARLBURY
Chilson
Shorthampton
Ascott-under-Wychwood
B4437
Finstock
Fawler
B4437
B4022
Leafield
88
59

Map 60 (middle left):
REDDITCH
A4023
Winyates
Ullenhall
Low
Henley-in-Arden
A3400
A4189
164
Mappleborough Green
Oldborrow
Preston Green
Morton Bagot
Studley
Wootton Wawen
Edsto
A448
A435
River Arrow
Little
Sambourne
Coughton
Coughton Court
Great Alne
Aston Cantlow
Newnham
New End
King's Coughton
Alne End
B4089
River Alne
Alcester
Dovecote
Walcot
Oversley Green
Haselor
Billesley
Arrow
Services
ROMAN ROAD
A46
Ragley Hall
Exhall
Temple Grafton
Binton
Dunnington
Wixford
Broom
Ardens Grafton
37
60

Map 61 (middle right):
Hall
Mere Green
Roughley
Four Oaks
Streetly
WATLING STREET
Sutton Park
A446
Toll
SUTTON COLDFIELD
M6
Wish
A4041
Kingstanding
Wylde Green
227
61
13

Map 62 (lower middle right):
Haywood
Cross
Walton-on-the-Hill
Milford
Colwich
A513
A51
Wildwood
Broctor
Valley
Etchinghill
Bednall
Cannock
Acton Trussell
Chase
M6
A34
Brereton
Brindley
Up
Lon
157
62
A460

Map 63 (bottom left):
Lye
A458
BRIDGE
HALESOWEN
Pedmore
Ille
Hagley
A451
Services
Hall
Clen
Frankley Services
Romsley
West Hagley
Holy Cross
63
6
315

Map 67 (bottom right):
Ewyas Harold
Howton
Orcop Hill
Pontrilas
Bagwyllydiart
owlestone
Kentchurch
Garway Hill
sway
Orcop
stone
Kentchurch Court
St W
Llangua
Afon Mynwy
Grosmont Castle
366
White Rocks
River Monnow
Hoaldalbert
Garway
B433
70
25
73
67

259

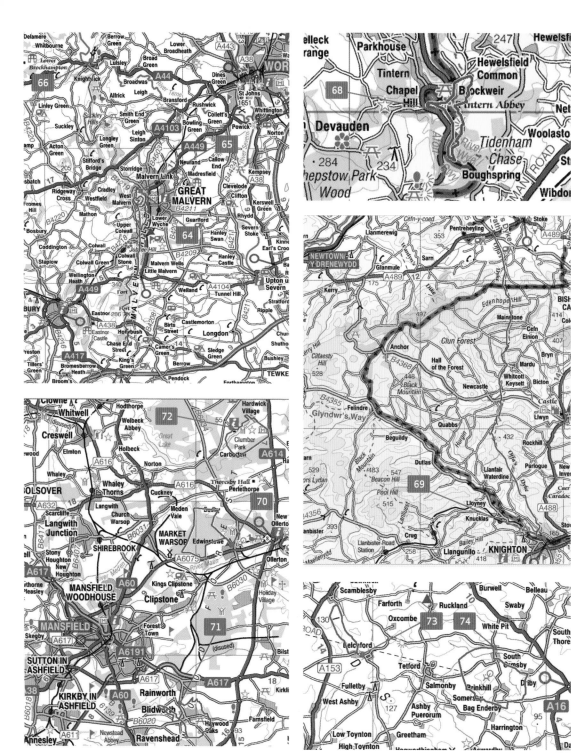

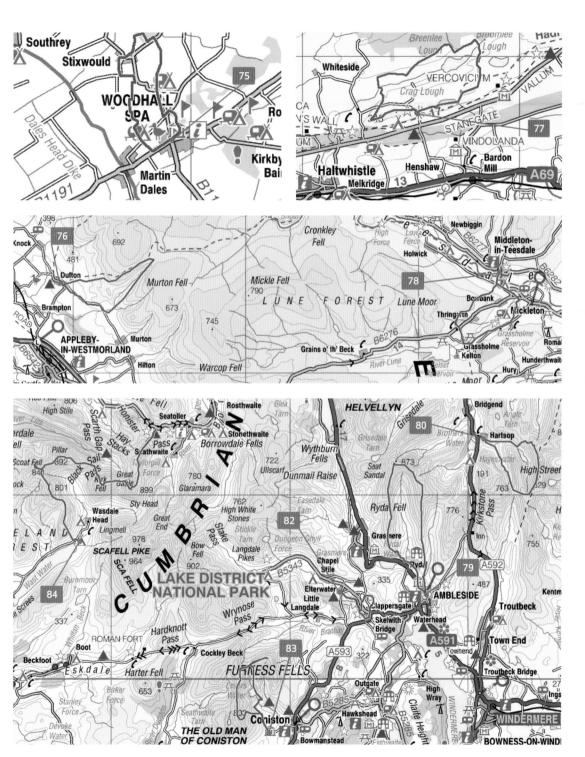

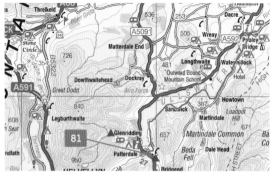

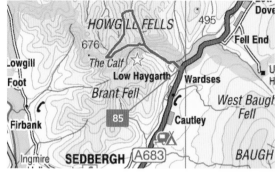

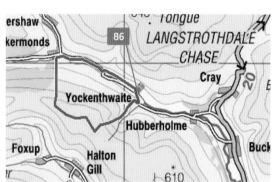

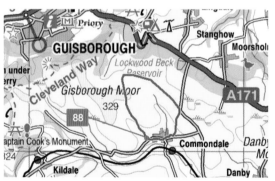

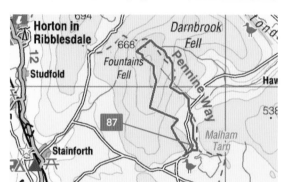

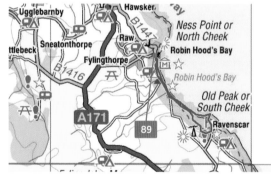

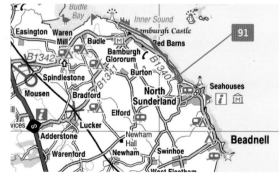

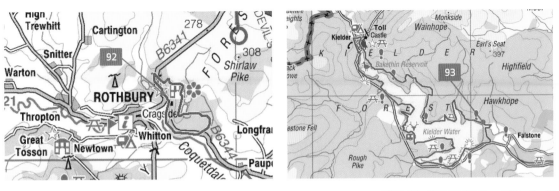

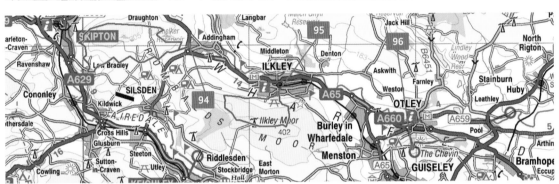

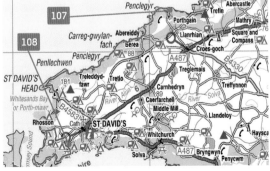

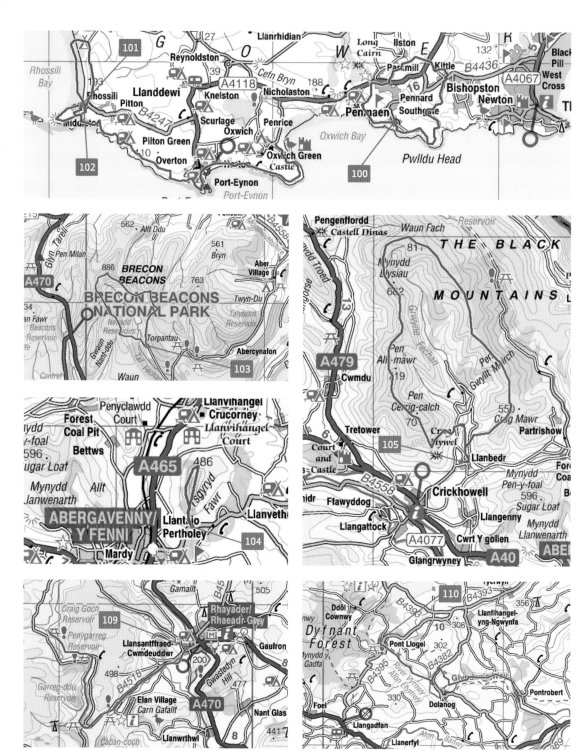

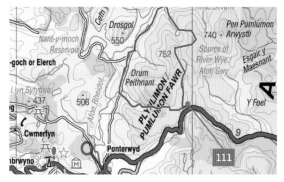

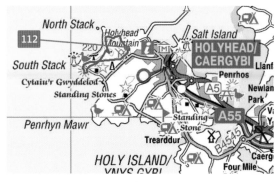

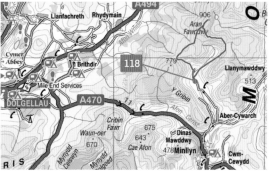

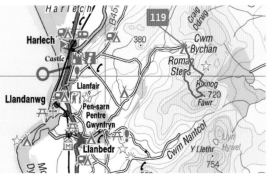

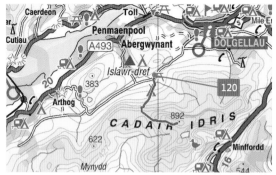

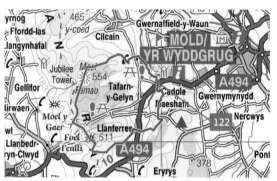

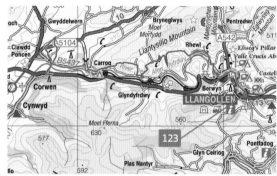

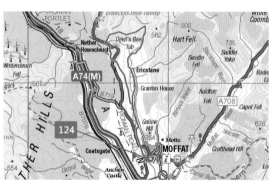

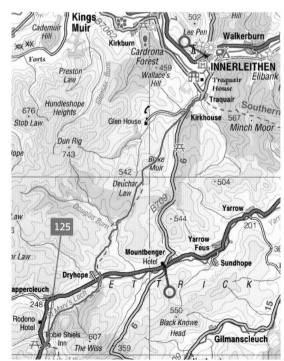

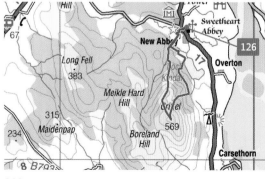

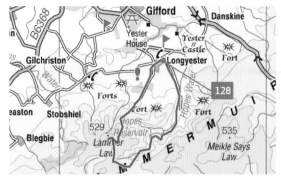

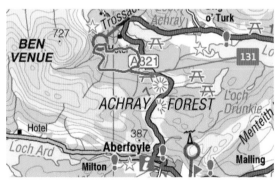
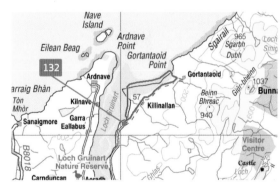
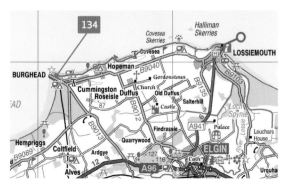
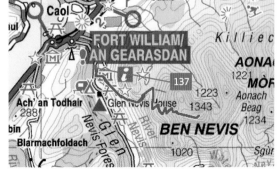

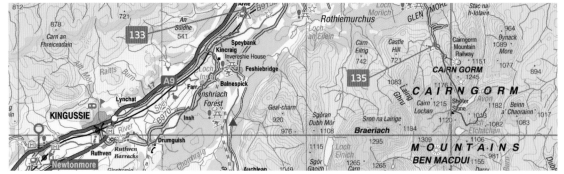

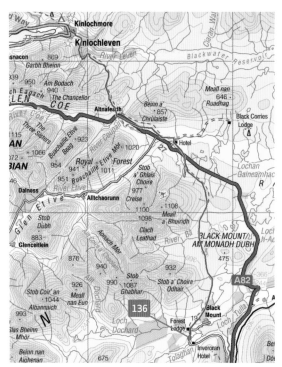

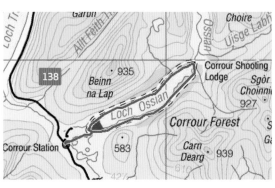

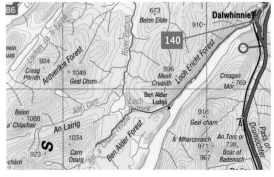

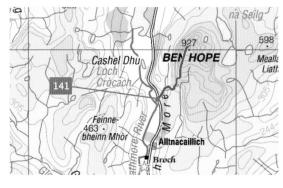

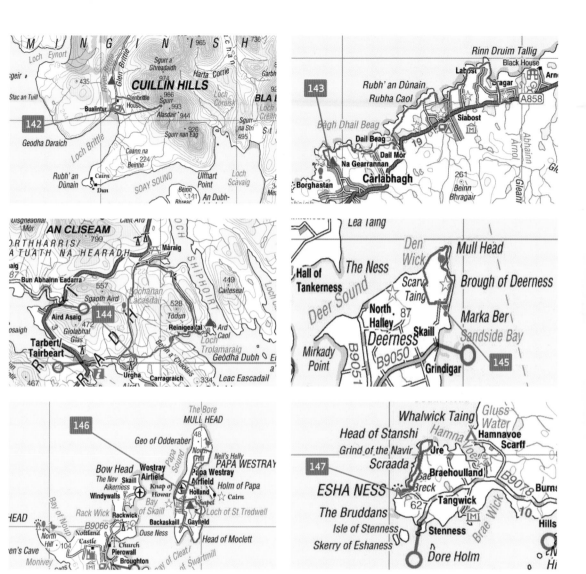

Grid squares represent 10 km. Maps are for guidance only and do not contain all footpaths or names. To help improve these maps for a future edition please contribute to Open Street Map. For more accurate mapping insert the Lat Long into *bing.com/maps* and choose the Ordnance Survey layer.

Ordnance Survey maps © Crown copyright and database right 2014. Superimposed paths © OpenStreetMap.org contributors. With thanks to 'UK Map App' for iPhone (Philip Endecott)

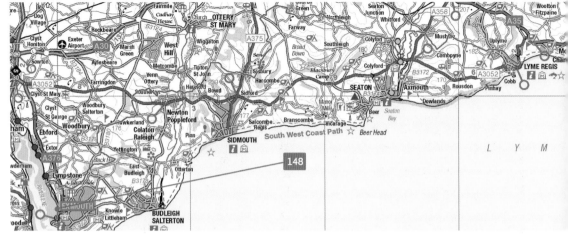

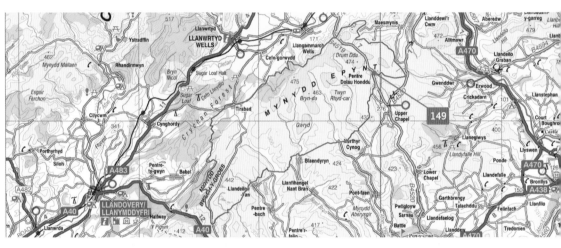

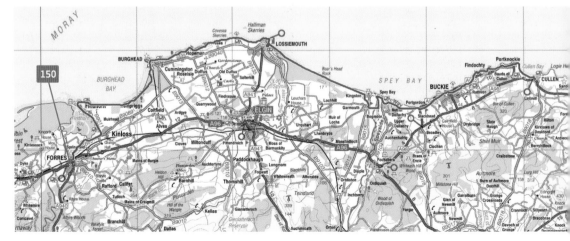

Grid References of start points

Run	Lat Long	Grid Ref	Run	Lat Long	Grid Ref	Run	Lat Long	Grid Ref
1	50.1647, -5.6703	SW3798435859	51	51.7774, -2.1786	SO8777508759	101	51.5693, -4.2886	SS4148788083
2	50.1213, -5.5324	SW4759630561	52	53.2002, -1.8661	SK0904367017	102	51.5693, -4.2886	SS4148788083
3	50.1420, -5.0141	SW8473231227	53	53.2174, -1.6684	SK2224168980	103	51.8505, -3.4064	SO0322217814
4	50.3323, -4.6474	SX1168251392	54	53.2144, -1.6711	SK2206468649	104	51.8421, -2.9763	SO3283416394
5	50.5138, -4.4557	SX2599271102	55	53.3648, -1.8154	SK1238385339	105	51.8769, -3.1060	SO2395720392
6	50.4828, -4.5591	SX1854667904	56	53.3793, -1.9284	SK0485786937	106	51.6250, -4.9033	SR9913395795
7	50.2788, -3.8709	SX6679243765	57	53.3168, -1.6014	SK2665580057	107	51.9479, -5.1807	SM8150832496
8	50.2147, -3.7099	SX7810136359	58	51.5594, -1.6103	SU2711284571	108	51.8707, -5.284	SM7402224222
9	50.2445, -3.8111	SX7096039852	59	51.8725, -1.4897	SP3523219446	109	52.2985, -3.5177	SN9660367799
10	50.6557, -3.3224	SY0662184842	60	52.2915, -1.7838	SP1484565952	110	52.7296, -3.4347	SJ0321215628
12	50.7171, -3.5305	SX9204691947	61	52.5641, -1.8337	SP1137196264	111	52.7296, -3.4347	SJ0321215628
11	50.7776, -3.0323	SY2731398066	62	52.7515, -1.9720	SK0198717095	112	53.3165, -4.6647	SH2259383264
13	50.5434, -3.9904	SX5906473408	63	52.4249, -2.0917	SO9386480767	113	53.1443, -4.3855	SH4054963454
14	50.7078, -4.0389	SX5613091781	64	52.1202, -2.3357	SO7711546929	114	52.8045, -4.7128	SH1723226445
15	50.5808, -3.7453	SX7653177126	65	52.1202, -2.3357	SO7711546929	115	53.1165, -4.1188	SH5828959801
16	51.1653, -4.6657	SS1372344050	66	52.2017, -2.3913	SO7335356012	116	53.1233, -4.0200	SH6492460369
17	50.9943, -4.5343	SS2225424712	67	51.9336, -2.8111	SO4432926435	117	53.1234, -3.9663	SH6851660281
18	51.2165, -3.9272	SS6549948136	68	51.6979, -2.6774	SO5328200124	118	52.7517, -3.700	SH8535918473
19	51.2301, -1.9592	SU0294647881	69	52.3471, -3.0499	SO2857672635	119	52.8637, -4.0134	SH6455531483
20	51.2895, -2.8699	ST3943854849	70	53.1978, -1.0674	SK6240167157	120	52.7194, -3.9293	SH6978515272
21	51.1163, -3.196	ST1638135902	71	53.1051, -1.1199	SK5902056792	121	52.9238, -3.4364	SJ0352737235
22	51.3809, -2.3455	ST7605064702	72	53.2652, -1.0643	SK6250774653	122	53.1547, -3.201	SJ1978562629
24	51.4566, -2.5867	ST5933273236	73	53.2606, -0.0642	TF2922575477	123	52.9715, -3.1709	SJ2146842213
23	51.4797, -2.3629	ST7489375698	74	53.2619, 0.0520	TF3696675845	124	55.3295, -3.4459	NT0836504894
25	50.7036, -3.0665	SY2478389872	75	53.1515, -0.2171	TF1932663085	125	55.4741, -3.2013	NT2416420687
26	50.5785, -2.4691	SY6687975519	76	54.6174, -2.4753	NY6940324803	126	54.9804, -3.6197	NX9644266291
27	50.6451, -2.3897	SY7254582894	77	55.0031, -2.3910	NY7508567679	127	55.8549, -3.227	NT2328463088
28	51.7318, 0.9257	TM0212907728	78	54.6239, -2.0830	NY9474125425	128	55.8806, -2.7212	NT5498165506
29	51.6414, 0.0543	TQ4224695624	79	54.4338, -2.9643	NY3754804689	129	56.0143, -2.8498	NT4712080477
30	51.4499, -0.2958	TQ1852073700	80	54.5088, -2.9124	NY4102112994	130	55.7635, -4.0126	NS7382054071
31	52.9631, 0.6370	TF7720943887	81	54.5351, -2.9353	NY3957815935	131	56.2132, -4.3940	NN5162504868
32	52.5327, 0.8596	TL9405796602	82	54.4336, -3.0372	NY3281704740	132	55.8549, -6.3118	NR3025970821
33	52.9664, 0.8144	TF8910144709	83	54.364, -3.0956	SD2891197049	133	57.1518, -3.8883	NH8586008356
34	52.2087, 1.6213	TM4750862896	84	54.456, -3.2633	NY1819807467	134	57.7023, -3.4880	NJ1142069031
35	52.2266, 0.7291	TL8649362215	85	54.3649, -2.4672	SD6974196697	135	57.1349, -3.6714	NH9893706124
36	52.4083, 0.7532	TL8736882485	86	54.2065, -2.1478	SD9045978985	136	56.5370, -4.8141	NN2705441875
37	51.2645, -0.1504	TQ2914553331	87	54.1033, -2.1762	SD8857867507	137	56.8113, -5.0764	NN1230373086
38	51.1695, 0.9732	TR0794745346	88	54.4857, -0.9877	NZ6567910508	138	56.7607, -4.6906	NN3561966462
39	51.3127, 0.8889	TR0143361023	89	54.4360, -0.5362	NZ9504505497	139	58.2381, -5.4009	NC0045932751
40	50.7414, 0.2532	TV5907695948	90	53.9606, -1.0867	SE6002251997	140	56.9327, -4.2469	NN6336784626
41	50.9008, -0.1051	TQ3334312963	91	55.586,0 -1.6674	NU2106532538	141	58.3903, -4.6327	NC4619847672
42	50.9751, -0.9486	SU7391620049	92	55.3154, -1.8862	NU0731802375	142	57.2033, -6.2919	NG4089220667
43	51.7622, -0.7479	SP8650807800	93	55.1879, -2.4622	NY7066788273	143	58.2964, -6.7909	NB1939544199
44	51.8076, -0.5928	SP9711813041	94	53.945, -1.9045	SE0636949876	144	57.9043, -6.7554	NB1839400457
45	51.8675, -0.5369	TL0083819782	95	53.9204, -1.8230	SE1171947159	145	58.9563, -2.7147	HY5898307894
46	50.7844, -1.3554	SZ4553798508	96	53.8926, -1.6982	SE1993444085	146	59.3513, -2.8984	HY4900952004
47	50.8727, -1.5683	SU3046908223	97	54.2958, -4.5340	SC3518991868	147	60.4895, -1.6266	HU2062278482
48	50.6914, -1.3123	SZ4867088194	98	54.0916, -4.7660	SC1920569722	148	50.6204, -3.4167	SX9988081031
49	52.0345, -1.862	SP0956337350	99	54.3203, -4.4126	SC4317894316	149	52.0746, -3.4664	SN9959642819
50	51.9431, -2.0169	SO9893827177	100	51.5669, -4.0878	SS5539587404	150	57.6095, -3.6262	NJ0293658885

Wild Running

150 Great Adventures
on the trails and fells of Britain

Words and Photos:

Jen Benson & Sim Benson

Editing and Proofing:

Michael Lee
Tania Pascoe
Candida Frith-Macdonald
Sarah Baxter

Design and Layout:

Oliver Mann
Marcus Freeman
Tania Pascoe

Distribution:

Central Books Ltd
99 Wallis Road, London, E9 5LN
Tel +44 (0)845 458 9911
orders@centralbooks.com

Published by:

Wild Things Publishing Ltd.
Freshford, Bath,
BA2 7WG, United Kingdom

WildThingsPublishing.com
WildRunning.net

Copyright © 2014 Jen Benson & Sim Benson

This first edition published in the United Kingdom in 2014 by Wild Things Publishing Ltd, Bath, BA2 7WG, United Kingdom. ISBN: 978-0957157361. The moral rights of the author have been asserted. All rights reserved. No part of this publication may be reproduced, stored in a retrieval system, used in any form of advertising, sales promotion or publicity, or transmitted in any form or by any means, electronic, mechanical, photocopying, recording or otherwise, without prior permission in writing from the publishers. Any copy of this book, issued by the publisher as a paperback, is sold subject to the condition that it shall not, by way of trade or otherwise, be lent, resold, hired out or otherwise circulated, without the publisher's prior consent, in any form of binding or cover other than that in which it is published and without a similar condition including these words being imposed on the subsequent purchaser.

Photographs © Jen & Sim Benson except the following (all reproduced with permission or with CC-BY-SA): front cover and front flap bottom left, Ben Winston; p32, p34, p35, p38-9, p54, p94, p184, p187-91, p196, p198, P222, p251 Daniel Start; p34 Endurancelife, Nilfanion; P42 Lewis Clarke; p46-7 Lewis Gillingham (lewisgillingham.co.uk); p50 Tony Atkin; p54 Gareth James; p66 Jim Champion, Philip Halling; p74 Nigel Chadwick; p75 Diliff; p82 Bob Jones, Evelyn Simak; p84 Robert Tilt, p86 Joe & Zana Benson, Ian Capper; p87 Javier Carcamo; p90 Dominic Alves; p96 Peter Trimming; p98 Jim Champion, Dave Pape, Markellos; p99 Jim Champion; p106 Philip Halling, Derek Harper; p114 Adam Tilt, Marcin Floryan; p116 Tim Heaton; p118 Kurt C, Andrew Bowden, Pam Brophy; p119, p122-3 Lucy Perkins/Sam Foggan; p126 Bob Embleton, Mantiuk; p127 markpeate; p130 Roy Parkhouse, Jeff Buck; p131 Philip Halling; p134 Marcin Floryan, James Hill; p136 Paul Stainthorp; p138-9 Chris; p148-51 High Terrain Events; p150 Diliff, Ben Gamble; p153 Eddie Winthorpe; p154 High Terrain Events; p155 Eddie Winthorpe; p161 Kreuzschnabel; p162 Philip Barker, rowanofravara, Mick Garratt; p166 High Terrain Events, Robert Tilt; p168 Heather Dawe; p172 Gregory J Kingsley; p174 Chris Gunns, Andy Stephenson; p175 Andy Radcliffe; p182 Gareth Lovering; p186 Phil Price, Geoff Perkins/Imogen Triner; p192 Barrie Foster; p194 Robert Tilt, Philip Halling, Nigel Brown; p195 Optimist on the run; p198 Ian Warburton, Eric Jones; p202 Kenneth Yarham, Llydrwydd, Gelboy; p206 Blisco, Nigel Brown; p209 Jeff Buck; p211 Espresso Addict; 212-3 Dave MacLeod; p216 Douglas Law; p218 Andrew Smith, Scothill; p219 Hugh Simmons; p222 Richard Webb, wfmiller; p226 Alistair McMillan, Elliott Stimpson, Stemonitis; p227 Gary Denham; p228 Paul Raistrick; p230 Mary & Angus Hogg, Bill Reid, Nick Bramhall; p231 Mick Knapton; p234 Dave MacLeod, John Lucas; p236 Paul Hermans; p238 Stuart Meek, Nick Bramhall; p239 GariochT; p240 Nick Bramhall; p242 John Allan, Dave Maclennan, Richard Barrett; p243 Lewis Clarke; p244 Bill Boaden; p246 Colin Park, Will Craig; p247 ThoWi; p250 Alan Richards, Lewis Gillingham (lewisgillingham.co.uk).

Author acknowledgements: We'd like to thank all of our wonderful running friends and acquaintances, many of whom we've met along this journey, for their company, advice and generosity. We would particularly like to thank: Eva & Bump; Dan & Tan for going for the idea and guiding us through; Chris & Clare for providing us with a loving home while we researched and wrote; Geoff & Imo; Lucy & Sam (getagripstudio.com); Joe & Zana; Rose & Toto; Sarah Baxter; Sarah Churchill; Jimmy, Sarah, Charlie & Elsie; Nick & Helen; Collette Pryer (Fit-2-U); Eryl; Mark Bullock; Endurancelife; Alicia Hudelson; Heather Dawe; Norma Anderson; Carnethy Hill Runners; the authors of the many books that inspired and informed our adventures; everyone involved in editing and production at Wild Things Publishing and the Flickr, Geograph and Panoramio community of photographers.

Health, Safety and Responsibility. Like any activity undertaken in the outdoors, particularly in remote and elevated areas, off-road running has risks and can be dangerous. Terrain, access and signage is subject to change and areas that were once safely and legally accessible may no longer be so. Runs should only be undertaken by those with a full understanding of these risks and the appropriate training, experience and equipment. The authors have gone to great lengths to ensure the accuracy of the information herein. They will not be held legally or financially responsible for any accident, injury, loss or inconvenience sustained as a result of the information or advice contained in this book. Running in the locations described is undertaken entirely at your own risk.

hello@wildthingspublishing.com